The Alps

The Alps

Europe's Mountain Heart

NICHOLAS AND NINA SHOUMATOFF

Ann Arbor
THE UNIVERSITY OF MICHIGAN PRESS

A CIP catalog record for this book is available from the British Library.

Library of Congress Cataloging-in-Publication Data

Shoumatoff, Nicholas.
  The Alps : Europe's mountain heart / Nicholas and Nina Shoumatoff.
      p.   cm.
  Includes bibliographical references and index.
  ISBN 0-472-11111-6 (alk. paper)
    1. Alps—History.   2. Alps—Civilization.   3. Alps—Description and
  travel.   4. Human ecology—Alps.   5. Mountain ecology—Alps.
  6. Human geography—Alps.   7. Alps—Social life and customs.
  I. Shoumatoff, Nina.   II. Title.

  DQ823.5.S332   2000
  949.4′7—dc21   00-62997

Due to the untimely death of Nicholas Shoumatoff while this book was in
production, some sources could not be identified. Although many people were
helpful in identifying sources, we apologize for any incomplete information.

Foreword

Can the earth be imagined without mountains, or Europe without the Alps? Instead of the great Alpine arch, which extends for more than a thousand kilometers from the western Mediterranean to Austria, there would be an empty plain and an empty sky.

The convulsions of the Tertiary era that built the Alps have given us an extraordinary gift: not fertile earth, rich for cultivating crops and for raising animals, but something perhaps much more than that—a vertical world.

For centuries, this world above the world has loomed over the fields, blotting out the sunshine and blocking the view of the horizon. Once, the mountains seemed to be intent on punishing people with avalanches, rockfalls, surging torrents and glaciers that flattened the villages. It was a forbidden world, made especially to be the domicile of dragons and legendary evil spirits. The rock spires and massive glaciers were but a piercing cry from the earth to the sky. The crevasses and seracs, the great layers of ice, the everlasting snows, all things in this accursed world inspired only fear and often terror into the minds of the fragile people who were overwhelmed below.

And then everything changed. People dared to venture into the mountains. Rock crystal and chamois hunters opened the way. The world of mountain climbing was born. The Alps quickly became "the playground of Europe," in Leslie Stephen's witty phrase. First the English, those great travelers, curious to see everything; scientists who wished to observe and study on site; poets, writers and painters: all came to Chamonix, to Grindelwald, to Lauterbrunnen. Then came the avid cragsmen, the real lovers of mountain climbing, who began to crisscross this immensity where peaks and spires abound. The climbers set off to ascend the Dolomites, the Engadine, from the southern Alps to the

Matterhorn range. Those "horrible mountains" became known as "sublime mountains."

"Because they are there." Such was the answer of George Leigh-Mallory when he was asked why people wish to climb mountains. It is appropriate to add to this a theory that was dear to my husband, Gaston Rébuffat: "Man is made of curiosity and daring, and keeps this instinct from childhood, to climb trees and fences to discover what is on the other side."

In the valley of Mont Blanc, if the earliest travelers were threatened by villagers with guns, it was because the villagers didn't trust the strangers. These valleys, which were cut off from the rest of the world during long, cold and inhuman winters, had been settled originally by people who wished to disappear, knowing they would never be found in these places that were as inaccessible as they were unattractive. Nevertheless, these inhabitants had the intelligence to understand that, by guiding the new arrivals into the mountains, they could generate income to relieve the dire poverty of their existence.

Thus was born the first, and still the most prestigious, company of mountain guides in the world, the "Compagnie des Guides de Chamonix." Following its example, other companies of guides were established in each of the villages located at the feet of buttresses in strategic places. The guides, each familiar with their own region of the mountains, for the most part worked within their own locations, although a few with exceptional mountaineering skills ranged more widely.

My husband was accepted as a member of the company of Chamonix, which, with rare exceptions, is reserved to natives of the valley. He had become acquainted with the high mountains by reaching them on foot from the shore of the Mediterranean, where he was born and spent his youth. I leave it for him to describe his experiences, in an account I found among his papers after his death in 1985:

> One day, with several companions, all 14 to 16 years old, I start out for Briancon, to walk toward Mont Blanc! To see it, the giant of the Alps, has been our dream for many years.
>
> One morning, we leave the sea to reach higher altitude. We rise with the sun, we walk, and we stop to contemplate and enjoy the view. We set off again. Little by little, we joined with each other into a closer friendship with nature. The colors change and we are astonished at their variety.

Our journey begins from our native Provence. It allows us to discover higher mountains each day, as we cross the Hautes Alpes and continue in the same direction till the end of our trek. We cross many tempting trails, but like mariners, we have our reference point. It is toward the Mont Blanc that we march. When we think of it, our hearts leap with emotion. To be sure, we could have taken the train, but that was for our trip back. Our long walk was primarily a pilgrimage. For the moment, we head to the north. Each evening, drunk with wind, heat, fatigue and hunger, we receive the night like a gift from the heavens.

Each evening, we are happier as we feel ourselves approaching our goal. Happier is the pilgrim as he marches toward Mecca than the shopkeeper already in the Holy City.

We gather wood for our evening fire, like inhabitants of the hills and valleys and of cirques in the mountains. With nightfall, the high summits of the Oisans, then the Maurienne and the Vanoise seem to be getting nearer. Within these isolated ramparts, all is silence. Yet it is not. A mysterious life in the air and on the ground can be deeply felt. We can hear nature living. Then comes the cold and a light wind that makes the fading embers glisten. Everything snuggles in and falls asleep.

Finally one day, the narrow valley opens abruptly. The dream that had filled our evenings becomes real and takes form: Mont Blanc is there! It is ideally beautiful, ideally pure. What strikes the eyes is its restrained architecture. In the symmetrical arrangement of the massif, the satellite peaks that surround the great summit keep their proper distance from it. They spring toward the sky despite the massiveness of their union of snow and rock.

What simplicity, what testimony in that name: MONT BLANC!

Gaston's excitement was that of a young guide and writer. And still, after a fifty-year career of "running" from summit to summit, he maintained the same youthful, heartfelt enthusiasm that he had as a young man. His writing evokes the diverse beauty of the Alps as though they were part of him.

The Matterhorn soars from Zermatt like a torch. This "marvelous stack of rocks," as a friend wrote to us after making its ascent, this upward jet of rock, is proud and haughty. The other peaks have beauty; the Matterhorn has presence. We are transfixed by the way it divides the wind and tears the clouds; it shows the evolution of time for those people in the valley who know how to read its message.

And the Dolomites? How many times have I traveled those roads of white earth (alas, now paved with asphalt) that were placed like ribbons upon the verdant pastures from which the limestone peaks soar, planted into the ground like monuments? The Dolomites' altitude is not very high: 3,000 meters on average. They have no glaciers, except Marmolada and Cristallo, and even those are not large. But the whole massif is of dazzling beauty, closely linked to pure and delicate vertical lines. The Dolomites' harmonious forms reflect their geological formation and the work of erosion by water unceasingly wearing away the rock. Their narrow spires crown the Veneto. In the evening, they reflect the sun as brightly as the brasses in a hotel kitchen.

Once, under a flawless autumn sky, Gaston and I, invited by a pilot friend, flew out of the Rhone Valley, leaving beneath us Mont Blanc and its granite retinue. By a circuitous route, we were going to fly over the Piz Badile, to leap over the Matterhorn and circle around its summit, and to see the wild valleys of the Grisons. This view of the Alps from the sky later inspired my husband to write some lovely lines that bear the mark of his poetic style:

> Such places on our planet are colored in ochre on the atlas, then in white; they are high, sterile, and useful for nothing. Nothing grows there that can be sold, and higher still, nothing can survive. They are among those places that are created exclusively for people's happiness, so that in a universe transformed and changing each day, one can still find a few gardens in a forgotten silence, a few gardens whose primary colors are so good for the eyes and for the heart.

Born, like my husband, in Provence, it is through marriage that I came to know the true high-mountain world. In the course of Gaston's activity as a mountain filmmaker, he and I sampled the heights of all the world's great mountain ranges, and the majesty of the highest summits placed us under an irresistible spell.

In *The Alps*, Nicholas and Nina share their lifelong fascination with the Dames Anglaises, the Jungfrau, Castor, Pollux, the Flames of Stone, the Gusela del Vescova, and so many others, as well as the flora and fauna, the villages and towns, and the lives and customs of the people in Europe's mountain heart.

What sort of people were Nicholas and Nina Shoumatoff? They were endowed with strong character and attractive personalities. The Shoumatoffs, who conceived this literary work that spreads its wings so broadly, and who explored and verified every detail, were a couple united and demanding of themselves.

I never met them in person, though we had the pleasure of corresponding for several years. Nevertheless, in the course of this epistolary relationship, a particular friendship developed between us, marked by a little mystery and curiosity.

Nicholas and Nina have departed from this world and will not see this book in print. But this book is a testament to the quality of their work, and also to their quality as people.

Françoise Rébuffat

Nicholas Shoumatoff translated the original version of the foreword a few months before his death.

Contents

Illustrations

Maps

Tables

Photographs

Following page 42

Nicholas Shoumatoff at Mont Blanc Brenva
North face of Aiguille de Bionnassay with hanging glaciers

Following page 202

Least primrose (*Primula minima*), Defereggental
Moth (*Panassius apollo*) on a mountain thistle in the Val d'Herens
Helicigona arbustorum (left) and *Gentiana clusii* (right), Kandersteg
Scarce copper (*Heodes virgauresa*) on Alpine goldenrod (*Solidago
    virgaurea*), Lötschental
Mountain fritillary (*Boloria pales*) on *Sanguisorba officinalis,*
    Oschinensee
Erebia sudetica on *Taraxacum alpinum* in the Kander Gorge
Snowfinch (*Montefrigilla nivalis*) in Gornergrat, with Monte Rosa
    in the background
Young and mature Capra ibex on the Col d'Entrelor, Val Savranche
Gasterntal goats returning to fold beneath Kanderfirn
Haflinger horses in Timmelsjoch in the Otztal Alps
André, David, and Werner Wandfluh in front of the Blümlisalp
    peaks
French shepherds and sheep above Ceillac-en-Queyras
Italian cowherds making cheese on the south slope of Monte Visto
Slovene group bringing hay to drying rack, Triglav south
Bregaglia hayfield with view of Sciora and Cengalo peaks
Austrian group raking hay below Kals, Grossglockner west
Grindelwald hay drying on racks beneath Mettenberg peak with
    base of Wetterhorn in distance
Man carrying hay below Lötschental avalanche trail
Nicholas and Nina Shoumatoff at a stone farmhouse in Val d'Isère
Bernese summer chalet with ranked cowbells, Gasterntal
Farmhouse and stable under one roof in Bohinj, Slovenia
Hay barn with diagonal drying bars in Bohinj, Slovenia
Houses and church with onion-dome steeple in Zug, Lechtal
Castle, church, barn, and house along a Roman road in Bregaglia
Heiligenblut church and hamlet with view of Glossglockner
Chatelard castle, church, houses, and gardens in Valle d'Aosta
Bled lake, village, and castle with view of Karawanken Alps
Halstatt and Halstattersee, Salzkammergut
Les Haudères and Dent Blanche, painted by Joseph Georges
Bernese chalet with carved and painted facade, Lauenen
Store selling house-carved ceremonial masks, Lötschental
Engadine farmhouse with "graffito" of Adam and Eve, Ardez

Chapter 1

The Alpine World

Entering the Alps

Their hundreds of snow peaks clustered near the meeting points of rich and developed countries comprise one of the ways that the Alps are unique among mountains. Another is their vast network of walking trails, with hundreds of strategically situated high-altitude huts, which provide food, bunks, blankets and good company. These huts make it possible for trekkers, skiers, climbers and lovers of nature in the mountains to explore the flowering slopes and to climb the peaks, crags and roadless glacier passes with light packs and without sleeping bags. These advantages attract many people, yet the Alps have preserved large areas of wildness where we always find the inspiration of mountain solitude, often not far from the beaten track.

Being at the heart of Europe, the Alps have developed a cultural heritage with two different branches. The first is the pastoral way of life, which also includes ethnic traditions, dialects, home life and legends. The second branch, which applies to literature, art, music and mountaineering, comes largely from the surrounding countries and is mostly of the cosmopolitan type, though inspired by the Alps. This book brings together these features of the entire upper Alpine region, including the natural and cultural histories and the relationships between them. It is not a guidebook but an essay, being an interpretive reference that can be read in any sequence, and a study of interdependence.

Attractive details emerge as we review the histories, diversities and interactions of the cultural niches just named; plus those of Alpine geography, geology, climate, snow, glaciers and ecology of plants and animals (both invertebrate and vertebrate); also folk arts, folklore, festivals, dancing, films, warfare, trekking, skiing and high-altitude emotions. It is an opulent panorama of a magnificent mountain world.

One Day in the Alps

No other region on earth can match what the Alps, in many of its places, have to offer to a trekker or climber in just one day. Starting from an ancient high-valley village, we climb through a dark forest with occasional sunlit clearings. Near the top of the forest, the trees become smaller and thin out or end abruptly. Above the tree line, the slope opens out into moors and meadows, where butterflies feed on miniature flowers. Here are the upland pastures for cows, sheep, goats and horses that have come up from the valleys for the summer. On these open slopes, we can often hear the yodeling of the herders. On the rocks above the meadows, we can watch the chamois and ibex play and listen to the piercing whistles of the marmots.

We then reach the zone of the year-round snow and glaciers, the larger of which often reach down into the forests. Near the threshold of the snow, on the terrace of a climbers' hut, we bask in the afternoon sunlight until it turns the snow peaks briefly crimson. Inside the hut, we enjoy a hearty supper and an evening of banter and song. Much-needed sleep arrives in an unheated coed bunkroom, under blankets marked "feet" at one end. Before dawn, it is time to set off again, through the thin air, beneath a dark blue sky. Within a few hours, we can reach a major snow summit or cross a glacier pass into an adjacent valley. With suitable snow conditions, we can also do much of this on skis equipped with sealskins for actual climbing.

Interactions

The Alps have been called the heart, the backbone, the playground and the natural or spiritual sanctuary of Europe. The lives of most people who live at these heights are still mostly or partly pastoral, which link them over years and generations with medieval and earlier times. Latin, Nordic and Slavic traditions, ancient and modern, are intertwined among them. Nowhere else on earth are the lives of ethnically diverse mountain peoples so richly integrated with each other, in spite of historic ethnic and religious tensions, which in the true Alps (though not in some of the Balkans) have now almost completely subsided. Despite encroachments from technological development, the upper Alps remain a vast sanctum of an authentic and complete mountain world.

Nevertheless, under present conditions in the Alps, when human ecology is included, the result, for better or worse, is a series of three-way interactions among indigenous and visiting peoples and the natural world. One important result is that local people have acquired more lucrative means of livelihood, as guides, innkeepers and shopkeepers. Partly because of the visitors' enthusiasm for penetrating the mountains, residents now see their heights in a more appealing way than they did in the past and explore them often as individuals, families and clubs. The visitors have also introduced a classical note into Alpine cultures and have inspired local people to do the same. Conversely, the residents have offered much to the visitors, through ethnic, linguistic, pastoral, domestic and mythical traditions. Thus, the aesthetic, intellectual and physical lives of both groups have been enriched.

Unfortunately, the mountains themselves have been adversely affected in many places, by excessive forestry, pastoralism, industry, construction and recreation, including carving up slopes for safer ski runs. In one sense, however, the mountains and their nonhuman denizens have benefited, because so many people, institutions and organizations now appreciate their natural treasures and protect them through various legal imperatives, including large numbers of Alpine nature reserves and sanctuaries. Programs for conservation of nature and protection of threatened species are for the most part effective and continually expanding. As a result of such measures, it is possible for people, both residents and visitors, to continue to benefit from this magnificent part of the natural world.

Past and Present

When approaching the Alps from the air, on a clear day, we look down on their highest point within the massive snows of Mont Blanc. We also identify the dark finger of the Matterhorn and the great north wall of the Bernese Alps. Beyond these familiar landmarks, virtually endless rows of snow peaks recede to a misty horizon. They resemble white-capped waves on a windblown sea. Millions of years ago, these mountains really did come out of the sea. On overcast days, the highest peaks protrude through the clouds as they did through the ice sheets thousands of years ago.

Since well before the Christian era, even more than 5,000 years ago, routes for travel, trade and warfare between the southern and northern countries have led across the Alps. Historically, the Alps have been a crucial hub on the rich but bloody road of European civilization. Military crossings began with those of the Celts before 380 B.C. and later included those of Hannibal, Julius Caesar, Attila, Alaric, Charlemagne, Suvorov and Napoleon. The Alps also bear the far more numerous peaceful trails of St. Bernard of Menthon, Petrarch, Leonardo, Rousseau, de Saussure, Goethe, Wordsworth, Byron, Shelley, Dumas, Dickens, Turner, Ruskin, Whymper, Mummery, Daudet, Agassiz, Huxley, Chopin, Liszt, Wagner, Brahms, Johann and Richard Strauss, Lehar, Bruckner, Nietzsche, Tolstoy, Freud, Jung, Klee, Kokoschka, Giacometti, Thomas Mann, Achille Ratti (who became Pope Pius XI), Harrer, Bonnatti and Rébuffat. For centuries, these men and countless other people less well known have carried the seeds of Western civilization by overland travel into and among the Alps.

Some places in those mountains reverberate with legendary names. There is Brünnhilde's Rock, probably on the Wetterstein, where she was awakened by Siegfried; two chapels, two monuments and a museum for William Tell near Lake Lucern; a Sherlock Holmes museum at Meiringen; and a Disney-style Heidiland in east Switzerland. On the Nibelung Strasse at Melk, at the feet of the Austrian Alps, the real and legendary realms appear to have converged, where Attila is said to have married Queen Brunhild of the original Burgundian saga (not the Wagnerian *Walküre*). A few miles away, in the castle of Dürnstein, the Hapsburg Duke Leopold incarcerated a returning Crusader, the royal troubadour Richard the Lion-Hearted.

A Wedding of Nature and Culture

Before this book addresses the principal categories of Alpine nature and culture, with specific examples and interactions of each, chapter 2 presents a geographical overview. This mainly applies to the locations and arrangements of the subsidiary ranges and their topography in terms of the heights that they attain. This chapter also indicates, interactively, the respective major points of human interest. Such places include the Winter Olympic sites at Grenoble, Albertville, Chamonix, Garmisch, Innsbruck, Cortina and Sarajevo, with other famous ski and climbing resorts at Zermatt, St. Moritz and Bad Gastein; the huge religious citadels at Grande Chartreuse,

Einsielden, Melk and St. Florian; the active monastic hospices at the St. Bernard and Simplon Passes; the sites of prehistoric cultures at Halstatt, La Tène and Mercantour, with hundreds of ancient petroglyphs; the romantic Bavarian castles of the "mad" King Ludwig II; the Passion play, frescoes and wood carvings at Oberammergau; the "mostly Mozart" festivals at Salzburg; the mountain of ore at Eisenerz, which supplies the Austrian steel mills; the crags of the Bregaglia, which inspired Leonardo da Vinci's art; and the Pass of Morgarten, where Swiss villagers decimated the Hapsburg knights at the origin of Western democracy.

Chapters 3 and 4 introduce the natural history of the Alps in terms of the earth sciences. Chapter 3 describes the formation of the two major types of Alpine mountains from their submarine and subterranean origins in sedimentary and igneous rocks, respectively, including their metamorphic transformations. Chapter 4 concerns their physical environment of climate, snow and ice, especially as a function of altitude, including temperature, pressure, radiation, precipitation, snow characteristics, avalanches, cornices and glaciers. Both of these chapters testify to the respective human interactions, including habitat formation, practical uses, hazards and disasters.

In the vertical direction, the Alpine region is loosely defined as beginning with the montane forest zone at approximately 600 meters (1,969 ft.), with the so-called alpine zone beginning at the upper tree line at about 2,000 meters (6,562 ft.), while the year-round snows generally begin at about 3,000 meters (9,843 ft.). Chapters 5 and 6 integrate this framework ecologically with the phenomena of chapters 3 and 4. The primary results are the survival strategies of high-altitude plants and animals of different major groups and the interdependence of these between and within the vegetable and animal kingdoms. These respectively range from miniature plants to forest trees and from mites to major mammals. Both chapters include and emphasize interactions with the human presence.

Chapters 7 and 8 focus explicitly on the cultural side of the human domain in the Alps, in its ethnic groups, customs, tensions, dialects, pastoral lives and home lives, including architecture, folk arts and festivals. The cultural panorama also combines external with indigenous sources in chapters 9 and 10, under headings of legends, fiction, visual arts and music and dance. The legends mentioned include those of Charlemagne, mountain names and gnomes, while the important fiction ranges from Rousseau to Troyat. The visual arts are historically extensive, from prehistoric cave paintings and petroglyphs to Roman, medieval, Renaissance, Romantic, Impressionist, Postimpressionist and contemporary paintings, engravings, illustrations, posters, cartoons, photographs and films. In Alpine music, we find the influence of pastoral, religious and knightly themes and of folk dancing on the works of major classical composers.

Chapters 11 through 13 review historic mountain warfare, summit climbing and exploration, all three of which involve what is generally called mountaineering, with likewise external and indigenous components. Alpine military history ranges from the crossing of the Alps by Hannibal to the major European wars. Recorded summit climbing begins with Petrarch's ascent of Mont Ventoux and continues through the landmark ascents of Mont Aiguille, Mont Blanc, the Matterhorn and the Eiger north face. De Saussure's ascent of Mont Blanc, though not the first, was the most influential event in the history of Alpine climbing. However, he was even more important as a scientific and cultural explorer. Other articulate Alpine travelers were Leonardo da Vinci, Goethe and Dumas.

In all the cultural chapters, the motivations and constraints of the natural context are explicitly identified. However, all of the interactions considered up to this point barely exceed the conventional limits of natural and human ecology. The book concludes in chapter 14 by powerfully expanding the scope of ecology into the large but less tangible realm of psychology, both human and nonhuman, which we can thus describe as psychological ecology. This type of interaction is most easily observed among the birds, mammals and other vertebrates, but recent microbiological findings show that lesser creatures, most visibly the butterflies, are also affected.

Most of chapter 14 reviews the well-recognized forms of Alpine psychology, namely, those that occur among human beings. These include not only the widely shared aesthetic emotions but also the rather common fear of the heights (acrophobia) and, conversely, attraction to them (acrophilia). The latter, on occasion, can be an explicitly fatal attraction. The chapter goes on to provide examples of Alpine emotion as expressed in poetry, poetic prose, art and spirituality. The book ends in this real but intangible psychological realm, which adds an important interactive dimension to the marriage between nature and culture in the Alps.

Chapter 2

Where Peaks and People Are

Mapping the Alps

Before embarking on a mental voyage through the relationships between the natural and cultural histories of the Alps, it is useful to have a brief look at where and what the Alps are and what points of interest are in them, in the context of the six major Alpine countries: France, Italy, Switzerland, Germany, Austria and Slovenia. This chapter aims to characterize the topography of the whole Alpine mountain complex and to link the mountains with major physical and human features of the region. Accordingly, the presentation begins with a set of ten maps that provide a visual framework for the ensuing text. Maps 1 through 6 locate the higher peaks in each main range in relation to significant passes, lakes, seas, national frontiers and towns, including health spas and recreational resorts. To facilitate spotting such places, these maps employ a widely used schematic style, leaving blank the intervening spaces. Conversely, maps 7 through 9 exemplify the overall and local topographical relief, with less emphasis on specific places.

Map 1 spans the Alps from end to end, from Grenoble in the west and Nice in the south to Vienna in the north and east. This map shows where three large rivers, the Rhone, Rhine and Po, have their sources in the Alps, from which they flow into the Mediterranean, North and Adriatic Seas, respectively. The map also shows the Alpine sources of four major rivers, the Inn, Mur, Drava and Sava, which flow to the Black Sea via the Danube. Maps 2 through 6 show the same region in greater detail in five contiguous segments.

Map 7 gives emphasis to the overall structure of the Alps through the medium of those areas that rise above 2,000 meters (6,562 ft.), in sharp contrast to the lower areas, which are left blank except for the rivers.

Curiously, the structure resulting from this procedure resembles the profile of an immense rock lobster, with a thick, straight thorax facing east and a relatively thin, curled-up tail that ends near the western tip of Italy. The vast Alpine region, with this strange suggestion of a marine creature, really did come out of the sea (see chap. 3).

Map 7 also vividly shows how the rivers, whether in their present form or earlier as glaciers, have sliced through the highlands and created the Alpine valleys, thus establishing the larger patterns of the mountain topography. On this map, one can see that westward or eastward flowing segments of the major rivers line up into a series that separates the northern chain of mountains from the main watershed crest, in a rift that cuts through the entire Alpine system from end to end. A similar series of river valleys, also shown on the map, likewise separates the southeast mountains from the main crest, which is continuous over the whole length of the Alps.

Maps 8 and 9 present the local relief of the three highest mountain groups in the more familiar idiom of contrasting light and shade. Map 8 represents the Mont Blanc range, which is especially impressive at the south face of Mont Blanc itself, with its three gigantic rock ridges rising to the highest summit in the Alps. Map 9 includes the two largest glaciated areas, namely, those of the Pennine and Bernese Alps, which the Rhone River separates. These two areas together comprise by far the largest number of those mountains that rise above 4,000 meters (13,123 ft.). Among the best-known peaks, the Pennine group includes the Matterhorn and Monte Rosa, while the Bernese group features the sweeping curve of the Great Aletsch Glacier, which originates at the summit of the Jungfrau. These two maps give an idea of how the south-facing slopes are generally steeper than those facing north, with the notable exception of the adjacent north walls of the Jungfrau, Mönch and Eiger.

The last map in the series, map 10, shows a geological scheme for all the Alps that is useful for comparison with the other maps here, though it relates mostly to chapter 3.

Alpine Gaul

Maritime Alps

The Alps rise abruptly from the narrow Mediterranean beaches of the Italian Riviera and the French Cote d'Azure. Between Monte Carlo, in the tiny principality of Monaco, and the Italian seashore resort of Ventimiglia,

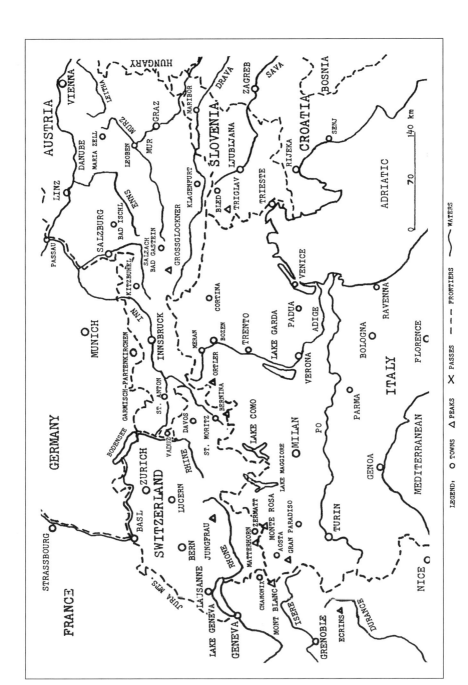

1. Alps from end to end

LEGEND: ○ TOWNS △ PEAKS ✕ PASSES --- FRONTIERS ⌒ WATERS

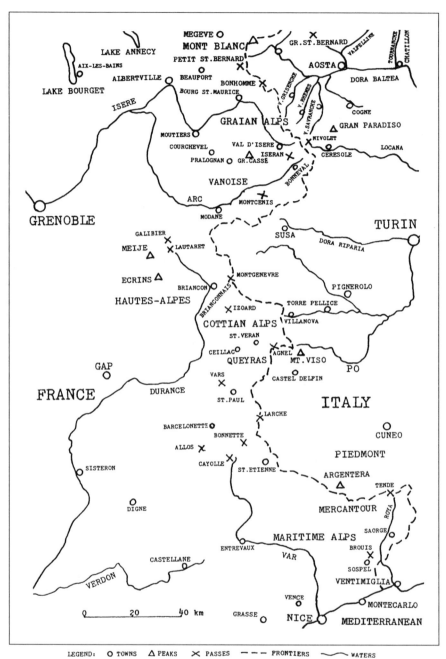

2. Nice to Mont Blanc

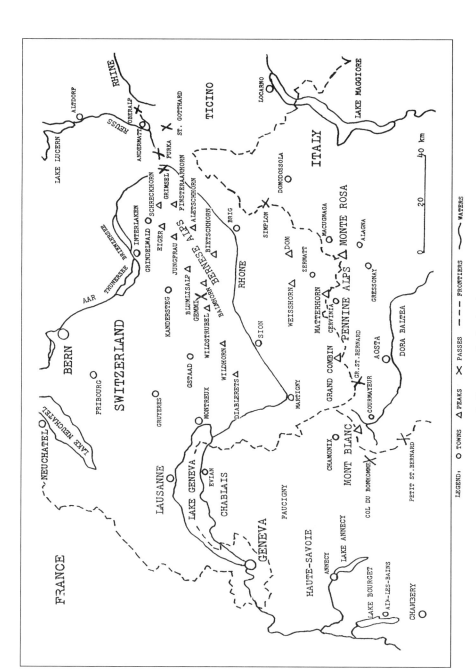

3. Geneva to St. Gotthard

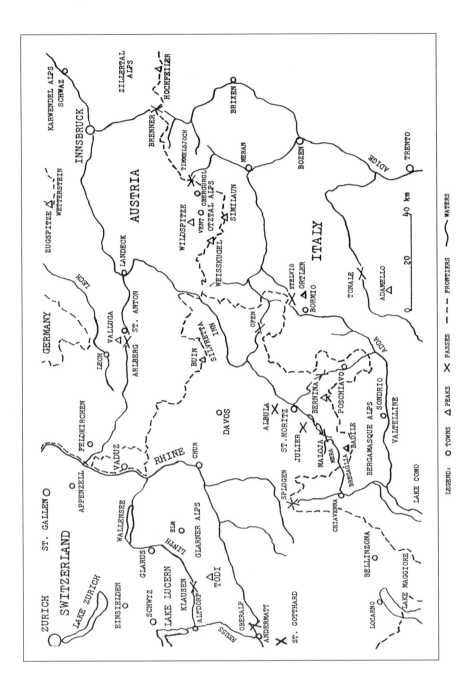

4. St. Gotthard to Innsbruck

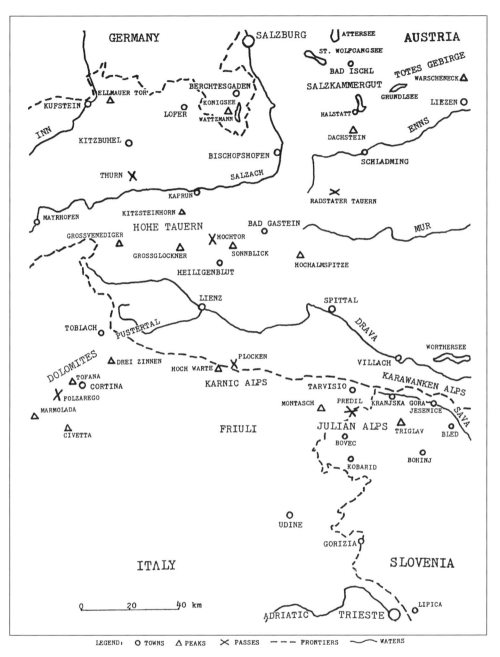

5. Salzburg to Trieste

6. Vienna to Ljubljana

7. Upper Alps, two-thousand-meter contours. (From Schaer et al. 1972.)

8. Range of Mont Blanc. (Reproduced by permission of the Swiss Federal Office of Topography, February 15, 1999.)

9. Bernese and Pennine Alps. (Reproduced by permission of the Swiss Federal Office of Topography, February 15, 1999.)

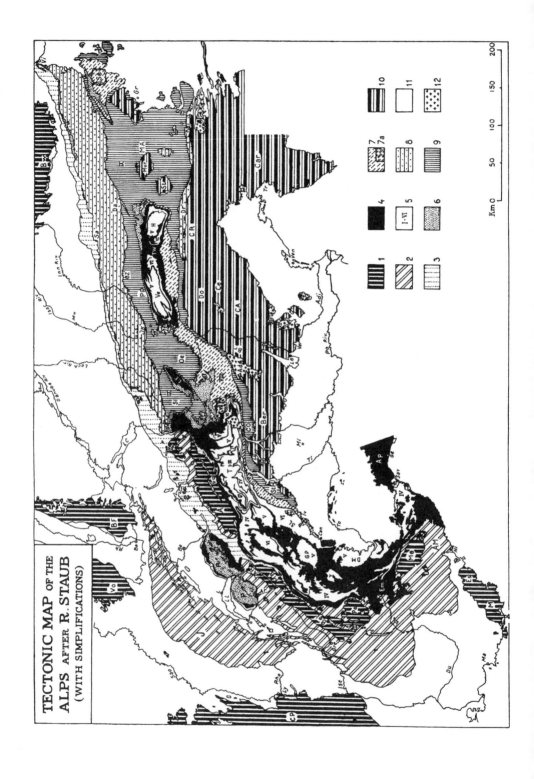

TECTONIC MAP OF THE
ALPS AFTER R. STAUB
(WITH SIMPLIFICATIONS)

Km 0   50   100   150   200

1, Crystalline Massifs of the Foreland.
2, Jura Mountains and sedimentary cover of the Foreland (Autochthon and Morcles Nappe).
3, Diablerets Nappe, Wildhorn Nappe and Upper Nappes of the High Calcareous Alps.
4, "Schistes lustrés" of the Pennine Nappes and Pennine elements of the Prealps.
5, Crystalline core of the Pennine Nappes.
6, Mesozoic of the Grisonides.
7, Crystalline core of the Grisonides.
7A, Crystalline core of the Bernina Nappe.
8, Mesozoic of the Tirolides.
9, Crystalline core of the Tirolides.
10, Dinarides.
11, Tertiary (Molasse) and Quaternary.
12, Eruptive Massifs of Post-Alpine age.

I-III, Simplon-Ticino Nappes.
IV, Great St. Bernard Nappe.
V, Monte Rosa Nappe.
VI, Dent Blanche Nappe.
VII, Err-Bernina Nappe.
VIII, Campo Nappe.
IX, Silvretta-Oetztal Nappe.

A, Aar Massif.
Ad, Adamello.
Adi, Adige River.
AM, Maritime Alps.
Ap, Apennine.
AR, Aiguilles Rouges.
Ar, Arve River.
Ba, Basel.
Bel, Belledonne Massif.
Be, Bern.
BF, Black Forest.
Br, Brenta.
Bw, Böhmerwald.
C, Campo.
CA, Cima d'Asta.
Can, Canavese.
Car, Carso.
Ce, Cadore.
CO, Catena Orobica.
CP, Central Plateau.
CR, Carnian Range.
Da, Dachstein.
Do, Dolomites.
DM, Dora Maira.
Dr, Drauzug.
Du, Durance.
Em, Embrunais.
Es, Esterel.
G, Geneva.
Ge, Genova.
Go, Gothard.
GP, Gran Paradiso.
Gr, Graz.
Gre, Grenoble.
GZ, Greywacke Zone.
H, Hochalm.
I, Insbruck.
Ise, Isère.
Iv, Ivrea.
IZ, Ivrea Zone.
J, Jura.
Ka, Karawanken.

L, Lausanne.
LC, Lake of Constance.
LE, Lower Engadine Window.
LG, Lake of Garda.
LL, Lake of Geneva.
Lu, Lugano.
Lg, Lyon.
M, Maures.
MA, Mur Alps.
Ma, Marseille.
Me, Mercantour.
Mi, Milano.
Mü, München.
Mur, Murau.
N, Neuchatel.
Ni, Nice.
Oe, Oetztal.
P, Prealps.
Pe, Pelvoux.
PP, Pinzgau phyllites.
Rh, Rhine.
Rho, Rhone.
Sa, Salzburg.
Sao, Saône.
Sav, Savona.
Se, Semmering.
Si, Silvretta.
SL, Sesia Lanzo Zone.
St, Stangalp.
Str, Strona.
T, Simplon-Ticino Nappes.
Ti, Ticino.
To, Torino.
Tr, Trieste.
TW, Hohe Tauern Window.
Ve, Venediger.
Ven, Venezia.
Ver, Verona.
Vi, Vienna.
Vo, Vosges.
Z, Zurich.

10. Geological scheme. (Reproduced from Collet 1974 by permission of Krieger Publishing Co.)

the main watershed crest of the Alps closely marks the French-Italian border northward, gaining altitude along the way. The crest first passes through the Maritime Alps, which are mostly in the region of southern France called Provence. In 121 B.C., the Romans conquered what they called Trans-Alpine Gaul, or simply the Provincia, which comprised the French Mediterranean strip, the lower Rhone Valley and part of the western Alps, all the way up to Lake Geneva. It was the first Roman colony outside of Italy. (In the fifth century A.D., it featured sybaritic villas equipped with swimming pools and lawns for a game resembling tennis, as described by the pleasure-loving St. Sidonius Apollinaris.)

The Maritime Alps form a group of relatively minor mountains, without glaciers or permanent snows, and with slopes largely denuded by centuries of excessive cutting of trees and grazing (though luxurious, tall fir forests still grow on the south side of the Col de Turini and in a few other places). In the mountains, the originally Roman villages, such as Vence, Sospel and St. Etiénne de Tinée, are now centers of a district that is much beloved by writers, artists and people of the arts.

Only seven summits of the Maritime Alps rise moderately above 3,000 meters (9,843 ft.), a crucial datum of the Alpine region where permanent snows usually begin. Six of these summits are in Italy, because in 1861, when Victor Emanuel II, then king of Sardinia and duke of Savoy, became the first king of Italy, he drew the frontier to retain his favorite hunting grounds. They are in what is now called the Natural Park of Argentières, which adjoins the French Parc Nacional de Mercantour. These two parks, one on each side of the border, form an island of granite in the predominantly limestone mountain range (see chap. 3). The Mercantour park includes the Vallée des Merveilles, a sanctuary of petroglyphs 4,000 years old. Not far to the west, from the village of St. Etiénne de Tinée, a steep road leads north to the Col de la Bonnette (2,692 m, 8,832 ft.) and from there, by a short detour, to the highest motor road in Europe (2,860 m, 9,383 ft.). This is a home of the glacier crowfoot, the creeping avens and other lovely, rare high-altitude flowers (see chap. 5). From la Bonnette, the road leads down north to the end of the Maritime Alps at the village of Barcelonette, which acquired its charming name because it once belonged to a younger brother of the count of Barcelona.

Queyras and Monte Viso

North of the Maritimes, the Cottian Alps are crowned by the craggy and snowy 3,841-meter (12,602 ft.) Monte Viso. On its French side, in the exceptionally unspoiled regional park of the Queyras, the lovely village of Ceillac lies below the Lac St. Anne and the snow-topped summit of the Font Sancte peak. Northward, tiny St. Véran is the highest village in Europe (2,425 m, 7,956 ft.). From there, a road leads over the steep Col Agnel (2,744 m, 9,003 ft.) into the Piedmont section of Italy. Beneath the Italian slopes of Monte Viso, Torre Pellice is the center of the oldest (twelfth-century) Protestant sect, the much persecuted Waldensians (Vaudois) (see chap. 11).

Hautes-Alpes

To the west, the precipitous Alps of Dauphiné are entirely within France. They include the Parc Nacional des Écrins, where the 4,102-meter (13,459 ft.) Barre des Écrins is the only 4,000-meter peak west of the Mont Blanc range. This region is known as Hautes-Alpes. Northward, across the Col d'Izoard from the Queyras, the walled town of Briançon is surrounded by a medieval moat and surmounted by seven forts built for Louis XIV by Vauban, his chief military architect. The forts shield the town from the nearby Montgenèvre, the easiest pass between France and Italy, which many believe was the route of Hannibal and his elephants (see chap. 11).

West of Briançon, below the Col de Lautaret, a hot chalybeate (ferrous) spring, now known as Le Monétier les Bains, was used by Roman soldiers for nursing their battle wounds. Across the pass, the peaks of the Meije soar to the Doigt de Dieu, "Finger of God" (3,983 m, 13,068 ft.) (see chap. 9). Farther west, through the desolate, partly industrial Oisans Valley, the large city of Grenoble is the home of a major university that is a renowned center for Alpine research. North of it, up a towering escarpment, the highland of the Grande Chartreuse, which has no easy access, holds the immense cloister where the monastic fathers made the herb liqueur of chartreuse green.

Vanoise and Gran Paradiso

North of Briançon in the Graian Alps, the Vanoise National Park of France adjoins the Gran Paradiso National Park of Italy. These parks include the 3,855-meter (12,648 ft.) Grande Casse in the Vanoise and the 4,061-meter (13,648 ft.) Gran Paradiso, the highest completely Italian peak (whose name ought to have been applied to all the Alps). Both parks have large areas remote from motor roads but with numerous trails and climbers' huts, among them the Refuge Savoie on the isolated Plateau de Nivolet, which was the hunting lodge of the Italian kings. Ibex and chamois, now well protected, abound in these parks (see chap. 6). A treacherous gorge between the two parks was formerly a smugglers' route. (Italian smugglers, one of whom we met in his later years, would leave home before dawn at Val Savranche and race 66 kilometers [40 mi.] over three difficult passes and through the gorge to the Pont St. Charles in France, where each would pick up a 50-kilogram [110 lb.] sack of contraband salt and return home the same day.)

Below the gorge, the ancient village of Val d'Isère is surmounted by a famous ski area (made more so by Olympic gold medalist Jean-Claude Killy). High above the village, the Col d'Iséran (2,770 m, 9,088 ft.) links the valleys of the Arc and Isère Rivers, which define the Vanoise on its south and north sides. At the top of the pass, the traveler finds no fanfare, no souvenir shops, not even a sign confirming that this is indeed the highest motor-road pass in the Alps. Instead, there is only a small, austere chapel where one can quietly pray.

The deepest penetration into the Vanoise by road is farther west, above the village of Pralognan, with a magnificent view of the Grande Casse peak, so named because its summit is split by a glacier. Near the road, a meadow features the rare (in the wild) "blue thistle," also known as the Queen of the Alps (it is not a thistle but a member of the parsley family; see chap. 5). The road to the west leads to the city of Chambery, capital of Savoie, and to the resorts of Aix les Bains and Annecy on Lakes Bourget and Annecy. (Lake Bourget is commemorated in Lamartine's wildly romantic poem "Le Lac.") This region is known as Haute-Savoie.

Valle d'Aosta

On the north side of the Gran Paradiso lies the densely populated Italian Valle d'Aosta, with its numerous medieval castles. Most of its inhabitants still speak French, in the local French dialect called Valdotain, because this was part of French-speaking Savoy until 1861. This valley also lies at the feet of the greatest peaks in the Alps, in the ranges of Mont Blanc and Monte Rosa. From Chatillon, the Val Tournanche leads up to Cervinia (formerly Breuil) at the Italian foot of the Matterhorn.

Between Gran Paradiso and Mont Blanc, the Petit St. Bernard Pass is said to have been a route of Julius Caesar into Gaul. At the top of the pass, a tall Roman column now bears a statue of St. Bernard, beside the ruined monastic hospice. Aosta, the main town in the valley, was founded by Caesar Augustus, and its modern name is a contraction of its Roman name, Civitas Augusti. A road from Aosta leads directly north to the Great St. Bernard Pass. (According to Isaiah Berlin [1957], the prominent Savoyard royalist and ultramontane philosopher Joseph de Maistre, a native of Aosta, provided Tolstoy's *War and Peace* with its title, with some verbatim conversations in French, and with aspects of its nonheroic view of history.)

Range of Mont Blanc

The village of Courmayeur (in Latin, Curia Major) at the upper end of the Aosta Valley gives access to the tunnel through the Mont Blanc range and to cable-car transport over it. From the outskirts of Courmayeur, one can see the sheer Italian face of Mont Blanc as it soars over ridges and glaciers to its 4,807-meter (15,771 ft.) summit, the highest in the Alps. It is a view that looks more Himalayan than Alpine. The great mountaineer Julius Kugy described it as "a cathedral borne on giant granite columns, an altar lit by the glory of heaven, a dome standing brilliant in the firmament" (1934, 236; for a more complete quotation, see chap. 14).

Across the mountain, Chamonix (in Latin, Campus Munitus) is an ancient, once-Roman village that became French in 1861 after belonging, at that time, to Sardinia. It lies in a deep valley at 1,017 meters (3,337 ft.). With its view of the Mont Blanc summit above a 12,400-foot slope of snowfields, glaciers and granite spires, it is unquestionably the most spectacular village in the Alps. Mont Blanc's largest glacier, however, which descends from the Col du Géant (3,359 m, 11,028 ft.) and the Vallée Blanche to the enormous Mer de Glace, is no longer visible from the village but offers a favorite, though crevassed, ski run. Chamonix is probably the most popular center in the Alps for all mountain sports and was the first of all the world's Winter Olympic sites.

Apart from Mont Blanc itself, its range includes only a handful of 4,000-meter peaks. All of these are famous and significant but much lower, except for Mont Blanc de Courmayeur, which, at 4,748 meters (15,577 ft.), is a shoulder rather than a summit. The others are Mont Maudit (4,465 m, 14,649 ft.), Dom du Gouter (4,304 m, 14,121 ft.), Mont Blanc de Tacul (4,248 m, 13,937 ft.), Aiguille Verte (4,122 m, 13,524 ft.), Pointe Walker of the Grandes Jorasses (4,110 m, 13,484 ft.), Aiguille de Bionnassay (4,051 m, 13,291 ft.) and Dent du Géant (4,013 m, 13,166 ft.). Readily accessible from Chamonix are some of the world's most challenging rock-climbing routes, such as the Walker Spur of the Grandes Jorasses, the Petit Dru, the Grepon, the Grand Capucin and the Route Major from the Brenva Face to the summit of Mont Blanc.

Hard as it is to believe, the frontier between France and Italy at the summit of Mont Blanc is not mutually agreed upon. The problem goes back to when the mountain was divided between the two countries by a boundary commission in 1861. The text of the commission's protocol states that the frontier follows the watershed (which passes through the summit). This is the version that the Italians show on their official maps of today. The official French version, however, adheres to the map that was attached to the protocol and that shows the boundary deviating below the summit to Mont Blanc de Courmayeur. Thus, walking from the main summit toward Italy, one cannot be sure which country one is in.

From the upper end of the valley of Chamonix, a road leads northward into Switzerland. (Above this road, where the snowy north slope of the Mont Blanc range drops sharply from France into Switzerland, a prominent rock, precisely at the frontier, is officially named Le Pissoire.) From Le Tour, which is the Chamonix Valley's uppermost hamlet, once the home of Whymper's guide, Michel Croz (see chap. 12), one can walk over the Col de Balme directly into Switzerland.

Swiss Alps and Adjacent Italy

Around Lake Geneva

The north chain of the Alps extends from the mountains of the Grande Chartreuse and the Haute-Savoie into the district of the Chablais south of Lake Geneva. The lake is in the shape of a southward-pointing crescent, the western tip of which is engulfed by the city of Geneva (which the Romans called Genava). On the south (French) shore of the lake, the town of Evian is famous as the source of one of the world's most popular bottled mineral waters.

Near the eastern tip of the lake, on its north (Swiss) shore, the town of Montreux features the medieval Chateau de Chillon, which projects out over the water, with the sharp peaks of the Dents du Midi forming its classical backdrop. (In literature, the castle is best-known through Byron's dramatic poem *The Prisoner of Chillon*. Clarens, a village adjacent to Montreux, was the site of Rousseau's novel *La Nouvelle Héloise* (see chap. 9). The city was the last home of lepidopterist-novelist Vladimir Nabokov, author of *Lolita.*)

The road from Aosta over the Great St. Bernard Pass leads down to the Swiss town of Martigny, where the westward-flowing Rhone turns sharply north toward Lake Geneva. On its way into the lake, the Rhone slices an opening more than 2,500 meters (8,200 ft.) deep through the northern chain, between the towering spires of the Dents du Midi (3,257 m, 10,686 ft.) and the Dents de Morcles (2,969 m, 9,741 ft.). From the north, this dramatic, gigantic gateway leads to all the highest peaks of the Alps—southward to the range of Mont Blanc and eastward up the Rhone Valley to the ranges of Monte Rosa and the Finsteraarhorn, on opposite sides of the valley. The vast south face of the Dents de Morcles displays eons of geological history in the language of stratified rocks (see chap. 3). From there the north Swiss Alps continue over the Rocher de Naye above Montreux; the upland Gruyère, whose cheese of that name is the chief ingredient of fondue; and the ominously named Diablerets peaks, which rise to 3,209 meters (10,528 ft.). The latter provide facilities for summer skiing on a large glacier called the Tzanfleuron, whose resonant name in Vaudois dialect means merely "a flowering pasture."

Bernese Alps

East of Lake Geneva, the northern section of the Swiss Alps rises to the immediate north of the Rhone and Rhine Valleys. There the Rhone Valley is divided in roughly equal lengths into French-speaking and German-speaking parts, which are joined into a single canton called the Valais or the Wallis. North of it, between the Diablerets and Lake Lucerne, the snow-capped north chain is known as the Bernese Alps or the Berner Oberland, not all of which is in the large canton of Bern. Its north slope is the idyllic Swiss chalet country that includes the fashionable Gstaad, the popular resort of Interlaken, and the mountaineering centers of Kandersteg and Grindelwald.

Kandersteg (when its weather is clear) glories in its view of the Blümlisalp peaks. It also provides the footpath, via the Schwarenbach mountain inn, south over the Gemmi Pass and steeply down to Leukerbad in the Rhone Valley. Leukerbad is an ancient, still popular spa of which Martin Zeiller wrote in 1642 that its hot springs were good for "melancholic humors and bleary eyes" (de Beer 1967). (Later, John Murray wrote of it that "many a fair nymph in extreme negligée, with stockingless feet and uncoifed hair, may be encountered crossing the space between the bath and the hotels" [1838, 107]. He would have been even more surprised to see what they do today, walking in bikinis all the way over the pass to Schwarenbach.) Kandersteg also gives access to the Lötschberg tunnel of the Bern-Lötschberg-Simplon (BLS) Railroad, with special cars for automobiles. The railway emerges into the Lötschental, crosses the Rhone Valley and continues through the Simplon tunnel to Milan.

Two noteworthy, mostly parallel valleys—the larger Valaisan Lötschental and the smaller Bernese Gasterntal—are hidden within the northern chain, on the south and north sides, respectively, of its crest. They are dominated, respectively, by the stately 3,934-meter (12,907 ft.) Bietschhorn and the massive 3,709-meter (12,169 ft.) Balmhorn. The two valleys are connected by a footpath over the glacier-bearing Lötschenpass, where, at its 2,690-meter (8,255 ft.) summit, battles were fought in the religious wars between Valaisan Catholics and Bernese Protestants (see chap. 11). (Even today, because of those wars, two pastures on the north slope of the Bernese Alps, across the Gemmi and Grimsel Passes, belong to the Valais rather than to Bern.)

The two valleys, though both German-speaking and so close to each other, differ in several ways. The Lötschental has five year-round villages and several upper seasonal hamlets, while the Gasterntal has no villages, hamlets or year-round residents (though it did in medieval times). The Gasterntal houses, in the Bernese style, have wood-shingle roofs, while those of the Lötschental, like those in most of the southern Alps, have wooden roofs covered with stone slabs. On Sundays, the pious Lötschental women, like other high-altitude Valaisans, wear traditional formal *Trachten* (folk costumes) to church, while the Bernese women do not. The Lötschental people, like most Valaisans, are more reserved in their demeanor than the typically Bernese Gasterntal people. (For Rousseau's romantic description of high-valley Valaisans two hundred years ago, see chap. 9.)

Grindelwald, a larger resort than Kandersteg, also offers a famous railway tunnel, this one actually through the Eiger, with two windows on its murderous north face (see chap. 12), on the way to the Jungfraujoch, the glacier pass east of the Jungfrau (see chap. 4). The Eiger, Mönch and Jungfrau (respectively, 3,976 m, 13,045 ft.; 4,099 m, 13,448 ft.; 4,158 m, 13,642 ft.) form the classical "north wall of the Alps," but they hide the two highest Bernese peaks—the 4,274-meter (14,022 ft.) Finsteraarhorn and the 4,195-meter (13,763 ft.) Aletschhorn. There the longest glacier in the Alps, the 25-kilometer (15 mi.) Grosser Aletsch Glacier, sweeps southward toward the Rhone Valley (see chap. 4). East of Grindelwald and of the Wetterhorn, the Reichenbach Fall was the site of the joint demise of Sherlock Holmes and Professor Moriarty, from which Holmes miraculously recovered (see chap. 9).

Northeast Switzerland

The large Rhone Glacier, which is that river's source, descends from between the Grimsel Pass and the Furka Pass, which jointly block off the upper end of the Rhone Valley. Eastward, the valley between the Furka and Oberalp Passes is drained by the Reuss River below the St. Gotthard Pass. This river, a tributary of the Rhine, plunges out of the valley through the narrow Schöllenberg Gorge, which it has sliced through the northern chain. In the gorge, it is spanned by the legendary Devil's Bridge (see chaps. 9 and 11). The river drops into the Vierwaldstattersee (Lake Lucern), named for the four "forest cantons" that founded the Swiss Confederation (see chap. 11). The eastern shore of the lake is the land of the legendary (but not historic) William Tell, which is a magnet for thousands of Swiss pilgrims and foreign tourists (see chap. 9).

Continuing eastward, the Glarner Alps are off the tourist-beaten track but are rich in political and scientific history as well as in their natural setting (see chaps. 3, 7, and 11). Northeast of the Glarner Alps, the Toggenburg district leads to the village of Appenzell, which has given its name to a breed of small dogs and a gamy type of cheese. It is also known for its quaint, brightly painted, high-priced hotels and for its traditional artists' colony, which specializes in a primitive folk-art style that, to Americans, is reminiscent of Grandma Moses. The Swiss part of the northern chain ends where it is cut through by the Rhine, beneath the rugged, rocky Santis peak.

Pennine Alps

South of the upper Rhone and Rhine rises the main chain of the Alps. In the northern part of the Mont Blanc range, above the Grand Col Ferret, Mont Dolent (3,823 m, 12,543 ft.) marks the triple border point of France, Italy and Switzerland. Here the frontier of Italy turns sharply eastward, in a district of quaintly named mountains, such as the Angrionettes (Milkless Goats), Grand Golliat (Goliath), Leisasses (Rocks) and Marmontains (Marmots, a name from the Latin *murem montanum*, "mountain rat"). This leads to the bleak Great St. Bernard Pass (2,469 m, 8,100 ft.), with its active monastic hospice and huge rescue dogs. Close to the pass on its Italian side, the Alpe des Baux is a spectacular flowering meadow partly surrounded by rock spires (which are much bigger than those of Les Baux in southern France that gave bauxite its name). The largest one is called La Tour des Fous (Tower of the Insane) because it leans precariously downhill toward Aosta, like a gigantic Tower of Pisa.

This is the beginning of the great Pennine range, the densest concentration of major peaks in the Alps, seventeen of which are higher than 4,270 meters (14,000 ft.). All except one (the Grand Combin, which is near the St. Bernard Pass) are clustered around Zermatt. They include the 4,634-meter (15,203 ft.) Monte Rosa and the renowned 4,478-meter (14,692 ft.) Matterhorn. Some, such as the Matterhorn and the Lyskam (4,480 m, 14,698 ft.), are on the frontier, while the Weisshorn (4,506 m, 14,783 ft.) and the Dom (4,545 m, 14,911 ft.) are north of Zermatt, entirely within Switzerland. A traditional cog railway climbs from Visp in the Rhone Valley to Zermatt (1,616 m, 5,302 ft.). Private cars are also allowed to drive to a parking lot at the entrance of Zermatt, but not into its narrow streets. From Zermatt, another cog railway rises to Gornergrat (3,131 m, 10,272 ft.). This offers a unique, 360-degree panorama of all the great Pennine peaks already mentioned and several others, including the Dent Blanche and the Zinal Rothorn. With these attractions (and despite lingering xenophobia; see chaps. 7 and 13), Zermatt has become one of the most popular mountain-sport centers in the Alps, almost rivaling Chamonix.

The classical High Level Route over the glaciers from Chamonix to Zermatt or on to Saas Fee (or vice versa), with huts along the way, is a challenging spring tour of seven or eight days for capable skiers, though it has been done by Olympic skiers in two days (see chap. 13). It is also a major mountaineering trek in summer. This section of the Alps gives birth to several history-laden valleys, among them, on the Swiss side, the Val Entremont, the Val de Bagnes, the Val d'Hérens, the Val d'Anniviers and the Turtmanntal; and on the Italian side, the Valpelline, the Val Tournanche, the Val di Gressonay, the Val Sesia and the Val Ansasca. In the upper parts of these valleys, which have their individual traditional customs, the main languages are French or German, rather than Italian, on both sides of the crest. These spectacular valleys offer magnificent trekking trails along them and between them. Just east of the Matterhorn, the snow-covered Theodul Pass (3,290 m, 7,940 ft.) has for centuries been a travelers' route between Zermatt and Cervinia (Breuil) in Italy (see chap. 13).

East Swiss-Italian Alps

East of Monte Rosa, across the Simplon and St. Gotthard Passes, the international border deviates to the south of the high mountains. The frontier meanders because this is merely where the Swiss invaders happened to be when they were defeated by the French in 1515 (see chap. 11). The area now included in Switzerland is the Ticino, the Italian-speaking canton of Switzerland. This popular lake district, partly Swiss and partly Italian, and much favored by vacationers and retirees, includes the well-known Lakes Maggiore, Lugano and Como (which are mostly in Italy). Due north of Lake Como, in the homeland of the ancient Rhaetians (see chap. 7), the road across the Splügen Pass (2,113 m, 6,932 ft.) into the Rhine Valley leads through the Via Mala which, "for a distance of more than 4 miles, is, without doubt or exaggeration, the most sublime and tremendous defile in Switzerland. . . . The precipices, which often rise perpendicularly on both sides of it, are certainly in some places 1600 ft. high, and, in many places, not more than 10 yards apart" (Murray 1838, 206).

Switzerland acquired three other Italian valleys, east of Ticino, through acts of piety rather than war. In 775, Charlemagne gave the Poschiavo Valley, below the Bernina Pass (2,330 m, 7,644 ft.), to the bishop of St. Denis near Paris, who transferred it to the bishop of Como, who transferred it to the bishop of Chur, which is now in Switzerland. The Bregaglia Valley below the Maloja Pass and the Münster Valley below the Ofen Pass were given to the bishop of Chur by Holy Roman emperors in the ninth and tenth centuries. Between the Maloja and Bernina Passes, a sumptuously glaciated area includes Piz Bernina (4,049 m, 13,284 ft.), the easternmost summit above 4,000 meters in the Alps, with its satellites, Piz Roseg (3,937 m, 12,919 ft.) and the lovely triple-folded Piz Palü (3,905 m, 12,812 ft.). In the Engadine, which is the Swiss part of the Inn River valley, the watershed crest is defined by the summits of the Bernina group.

East of Maloja, St. Moritz is now an elegant ski resort, at an altitude of 1,768 meters (5,801 ft.)—much higher than Chamonix. It is also an ancient, traditional spa. The renowned alchemist Paracelsus (Theophrastus Bombastus von Hohenheim, aka Phillipus Aureolus Paracelsus, 1493–

1541) recommended its hot springs as a cure for "stone or gravel, gout or arthritis" (de Beer 1967). St. Moritz is in the Engadine (Inn Valley), which is in the Grisons (Graubünden, or "Gray Leagues"), Switzerland's largest canton. Its chief town is Chur, where the Rhine turns from east to north. It is a region whose Romanche is one of the four official Swiss languages, but it is struggling to survive (see chap. 7).

The Lower Engadine, east of St. Moritz, features houses painted with elaborate murals called "graffiti," notably at the village of Ardez. This is a narrow, eastward projection of Switzerland, between the Silvretta group on the Austrian frontier to the north and the Italian frontier to the south. The Swiss National Park, which is an important nature sanctuary and a center for ecological research, lies close to the end of the border between Switzerland and Italy. South of it, entirely within Italy, rise the peaks of the Ortler (3,905 m, 12,812 ft.). In the days of the Austrian Empire, the Ortler was its highest point. It is separated from the main crest by the Stelvio, which is the second highest motor-road pass in the Alps (2,758 m, 9,049 ft.), now infested by a dense concentration of souvenir shops.

Austrian and Southeast Alps

Austro-Bavarian Alps

East of the Rhine, the northern chain generally marks the boundary between Austria and Bavaria, with no summits higher than 3,000 meters (9,843 ft.). In the Lechtaler Alps, above the Arlberg Pass, the slopes of Valluga are Austria's best-known skiing area. From there the Inn River flows on through Innsbruck, a lovely, historic, truly Alpine town, which is the capital of Tirol. The Bavarian side of the mountains is famous for the castles of the "mad" King Ludwig II and for the village of Oberammergau, with its Passion play, its skilled wood-carvers and its houses decorated with religious murals. The soaring rocks of the Wetterstein group, on the frontier south of Garmisch-Partenkirchen, were probably the inspiration for the mountain scenes in Wagner's operas (see chap. 10). Also on the frontier are the Karwendel Alps, whose Lalider Wand is a favorite challenge for rock climbers.

Farther east, the northern chain is cut through by the Inn River below the medieval Kufstein fortress and the much climbed Wilde Kaiser crags, north of the ski resort at Kitzbuhel. In the Berchtesgadener Alps, overlooking Salzburg, the Watzmann (2,713 m, 8,901 ft.) is the highest peak entirely within Germany, though almost completely surrounded by Austria (because of a historical oversight in defining the border). Below it, at the south end of the Königsee, which can be reached only by boat or over the crags on foot, the St. Bartholomä Chapel, with its twin red domes, is "Motif no. 1" of the Alps, which thousands of visitors come to see.

South of Salzburg—the city of Mozart, an annual music festival and the powerful medieval archbishop's fortress—the Salzkammergut Lakes lead to Bad Ischl, where Emperor Franz Joseph, "the Good Old Kaiser," ruled the Austrian Empire from an office in his hunting lodge (which is more like a palace), while his entourage enjoyed the superlative pastries at Zauner's café. The ancient village of Halstatt is partly built on piles over its eponymous lake and has for centuries been important because of the salt mines for which it is named. It is a sensationally beautiful village at the foot of the craggy snowcapped Dachstein (2,995 m, 9,026 ft.), a major peak of the northern chain. The Halstatt culture, at the beginning of the Iron Age 4,000 years ago, first provided ax heads for carpentry, iron weapons for warfare, and artifacts exported to western Europe, the Balkans and even China (see chaps. 7 and 8). The Salzkammergut also includes Lakes Mondsee, Wolfgangsee and Aussee, the charming Grundlsee and, most picturesque of all, the Traunsee.

From these lakes, the northern chain continues eastward with a series of sinister and sacred names. Beginning with the Höllen Gebirge (Mountains of Hell), it rises to 2,389 meters (7,838 ft.) at the Warscheneck peak in the bare-rock Totes Gebirge (Mountains of Death). This is the high point of the remaining northern chain, which goes on through the attractive Alpine villages of Windischgarsten and Altenmarkt to the Lourdes-type shrine of Mariazell, on whose surrounding slopes "everyone in Vienna" is supposed to have learned to ski. North of it, where a swing of the Danube bathes the feet of the Alps, the massive Benedictine cloister of Melk overlooks the Nibelungstrasse (see chap. 1). The Alps make one more surge at Vienna's "house mountains"—the Schneeberg (2,076 m, 6,811 ft.) and the Rax (2,007 m, 6,505 ft.). They are separated from each other by the deep Höllental (Valley of Hell). The northern chain gradually ends in the idyllic Vienna Woods of Strauss waltz fame and, within the city limits, at Grinzing, which is famous for its "Heurigen" (meaning "this year's") wine.

West Austrian Main Crest

From the eastern tip of Switzerland, the main crest continues over a series of snowcapped mountains that divide Italy from Austria, along the Ötztal and Stubai Alps, and across the Brenner Pass to the Zillertal Alps. The

Ötztal Alps are Austria's largest glaciated area. Its major peaks include the Weisskugel (3,739 m, 12,267 ft.), the Wildspitze (3,772 m, 12,375 ft.) and the graceful 3,599-meter (11,808 ft.) Similaun, the most popular climb in this area. Near it, the discovery of the 5,000-year-old body of the "Ice Man," the earliest well-preserved human body ever found, has attracted worldwide attention (see chap. 7).

Nearby Obergurgl, with its onomatopoetic name, is the the highest village in Austria (1,927 m, 6,322 ft.). Its high-rise accommodations for skiers give an unfortunate first impression of the village. In contrast, at the lower end of the Similaun Glacier's valley, the village of Vent, the second highest in Austria, is one of the most charming in the Alps. A few miles above these two villages, the main road crosses the Timmelsjoch Pass (2,478 m, 8,130 ft.) on its way to the pleasant resort city of Meran in Italy. The Zillertal Alps are a wilderness area of classical mountaineering, with its highest summits along the Italian border, crowned by the impressive triple folds of the 3,509-meter (11,512 ft.) Hochfeiler.

Tauern Peaks

At the eastern tip of the Zillertal peaks, the Italian frontier turns south from the main crest, which continues eastward along the Hohe Tauern, Austria's highest range. In its southern valleys, still within Austria, the villages and landscapes of the Defereggental and Virgental, leading up to the 3,674-meter (12,054 ft.) Grossvenediger, are exceptionally appealing. Farther east, the village of Heiligenblut (Holy Blood) boasts the soaring perspective of its tall, thin-spired church (opened on October 11, 1492) beneath the skyline of the 3,797-meter (12,457 ft.) Grossglockner, now Austria's highest summit. Despite the commercial temptations of its strategic location, the elders of the village have wisely protected its authentic simplicity, even retaining a cow stable and a large outdoor manure pile close to the historic church.

The impressive Pasterze Kees Glacier below the northeast face of the Grossglockner, which is the center of a national park, is a mecca for tourists, who come in cars and buses over a spectacular road that crosses the main crest at the 2,505-meter (8,219 ft.) Hochtor Pass. In the northern valleys of this region, the traditional spas of Mayrhofen and Badgastein offer nineteenth-century-type ambience for the affluent. The main crest continues eastward with diminishing height through picturesque backroad villages, past the huge Erzberg iron-ore mountain, the steel mills of Donawitz and the university town of Graz, capital of Steiermark (Styria), then on to the Semmering Pass, which the Südbahn railway crosses on its way from Vienna to the south. In the rocky hills east of Semmering, the main watershed crest gradually ends near the Hungarian border.

Dolomites

East of Lake Como, the two-chain structure of the Alps abruptly changes with the addition of a third series of mountains across northeast Italy, from the Bergamasque and Adamello Alps and the Dolomites to the ranges of southeast Austria and Slovenia. The region of the Italian Dolomites formerly belonged to Austria, where it is still called South Tirol. It was actually the cradle of the former Tirolean nation, named for the castle and village of Tirol just outside the city of Meran. In Italian, the region is called Alto Adige, for the river flowing through it to the Adriatic. It is an area of spectacular limestone spires where tourism has approached the saturation point, but it still offers much for mountaineers and lovers of nature, especially rare, local alpine flowers, such as *Primula daonensis*.

In this area, German is the predominant language and is officially taught in schools along with Italian, but the Ladin form of Romanche is mainly spoken by the indigenous pastoral people. The Germanic influence is especially evident in Val Gardena, where wood carvings of the Madonna and other saints, of cherubs and floral objects and of animals, such as chamois and ibex, are offered in great variety by the prolific handcrafts industry, which rivals that of Oberammergau in Bavaria. Val Gardena gives access from the west to the major spires of the Dolomites, including the Sella group, the Langkofel (Sassolungo), the Marmolada (3,342 m, 10,945 ft.) and, farther east, probably the best-known peak of the region (though not its highest), the 2,999-meter (9,839 ft.), formidable Tre Cime de Lavaredo (Drei Zinnen). Across the border in Austria, Lienz, the capital of Austria's East Tirol, is a pleasant town off the tourist-beaten track. It faces a mountain panorama of jagged spires that are known as the Lienzer Dolomiten.

Slavic Alps

The series of southern mountains continues eastward to the Karnic, Karawanken and Stein Alps along the southern frontier of Austria. It is a region of authentic traditional life on both sides of the border. The Julian Alps of Slovenia, near the eastern end of the southern chain, are a group of limestone pyramids whose highest is the 2,864-meter (9,396 ft.) Triglav, for which the Slovenian national park and a rare local gentian (*Gentiana triglouensis*) are named.

On the Karawanken crest north of the Triglav National Park, between the Slovenian resort of Kranjska Gora and the Italian town of Tarvisio, the triple border point of Italy, Austria and Slovenia also brings together geographically the three great branches of European culture— Latin, Teutonic and Slavic—which blend together around that point. Between Kranjska Gora and Jesenice, an old, smoky steel-mill town to the east, the Sava River, a tributary of the Danube, passes through a narrow portion of its valley, between the Karwanken and Julian Alps. Also between these towns, the Vrata (Gateway) is a deep canyon that pierces the Julian Alps for several miles southward, ending at the foot of Triglav's great north face (see chap. 11).

Near the southwest corner of the Triglav National Park, Kobarid (Caporetto), on the Soca (Izonzo) River, which flows directly into the Adriatic, was the site of one of the bloodiest battles of World War I, between Italy and Austria (see chaps. 9 and 11; Hemingway 1929). East of the park, the fashionable resort at the lake of Bled is surrounded by a pastoral area with characteristic architecture in its farmhouses, barns and hay-drying racks (see chap. 8).

As a former, well-established part of the Hapsburg empire, Slovenia retains an Austrian character in both its villages and towns. In addition to Ljubljana, its capital, it includes the outskirts of the major, now Italian city of Trieste, which is locally spelled Trst. It was once Austria's main Adriatic seaport. Nearby is the region of the Karst limestone pits, whose name geologists use as a generic term for comparable phenomena throughout the world. Also nearby, the village of Lipica is the original but still active source and training ground for the magnificent white Lipizzaner horses of Vienna's Spanish Riding School.

Slovenia has its own Slavic language (see chap. 7), differing from the Serbo-Croatian that prevails in the lands to the south. There, in Croatia, Bosnia and what remains of Yugoslavia, the so-called Dinaric Alps, though not high enough to be considered an actual part of the Alps, are geologically continuous with those of the Dolomites and Julians (see chap. 3). The Dinaric Alps are a rugged region where the 1984 Winter Olympic Games took place at Sarajevo, in the placid days before the murderous Yugoslav wars of 1991–95 (see chap. 11). Northeast of the Julians, the Stein Alps, on the border with Austria, lead to the Slovenian town of Maribor and to the plains of Hungary.

Chapter 3

How Peaks Got There

Mountain Formation, Part 1

Overall Structure of the Alps

The Alps are the highest mountains of western Europe. As a setting, they are magnificent and powerful. They dominate the habitats, homes and habits of all local living things. The mountains are a good place to start in an approach to understanding the richness (and complexity) of the region's natural and human domains, especially in their relationships to each other.

The length of the Alpine chronology is impressive, exceeding 350 million years. Some of the mountains came up through the earth 40 million years ago, after others had emerged from the sea 65 million years ago; still others go back through the Jurassic, Triassic and Carboniferous periods to more than five times that many years ago (see table 1).

Geographically and geologically, the Alps differ markedly according to three major groups: western, eastern and southern. The first two of these groups further separate into two roughly parallel chains, one of which is the northern chain while the other is the main crest of the Alps. The western mountains form an arc around the northwest border of Italy, while the eastern ones run straight to the east. The southern group is in a world apart, sharply cut off from the other two groups, but geologically continuous with the Dinaric Alps of the western Balkans. Map 10 shows these differences in the language of geological characteristics.

Between the northern and main-crest chains, one of the largest tectonic features of the Alps as a whole is a discontinuous west-to-east rift that extends over the entire length of the Alpine system, from Grenoble through the valleys of the Isère, Arve, Rhone, Reuss, Rhine, Inn, Salzach, Enns, Salza and Leitha Rivers, reaching all the way to the Danube east of Vienna.

All of these rivers escape from the rift by cutting through the northern chain or, finally, through the right bank of the Danube. Leonardo da Vinci took note of this when he wrote that "rivers which cut through them [the mountains] flow towards the north" (1938, 1:356). The reason for this is that the northern chain is lower and more easily breached than the main watershed chain. The latter is composed of harder rocks and is continuous over the entire Alpine range, in the sense that it is not cut through by any rivers.

Types of Alpine Mountains

All mountains, though of different ages, develop in three overlapping stages: rock origin, upheaval and erosion. In the Alps, the mountains are mainly of two basic types: most of the older ones are of the igneous type, which emerged from the molten magma deep inside the earth; most of the younger ones are of the sedimentary, stratified type, first formed on the earth's surface but under the sea. The igneous rocks, being composed mostly of silicon compounds, have a slightly acid chem-

TABLE 1. Geological Chronology

Era	Period	Began Years Ago	Alpine Event
Cenozoic	Quaternary		
	Holocene	100,000	Würm glaciation
	Pleistocene	2,000,000	Other ice ages
	Tertiary		
	Pliocene	7,000,000	
	Miocene	20,000,000	Adamello eruption
	Oligocene	38,000,000	Bregaglia massif
	Eocene	54,000,000	
	Paleocene	65,000,000	Alps emerge ex sea
Mesozoic	Cretaceous	140,000,000	Alp uplift starts
	Jurassic	195,000,000	Dolomites formed
	Triassic	230,000,000	Geosyncline starts
Paleozoic	Permian	280,000,000	Hercynian massifs
	Carboniferous	345,000,000	Briançonnais
	Devonian	395,000,000	Karnic Alps
	Silurian	435,000,000	
	Ordovician	500,000,000	
	Cambrian	570,000,000	
Precambrian			

istry, while the sedimentary rocks, being mostly limestones, are more strongly alkaline. This difference is vital for the distribution of the Alpine plants (see chap. 5). A small number of the mountains are volcanic (now dormant); their rocks are products from erupting lava after it reached the air.

The sedimentary mountains are the most prevalent ones in all parts of the Alps, and the three stages of their formation are most clearly known, so even though they are not the oldest ones, they are a good place to start. One should remember, however, that during most of this lengthy process, the older mountains, though not yet completely formed, were already "there" and much farther along in their development.

Early Insights into Rock Formation

Others before Leonardo da Vinci, such as Ovid and Boccaccio, have noted that marine fossils found far from the sea in Italy meant that the sea was formerly there, but Leonardo was the first to extend this finding to the Alps. In one of his simpler statements, he wrote that "the ancient beds of the sea became chains of mountains" (1938, 1:341). Not satisfied with then-current theological concepts, he was passionately interested in how the mountains came into existence. At the risk of becoming a victim of the Inquisition, he explored the Alps extensively (Uzielli 1890) and recorded his insights, some of which were four centuries ahead of his time. During his Alpine travels and in his workshop, he studied the rock strata and fossils that he and others found, as clues to his search for theories of mountain formation.

Among his findings, he wrote, "Marine shells that are seen on high mountains, which have formerly been beneath the salt waters, are now found at so great a height, together with stratified rocks, once formed from layers of mud carried by the rivers" (1938, 1:374). This single short sentence spans an enormous range of today's geological knowledge: (1) that the rivers were the major sources of the rocks, (2) the formation of the rocks into strata, (3) the mechanism whereby they were formed, (4) the briny venue where this occurred, (5) the ensuing uplift and (6) the evidence for it in the form of fossils. He also explained the origin of the fossils: "When the floods of the rivers which were turbid with fine mud deposited this upon the creatures which dwelt beneath the waters near the ocean borders, these creatures became embedded in this mud" (1938, 1:330).

Theories of Stratified Rocks

We may now compare these early insights with the understanding of the same phenomena today, which, incidentally, still greatly depends on the study of rock strata and fossils (Heierli 1983; Schaer 1972; Collet 1974). The fossils interested Leonardo especially for proving that the Alps came out of the sea. He noted that the fossils were of many different kinds. Today their main interest is in paleontology, in the classification of their hundreds of species as gastropods, cephalopods, ammonites, nautiloids, trilobites and so on, and in their uses for the chronology of the geological ages.

The history of the stratified mountains, in the light of modern knowledge, goes back to the beginning of the Triassic period, about 230 million years ago, when rivers began to deposit silt from what was then the south coast of Europe into the northern part of the large Tethys Sea. (Named after a Titaness who was the wife of Oceanus, its local remnant is the Mediterranean.) Under the gradually increasing weight of the incoming sediments, the supporting section of the earth's crust, which is thinner under the seas than under the continents, began to sag. After a time, it sagged even more rapidly than the sediments were being added. The result was a large depression called a geosyncline, which trapped enormous further sediments instead of their spreading out widely over the bottom of the sea. That was how the raw material for the Alps accumulated and formed into layers.

The geosyncline process occurred not in a simple basin but in several basins that grew or shrank with the passage of time, within the changing outlines of the Tethys Sea. The idea of the geosyncline was first proposed by J. Hall in 1859; it was given its name by J. D. Dana in 1873; and the concept was fully developed, almost in its present form, by E. Haug in 1900 (Collet 1974).

Under their own weight, the layers of deposited silt within the geosyncline were petrified into sedimentary rocks, such as sandstones and limestones. Some of the older strata, being at greater depth and under more pressure from above, along with higher heat from below, transformed into crystalline metamorphic rocks, such as gneiss, schist and marble, or even sank back into the molten magma.

The sedimentary rocks remaining untransformed were those in the upper layers of the geosyncline and are thus of more recent origin. In the Alps, these are mainly limestones (calcium carbonates), though some, which include oceanic components, are dolomitic limestones, which also contain magnesium. The metamorphic rocks of the limestones are marble. Marble is less common in the Alps than gneiss and schist, which were more prevalent in the lower, older strata and derive from sediments rich in silica (the sandstones). Some of the gneiss, however, comes from igneous rocks.

Stratified Mountain Uplift

The next stage of the process was the upheaval of the Alps, which began under the sea during the middle of the Cretaceous period, about 100 million years ago, when the sediments were still being added. The mountains began to emerge from the sea near the end of that period, about 65 million years ago, having spent most of their existence entirely underwater. Remarkably, this means that, for 160 million years, the complex gestation process of the Alps was in process before the summits first came up for air (and this only for the average chronology, while at some locations, such as the Dolomites, even the limestones have much longer geological histories). Underwater rock formation continued until the end of the Oligocene period, about 20 million years ago.

Already in the nineteenth century, geologists understood, from the topography of the Alps, that the uplift of the mountains was a response to some form of pressure from the south (Lubbock 1896). Geologists speculated that this thrust occurred for various reasons, such as shrinkage of the cooling earth (the "baked apple" theory) or concentration of the continents in the northern hemisphere, of which the latter is a more valid reason. Since the 1960s, the geologists have generally agreed, in principle at least, that convergence of the African and European lithospheric plates, which support the respective continents, pushed the smaller Italian plate northward between them and thereby lifted the Alps out of the geosyncline, with peripheral lesser thrusts through the western Balkans and eastern France. This horizontal force then squeezed the strata upward, out of the geosyncline. That was the basic, prevailing process for the uplift of the stratified mountains, which is known as plate tectonics.

It is evident that the great longitudinal rift through the Alps from Grenoble to Vienna, which is situated between the main and northern crests, is part of the overall folded structure of the Alps in response to the thrust from the south. This suggests that the overall structure resulted from a fundamental tectonic process that occurred over the entire length of the Alps, even though the geological compositions and even the local mechanisms of the folds are not homogeneous throughout.

Leonardo da Vinci struggled mightily but unsuccessfully, as did all others for more than the next 500 years, with trying to explain how the mountains were lifted out of the sea. Leonardo did, however, come up with two ideas, namely, drying up of the sea and buoyancy: "The earth and the mountains will emerge out of the sphere of the water lightened by this part, and will also make itself lighter by the weight of the water that rested upon it, and will come so much the more to raise itself towards the sky" (1938, 1:373). Both of these ideas have some relevance to the Alps, though buoyancy applies mainly to rocks emerging out of the magma, rather than mountains emerging out of the sea.

Mountain Formation, Part 2

Deformation of Strata

Before the Alps began to emerge from the sea, most of their strata had become solid rock, resistant to deformation, though the lower ones were more pliable because of heat from inside the earth. The plate-tectonic force was so great that the rocks, whether rigid or not, were drastically deformed, being folded, crumpled, upended, ruptured, transported or slid over each other, as revealed by exposed strata in various parts of the Alps. This did not escape the sharp eyes of Leonardo, who wrote, in the course of his mountain climbing, "In every hollow at the summits of mountains you will find folds of rock strata" (1938, 1:332).

A large and historic example came to light in 1841 near Martin's Loch in the Glarner Alps of eastern Switzerland, when Escher von der Linth first found large areas of older strata, up to 50 kilometers long, lying above younger ones. He did not publish this sensational discovery, for fear of being called insane, but he took his students on field trips there, and after Albert Heim published the finding in 1870, it virtually revolutionized Alpine geology (Collet 1974; Neustadtl 1990). Today, the most accessible part of the overthrust is restricted to those who have special permits and is an unusual example of a purely geological nature sanctuary (Neustadtl 1990).

In the northern Swiss Alps, especially in their prevalent limestones, one can see the great variety of deformations of strata. At the upper end of the Üschinental, the east ridge strata are mostly tilted upward away from the valley, while those of the west ridge are contorted in irregular ways. Yet at the very top of the latter, the spectacular Tschingeloch-tighorn, with its row of spires as jagged as its name, is built up with perfectly horizontal layers, in this case of shale. Farther west, near the Diablerets hamlet of Anzeindaz, the Pierre Q'Abotze is a narrow spire with prominent strata pointing almost straight up and cut off squarely across the top. The folded and eroded limestone mountains continue through most of the northern chain to the eastern border of Switzerland at the Santis, a peak with rough, rocky slopes overlooking the Rhine.

Peripheral Limestones

East of the Rhine, the structure of the northern chain of the Austrian Alps differs markedly from the north Swiss chain by the strata being more horizontal and less disturbed. Most geologists agree that the northern Austrian chain, which partly borders Germany, traveled as an entire unit, virtually intact, from somewhere to the south. The location from which this transport started, whether from near the central chain or all the way from the Dolomite region, is undecided. Either way, the distance traveled, without significant contortion, is impressive.

The limestone Alps of France include those of the Maritime Alps and those of the western Dauphiné and Savoy. Most of these, like those in Austria, being peripheral to the main tectonic thrust through the axis of Italy, are relatively free from violent folding. However, in the region of the Grande Chartreuse, some of the ridges have sharp summits. These are the result of erosion cutting through the flat upper parts of the relatively undisturbed strata. The Maritime Alps also offer examples of powerful erosion, where the strata are cut through by the rivers. Of these, the gorges of the Roya, Var and Verdon Rivers, with locally vertical sides, are particularly spectacular.

Below the fortress of Entrevaux, the V-shaped Var Valley is crossed by an unusual structure that resembles a segment of the Great Wall of China. It descends to the river from the ridges on both sides, with a rectangular opening at the bottom through which the river flows. This structure of harder rock above the limestone matrix provides a natural fortification, which is enhanced by the military fortress that is built on it, high above the eastern side of the valley. Such valleys with a V-shaped cross section are the long-term result of erosion by rivers, as distinct from U-shaped valleys produced by glaciers (see chap. 4). Since the Maritime

Alps, being the most southern of all the Alps, had little or no glaciation, the V-shaped valleys predominate in that region.

The Folded Mountains of the Main Crest

The mountains that form the main crest of the Alps incorporate several important differences from those described up to this point. The great peaks of the Zermatt group, between Monte Rosa and Mont Blanc, are remnants of a major fold (or group of folds) in the sedimentary and metamorphic rocks, which is called the Pennine nappe.

In the Pennine nappe, the dominant rocks are metamorphic, mainly crystalline schists produced in the lower strata of the geosyncline, from which most of the overlying sedimentary rocks have vanished by a combination of erosion and transport. Geologists estimated that the average thickness of former rocks above the existing Pennines was about 3,000 meters (9,843 ft.). The sharp ridges of the peaks resulted from erosion between adjacent glaciers, of which the classical example is the four-sided Matterhorn. In addition to erosion, huge masses of the upper strata moved bodily northward and deformed in the process under the thrust from the south, thereby forming most of the Bernese Alps.

In Austria, the rocks of the main crest are crystalline types called Austrids or Tirolids. At the highest part of the Hohe Tauern, on the Austrian crest, geologists found a "window" where rocks resembling those of the Pennines emerge to the surface. The area involved, which centers at the Grossglockner, measures 180 kilometers from west to east and 30 kilometers from south to north (see map 10). After geologists found the Tauern window in 1903 and a smaller one in the lower Engadine, they thought that the Pennine nappe reached all the way eastward to these windows, where it protruded through overlying rocks that had not yet eroded away (Collet 1974). Since then, more detailed studies have revealed that the Pennine and other nappes are much smaller and less uniform than previously thought and that the Pennines as such do not actually reach into Austria (Rutten 1969).

The Southern Alps

The southern Alps include the Bergamasque, Adamello and Brenta groups; the Dolomites of Italy; the Julian Alps of Friuli and Slovenia; and, north of them, the Karnic, Karawanken and Stein Alps on the south-

Nicholas Shoumatoff at Mont Blanc Brenva. (Photograph by N. and N. Shoumatoff.)

North face of Aiguille de Bionnassay with hanging glaciers. (Photograph by N. and N. Shoumatoff.)

North Slope of Mont Blanc with seracs and snow strata. (Photograph by N. and N. Shoumatoff.)

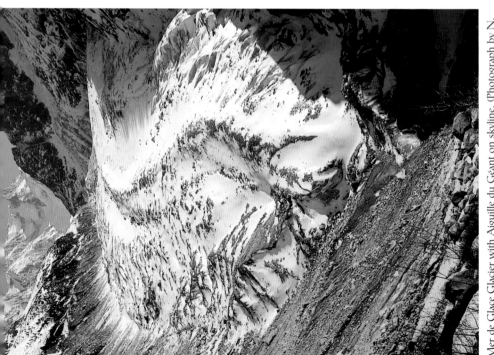

Mer de Glace Glacier with Aiguille du Géant on skyline. (Photograph by N. and N. Shoumatoff.)

Aiguille du Midi with cable cars crossing Mont Blanc range. (Photograph by N. and N. Shoumatoff.)

Nicholas Shoumatoff, Jr. at Breithorn and Upper Theodule Glacier with crevasse. (Photograph by N. and N. Shoumatoff.)

Matterhorn and Dent Blanche from Monte Rosa summit. (Photograph by N. and N. Shoumatoff.)

Monte Rosa Nordend with view of Bernese Alps. (Photograph by N. and N. Shoumatoff.)

Matterhorn Glacier and north face of Matterhorn. (Photograph by N. and N. Shoumatoff.)

Spectators investigating blue ice under rock debris on Glacier du Mont Miné. (Photograph by N. and N. Shoumatoff.)

View from Monch of lenticular clouds over Aletschhorn and Aletsch Glacier. (Photograph by N. and N. Shoumatoff.)

Nicholas Shoumatoff, Jr. (age 16) and Alex Shoumatoff (age 11) viewing Finsteraarhorn from Grunegghorn. (Photograph by N. and N. Shoumatoff.)

Snow cornices on the Monch (foreground) and Jungfrau (background) seen from the west ridge of Eiger. (Photograph by N. and N. Shoumatoff.)

Eiger north face and Wetterhorn from the west ridge of Eiger. (Photograph by N. and N. Shoumatoff.)

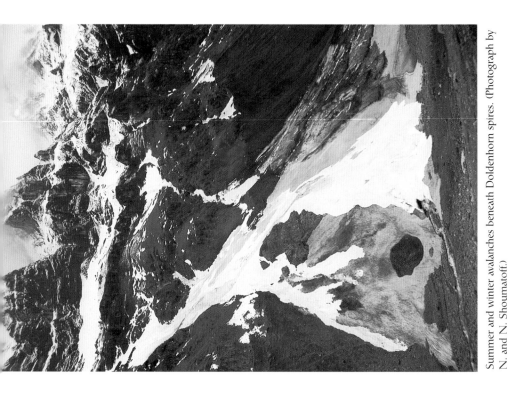

Summer and winter avalanches beneath Doldenhorn spires. (Photograph by N. and N. Shoumatoff.)

Gasterntal cows beneath Balmhorn buttress with folded strata (recumbent fold). (Photograph by N. and N. Shoumatoff.)

Francis Chaux on Glacier Blanc, Écrins. (Photograph by N. and N. Shoumatoff.)

Martin Busch Hut at the base of Mutmalspitze, Ötztal. (Photograph by N. and N. Shoumatoff.)

Summer glacier skiers at Piz Bernina and Piz Roseg. (Photograph by N. and N. Shoumatoff.)

Ancient lateral glacial moraines beneath Similaun peak. (Photograph by N. and N. Shoumatoff.)

Nina Shoumatoff at north face of Hohe Tauern from Kitzsteinhorn. (Photograph by N. and N. Shoumatoff.)

Abandoned stone hamlet and Vanoise peaks, upper Arc Valley. (Photograph by N. and N. Shoumatoff.)

Avalanche trails and pastures alongside Bietschhorn, Lötschental. (Photograph by N. and N. Shoumatoff.)

Arid peaks, creeping avens, and glacier crowfoot in the Col de La Bonnette. (Photograph by N. and N. Shoumatoff.)

Lichen *(Rhizocarpon geographicum)*, Oschinensee. (Photograph by N. and N. Shoumatoff.)

Larches and Vaccinium shrubs in fall colors, Chamonix. (Photograph by N. and N. Shoumatoff.)

Alpine buttercup (*Ranunculus alpestria*) on Almenalp. (Photograph by N. and N. Shoumatoff.)

Alpine willowherb (*Epilobium anagallidifolium*) and Glacier de Ferpecle in the Val d'Herens. (Photograph by N. and N. Shoumatoff.)

Spring anemone (*Pulsatilla vernalis*) in the Sexten Dolomites.
(Photograph by N. and N. Shoumatoff.)

Mountain houseleek (*Sempervivum mortanum*) on Bietschhorn.
(Photograph by N. and N. Shoumatoff.)

Moss campion (*Silene acaulis*) near Martin Busch Hut. (Photograph by N. and N. Shoumatoff.)

Edelweiss (*Leontopodium alpinum*) in upper Val d'Isère. (Photograph by N. and N. Shoumatoff.)

ern frontier of Austria. They are limestone and crystalline rocks with special characteristics that distinguish them from others of these general types to the north and west. In the southern Alps, these differences include (1) a wider range of geological ages, (2) more dramatically eroded shapes, (3) overlying coral reefs, (4) significant volcanic deposits and (5) separation from the main Alpine crest by a long, visible fault. The southern Alps are not a coherent chain of peaks but a collection of mountain groups that differ markedly from each other as well as from other Alpine mountains. In one way, however, the southern Alps resemble the northern chain of Austria, namely, in their relatively horizontal strata without significant deformations.

Such undisturbed strata are surprising in the famous jagged spires of the Dolomites, which resulted from an erosion process closely associated with coral-reef activity. Requiring shallow water, the reefs, once started, kept growing above the stratified rocks, just below the surface of the water, while the underlying strata were still sinking in the process of the geosyncline. This was a long, slow process. The vertical span of the reefs is as much as 1,000 meters (3,281 ft.), within which no sedimentary strata are visible. This indicates the great age of some of the reefs and of the limestone strata beneath them, going back more than 200 million years, to the Triassic period (Schaer 1972).

Because of these reefs, which are more resistant to erosion than the other limestones, some of the major towers, especially those in the western Dolomites, such as the Sella group, have characteristic flat tops while the sides have almost vertically eroded beneath them. The chemistry of the corals derives from the sima (magnesium silicates) of the oceanic crust, which thereby introduced magnesium into the dolomitic limestones, in addition to the calcium that is basic to all limestones. (Throughout the world, limestones that include magnesium as well as calcium are called dolomitic, named after the eighteenth-century French mineralogist Dcodat Gratet de Dolomieu, who first analyzed these rocks, and who was also keenly interested in volcanoes. The author of the name of the Dolomites was Theodore de Saussure, son of the great Horace-Bénédict de Saussure, who is called the father of Alpine geology [see chap. 13].)

North of the eastern Dolomites, the Karnic Alps are an outcrop of ancient (Paleozoic) crystalline rocks from beneath the strata of the geosyncline. They are among the oldest mountains in the Alps. Farther east, in the Julian Alps, the limestone peaks have eroded, in the absence of coral activity, into the form of pointed pyramids with sloping sides.

Great Subduction Fault

In addition to the upheaval of the mountains by compression in the geosyncline, a major part of the mountains south of the main crest in all of Austria and much of Switzerland rose up in a process more typical of plate tectonics, namely, subduction of one lithospheric plate under another. What occurred in the Alps was the subduction of the Italian plate and of its Balkan extension under the more rigid European plate to the north. The evidence for this is a continuous fault that begins at Ivrea at the outlet of the Valle d'Aosta, directly south of Monte Rosa, and reaches eastward for 700 kilometers (435 miles) north of the Italian lakes, of the Dolomites and of the Bergamasque, Karnic, Karawanken and Stein Alps, through the Pustertal and the Gailtal, to the eastern tip of all the Alps (see maps 7 and 10).

At the Tonale Pass, north of the Adamello peaks, within a few hundred meters along the surface of the ground, one can move from rocks 20 million years old to others 300 million years old on the north side of the fault. The older rocks were lifted out of the fault as much as 6,000 meters vertically, but their upper, younger strata have eroded away (Schaer 1972).

The fault is bifurcated in two places, where important geological changes occur. One of these is just east of the Tonale Pass, where the southern branch is relatively short. Here the Adamello peaks are situated between the fork's two branches and are the largest formation of volcanic (now dormant) activity in all the Alps. The other volcanic deposits in the Alps are also located close to the fault. This indicates that the breach in the earth's upper crust, caused by the fault, facilitated the release of lava.

The other bifurcation in the fault occurs at the northern tip of Lake Maggiore, where the northern branch heads up toward the Simplon Pass and the southern one to Ivrea. Just north of this bifurcation is the location of the anomalous massif of the Alpe Arami (anomalous massifs are discussed in a later section of this chapter). Throughout the length of the fault, the geological histories are dramatically different on its opposite sides. It is presumed that major movements of the land have occurred both along the fault and into it. The fault thus forms a major break between the southern and main chains of the Alps.

Both the geosyncline and the subduction processes depend on a concept of plate tectonics that became generally accepted in the 1960s. The definitive, convincing evidence was the spreading of the ocean floors from midocean rifts, rather than mountain building. This also involved a belated recognition of the theory of continental drift as formulated by Alfred Wegener in 1910. Before 1935, Collet (1974) explicitly applied this concept to the formation of the Alps.

The rate of movement between the plates is uncertain, but geophysical measurements indicate that the uplift of the Alps is continuing and responding to the pressure from the south. On the Italian side of the St. Gotthard Pass, the recent rate of upheaval (since 1900) was 0.7 millimeters per year, practically the same as the average for the past twenty million years, while north of the pass, between Altdorf and Lucerne, it is virtually zero (Schaer 1972).

Mountain Formation, Part 3

Granite Massifs

The highest of all the Alpine peaks, namely, Mont Blanc and several others that dominate their respective ranges, resulted from another, distinct process not directly related to plate tectonics. These are the several granite massifs, whose presence is restricted to the western and central Alps. The granite massifs are of subterranean, rather than submarine, origin. Their rocks formed before the beginning of the geosyncline, near the beginning of the Permian period, about 280 million years ago. They are autochthonous in the sense that they are still at the same geographical location where they originated. Unlike the stratified mountains, they did not move with the thrust from the south. With roots reaching far into the depths of the earth and with relatively small exposed parts, like the tips of icebergs, the massifs were essentially immovable horizontally.

What made them rise to such heights, geologists believe, was primarily the force of buoyancy, because the granite that composes them is lighter than the surrounding basalt within the molten magma. Before rising to their present heights, the massifs lay beneath several thousand feet of sedimentary strata, which are no longer there. Attempts to reconstruct the original strata show that Mont Blanc, when it was not as high as it is today, lay beneath 3,700 meters (12,000 ft.) of sedimentary rock that has almost completely eroded away (Lubbock 1896). The resulting loss of weight increased the effective buoyancy.

The massifs of Mercantour, Argentera, Mont Blanc and St. Gotthard are on the main crest, while those of Pelvoux, Belledonne, Aiguilles Rouges, Gran Paradiso and the Aar are in the lateral ranges. Those that are on or around the main crest seem to form a backstop against the northward movement of the stratified mountains under the thrust from the south. The highest peaks of the Bernese Oberland, including the Jungfrau and the Finsteraarhorn, belong to the Aar massif, with the exception of the Eiger, which is a limestone mountain.

Other massifs of similar type and age are those of Sardinia, Corsica, central France, the Vosges, the Black Forest and Bohemia, all of which, including those in the Alps, are called Hercynian. (This appears to be a misspelling. They were not named for Hercynia, a nymph who was a playmate of Zeus's daughter Persephone. The spelling apparently should have been *Orcynian*, the old Greek name for the large forest between the source of the Danube and Bohemia [Caesar 51 B.C.], where geologists first identified mountains of this type.)

Anomalous Massifs

Not all of the massifs in the Alps are from the ancient Hercynian period. The granite peaks of the Bregaglia group, including the Sciora, Cengalo and Piz Badile, are much younger, dating from the Eocene period, about 40 million years ago. They emerged through the geosyncline after the sedimentary rocks had formed. The Sciora group is one of the few places in the Alps with narrow, needlelike granite spires resembling those of the Mont Blanc range.

Another anomalous small massif, a satellite of the St. Gotthard, is the Alpe Arami near the north end of Lago Maggiore and near the fork of the great subduction fault. Geologists have recently identified titanium crystals at the Alpe Arami, of a type that is estimated to have formed as much as 200 miles below the surface of the earth, based on laboratory studies of the temperature required to form them (Broad 1996; Dobrzhinetskaya, Green and Wang 1996).

The Hercynian massifs are not the oldest parts of the Alps. Among older ones are the Karnic Alps of Friuli and a coal-bearing ridge called the Briançonnais, near the French-Italian border between the Montgenèvre and Izoard Passes. Its origin goes back to the Carboniferous period, some 350 million years ago. It never sank into the geosyncline, and it was free from sediments entirely.

Erosion

Previous sections refer to the removal of significant amounts of material by erosion from the Alps. After rock origin and upheaval, this is the third and final stage of mountain formation. It involves various processes of erosion that have sculpted the mountains into their present shapes. The agencies of erosion are numerous, including glaciers, rivers, rivulets and waterfalls; avalanches of snow, mud, earth and rocks; expansion from frost and the melting thereof; softening of the earth by patches of late-melting snow, which can result in soil creep (solifluction); and wind and electric storms. Such human activity as deforestation, quarrying and road building can accelerate erosion, while reforestation and avalanche barriers can retard it.

Stratigraphy

In the matter of erosion also, Leonardo da Vinci had accurate early insights: "The rivers that wear away the sides of these mountains lay bare the strata of the shells. . . . The rivers have sawn through and divided the great Alps as revealed by the order of stratified rocks on one side of the river corresponding with those on the other" (1938, 1:340, 357). Not only was he aware of the role of the rivers in sculpting the mountains and exposing their strata, but he also identified the sequence of the individual strata, which is called stratigraphy.

Centuries later, stratigraphy became a key to geological chronology, and it still is, along with fossil evidence and the more recent development of radioactive-dating techniques. Correspondence between strata on opposite sides of a valley was one of Leonardo's major discoveries. One can verify it, even without laborious stratigraphy, at the lower end of the Gasterntal in the Bernese Alps, where a large Z-shaped fold in the exposed rocks of the Doldenhorn dramatically corresponds with the folds on the face of the Balmhorn across the valley. Here, several powerful jets of water shoot out between the strata and indicate that the interior of the mountain is under pressure, even well above the valley floor.

Leonardo also wrote about erosion "wearing away the sides of these rivers until the intervening banks become precipitous crags" (1938, 1:329). This can be seen in a number of places throughout the Alps, and map 7 shows how rivers have cut through the entire mountain region. A dramatic example is on the south face of the Dent de Morcles, at the point where the upper Rhone makes a sharp turn from the west to the north, on its way into Lake Geneva (map 3). Collet (1974) identified thirty-five different strata on this great cliff, according to their composition, and according to nineteen different geological periods from the Paleozoic to the Eocene. This single rock face spans almost the entire stratigraphic history of the Alps, as a result of erosion by the great Rhone River.

Such stratigraphy of the cliffs in different parts of the Alps indicates major differences in ages between the western strata and those in the east and south. In the Pennine and north Swiss Alps, about two-thirds of the strata are from the Jurassic period or younger, less than 190 million years old; while in the eastern and especially in the southern Alps, the proportion is reversed, with most of the strata being from the Triassic period, up to 230 million years old (Schauer and Caspari 1975). In all of these stratigraphies, the bases of the cliffs reach into the ancient, pre-Alpine, pre-Carboniferous strata, which have been exposed by erosion.

Practical Geology

Natural and Other Disasters

The larger features of the Alpine peaks break up into side valleys, large and small, and into thousands of streams, waterfalls and glaciers that are slowly but steadily wearing away the buttresses and slopes of the peaks. These lesser features of the landscapes add much to the beauty of the Alpine world and also to its ecology, being important components of the local environment (see chap. 4). Unfortunately, the great differences in altitude between the peaks and the valleys correspond to tremendous potentials for traumatic impact from rockfalls and landslides and from avalanches and glacier breaks, not all of which are natural (see chap. 4).

Leonardo da Vinci made special note of such disasters: "Fragments of mountains, which have already been stripped bare by the rushing torrents, fall headlong into these very torrents and choke up the valleys, until the pent-up rivers rise in flood and cover the wide plains and their inhabitants" (1938, 2:288); "these floods occur at the time when the sun melts the snow on the high mountains" (1:363). He also observed, however, that people living in the Alps can cause damage to the mountains: "The rivers make greater deposits of soil when near to populated districts than they do when there are no inhabitants. Because in such places the mountains and hills are being worked upon, and the rains wash away the soil that has been turned up more easily than the hard ground which is covered with weeds" (1:328).

Fourteen glaciers hang above the Italian Val Ferret on the Mont Blanc side, cutting into the steep, mostly barren slopes that rise 8,000 feet above the valley. Piles of gravel below the glaciers reach not only down to the valley floor but also most or all of the way across it. They block the Dora Baltea from its normal riverbed and make it flow in a twisted, snakelike course. For years, these rock piles were thought to be terminal moraines formed by the processes of glacier movement and erosion, but some of them happened in a far more violent way (Parker and Orambelli 1981). In November 1920, a large mass of rock detached itself from the Peuterey Ridge below the Mont Blanc summit and fell to the Brenva Glacier. When it hit the glacier, it shattered and spread gravel and boulders across the lower end of Val Ferret. In 1717, two hamlets in the upper part of the valley, with their people, houses and cattle, were buried by a similar rockfall from the Aiguille de Talèfre, which pulverized when it hit the Glacier de Triolet. Exceptionally beautiful alpine flowers now bloom on the piles of rock debris under which the hamlets are entombed. Large boulders from this rockfall are also scattered over the valley floor.

On opposite sides of the Rhone, destructive landslides have occurred from the Dents du Midi and from the Diablerets at Derborance (see chap. 9). A mountain close to the village of Elm collapsed and buried half the village when a slate quarry undermined it (see chap. 13). In the Gran Paradiso Park, a road being built from the Val Savranche to the Col de Nivolet was abandoned, after emerging from a tunnel, because falling boulders destroyed the roadway faster than it could be repaired. We have seen major landslides in the Val Veni and in the Dolomites, where the pile of fallen rock stopped a few feet from a house. The immense potential energy stored in these mountains, as a result of their upheaval, can and occasionally does spell tragedy.

Mining in the Alps

The minerals that the Alps have made available from inside the earth are valuable in various ways, both natural and technological. The rivers that have sources or tributaries in the Alps carry products of high-altitude erosion back to the lowlands from which earlier rivers had delivered these same materials to the mountains as erosion debris, through the medium of the geosyncline, in a segment of a very long-term natural cycle. As part of this process, erosion of the granite massifs brings valuable minerals to the lowland plains from deep inside the earth. With the arrival of human populations in the Alps, the availability of such minerals has increased by direct extraction through mining.

Alpine people have a 4,000-year-old tradition of mining and metallurgy, from the Bronze Age and the Halstatt period onward. This tradition is still alive in the Alps of eastern Austria. There, next to the Styrian village of Eisenerz, the Erzberg, which is an entire mountain of iron ore, provides raw material for major steelworks in the nearby town of Donawitz. The removal of the ore from the Erzberg has produced spectacular spiral steps going all the way around the mountain from bottom to summit, making it look like a gigantic Babylonian temple of the ziggurat type. Its supply is expected to last another century. The ore is converted to steel at Donawitz by the oxygen-blowing process that was developed there and at Linz in Upper Austria. This process now makes almost half of all the world's steel.

Sites for mining other metals, such as copper, tin, zinc, lead and gold, also go back to pre-Roman times. The gold mines of the Hohe Tauern, high on the slopes around Heiligenblut and the valley of Badgastein, were a major source for gold coins of the Roman Empire. These mines were commercially active until the early twentieth century, when their yield became insufficient to pay for the cost of operation at their relatively inaccessible places. They are still available as a tourist attraction and for nugget-finding contests by international teenage and adult groups. Rousseau mentions gold mines in the Swiss Valais; de Saussure visited some still functioning at Alagna south of Mont Rosa at the end of the eighteenth century; and Achille Ratti (later Pope Pius XI) visited one started up by a British company below the east face of Monte Rosa in the 1880s.

Useful Alpine Minerals

The geological richness of the Alps is indicated by the great variety of their rocks and minerals. These are the building blocks from which the mountains are built. They include not only the prevalent limestones, granite, porphyry, pegmatite and other crystalline rocks but also a wide assortment of valuable minerals and of semiprecious and precious stones. Among these are magnificent large, natural emerald crystals (a form of beryl), tourmalines, garnets, cinnabar, amethysts, smoky quartz and clear rock crystals (see chap. 13). Three hundred years ago, one location in Switzerland yielded 50 tons of clear rock crystals before the lode was effectively exhausted. People have been using various Alpine rocks for the construction of houses, roads, bridges and dams. In the southern Alps especially, stone slabs are the most common cover for roofs.

Table 2 gives a partial list of Alpine minerals containing the

TABLE 2. Alpine Minerals

Element	Minerals
Aluminum	bauxite, cryolite, corundum
Antimony	stibnite
Arsenic	arsenopyrite, realgar
Barium	barite
Beryllium	beryl, chrysoberyl, phenakite
Bismuth	bismuthinite
Cadmium	greenockite
Calcium	calcite, aragonite, limestone
Carbon	graphite
Chlorine	halite
Chromium	chromite, uvarovite
Copper	covelite, cuprite
Fluorine	fluorite
Iron	magnetite, hematite, pyrite
Lead	galena, wulfenite
Magnesium	dolomite, epsomite, magnesite
Manganese	hausmanite, milarite, pyrolusite
Mercury	cinnabar
Molybdenum	wulfenite
Nickel	nickeline, millerite, annabergite
Niobium	betafite
Potassium	orthoclase, muscovite, biotite
Silicon	quartzite, chalcedony and many silicates
Silver	argentite, proustite
Sodium	halite
Sulfur	pyrite, glauberite
Tin	cassiterite
Titanium	ilmenite, rutile, titanite
Tungsten	scheelite
Uranium	uraninite
Vanadium	vanadinite
Yttrium	gadolinite
Zinc	smithsonite, zincite, hemimorphite
Zirconium	tonalite

Location	
Adamello	cummingtonite, tonalite
Aosta	uvarovite
Bavaria	pyrolusite
Bergamo	zincite
Binnental	realgar
Bleiberg	wulfenite

TABLE 2—Continued

Location	Minerals
Carinthia	vanadinite, hemimorphite
Como	beryl, chrysoberyl, dolomite, epsomite, annebergite, cassiterite, uraninite
Dauphiné	quartzite
Erzberg	magnetite
Glarus	slate
Grisons	hausmanite, orthoclase
Idria	cinnabar
Ossola	phenakite, covelite, betafite
St. Gotthard	fluorite, hematite, ilmenite, rutile
Salzberg	glauberite
Salzkammergut	halite
Schwaz	pyrite, proustite
Sondrio	serpentine, rhodochrodite
Styria	aragonite, talc
Ticino	garnet
Trento	calcite, chalcedony, biotite
Val Anzasca	arsenopyrite
Val Sesia	cryolite, corundum
Zermatt	lasulite
Zillertal	magnesite

aforementioned and other useful chemical elements, as well as some of the locations where they occur. In addition to those in the table, other Alpine rocks and minerals that are valuable or useful in themselves include talc, gypsum, gneiss, slate, serpentine, marble, sandstone, hornblende, zeolites and rock salt. Leonardo was most interested in the rocks that sculptors could use: "Monbracco above Saluzzo, a mile above Certosa, at the foot of Monte Viso, has a mine of stratified stone, white as marble of Carrara and flawless, and hard as porphyry or even harder. My gossip the master Benedetto, the sculptor, has promised to send me a tablet for the colours" (1938, 2:564). To give an idea of the complexity of the various Alpine silicates, the chemical formula for one of them, zoite, is $Ca_2Al_2CO(OH)(SiO_2SiO_7)$. Oxygen is the most prevalent element of the Alpine minerals, at 50 percent, and silicon is the second, at 30 percent, which does not leave much for all the other elements.

Most of the localities for these minerals are in or near the granite massifs, the subduction fault and other parts of the main crest, in places that have had access to the deeper parts of the earth. The St. Gotthard massif is an especially rich source. The concentrations of different minerals vary with irregularities in the earth's crust, in the magma and in the outer mantle. Some of the most interesting mineral specimens have been found not only through prospecting and mining but also in the construction of railway, roadway and aqueduct tunnels, dams and other excavations. The cinnabar mines at Idria in Slovenia are one of the earth's three most important sources of mercury, thus a treasure for the world's dentists and their patients, for the makers of thermometers and for the Chinese craftspeople who produce exquisite cinnabar carvings.

Chapter 4

Alpine Climate, Snow, and Glaciers

Climate

Elements of Environment

The hundreds of magnificent glaciers and year-round snowfields that are so visible and accessible in the Alps are there because the local climate allows them to exist. The avalanches and glaciers that descend from the peaks transfer snow and ice from upper to lower slopes. This transfer has a moderating effect on the entire Alpine climate. Climate, snow and glaciers are thus mutually linked as key elements in the Alpine physical environment.

Snows, glaciers, their outlet streams and the clouds from which they derive are all forms of water. Leonardo da Vinci, who was keenly interested in the behavior of water, expressed this vividly: "Now rushing on with headlong course, now appearing bright and calm; now mingling with the air in a fine spray, now falling down in tempestuous rain; now changed to snow or storms of hail, so also now turning to ice. . . . At one time it becomes changed to the loftiest clouds, and afterwards it is pent up within the deep caverns of the earth" (1938, 2:101).

The situation of the Alps, between the latitudes of 44° North and 48° North, is midway between the tropics and polar regions. The longitude of the Alps is also intermediate between the oceanic lands to the west and the deeply continental Eurasian heartland. Between these extremes, some characteristics of both oceanic and continental climates occur in the Alps. The main difference is that the ocean, like snow and ice in the mountains, smooths out the seasonal cycle and thereby effects a moderate local climate, which does not occur in the continental heartland.

However, the most significant difference within the Alpine region is that between the temperate conditions in the valleys and the arctic-type conditions on the year-round snows, which are made more pleasant by the power of the high-altitude, temperate-zone sunlight (which can also be harmful to exposed skin). In many places, this facilitates skiing and climbing at all seasons. The most controlling dimension of climate in the Alps is neither latitude nor longitude but altitude.

Temperature and Atmosphere

Travelers to the upper Alps soon become aware that the air gets colder at higher altitudes. For example, in the eastern Alps, as one rises from 300 to 3,000 meters, the average temperature changes from 9°C to −6, which is a drop of 15°. In July it drops from 19 to 2 for a difference of 17°, while in January it drops from −2 to −12 for a difference of 10°. Thus the decrease is less in winter than in summer, because of the moderating effect of winter snow. Moreover, as these figures show, at 300 meters the average decrease from July to January is 21° compared to 14° at 3,000 meters, so that, at the higher elevation, the year-round temperature is more stable too. (Table 3 summarizes and gives the sources of climate data in this chapter.)

The difference between years of maximum and minimum January average temperatures is 24° at 582 meters and 22° at 3,106 meters, while in July these differences are 25° and 16°, respectively. These data show that, at higher altitude and in winter, average temperature changes less between years. These tendencies for the higher-altitude and winter temperatures to be more stable also apply between hours within a day. At Innsbruck, at 582 meters, the temperature changes from −5°C at 9 A.M. to +1 at 2 P.M. in January, which is a rise of 6°, and it changes from 13 at 5 A.M. to 24 at 3 P.M. in July, which is a rise of 11°. Meanwhile, on the Zugspitze, at 2,963 meters, it rises from −11.5 at 6 A.M. to only −10 at 1 P.M. for a difference of 1.5° in January and from +0.5 at 4 A.M. to 3 at 2 P.M. for a difference of 2.5° in July.

In contrast to these ambient air temperatures, which are measured above the ground, the surface temperatures can be quite different, especially at upper elevations. The high crags, where they are free from snow or ice and exposed to the sun, can reach a temperature hotter than 38°C (100°F) even where it drops below 0°C (32°F) every night. (At 3,000 meters, the average above-ground temperature is below freezing for ten months per year, versus three months per year at 300 meters.) Such wild daily swings in surface temperature are a challenge to which

TABLE 3.   Climate Data

A. Average Climate Data—East Alps (Turner 1970)

Altitude meters	300	1500	3000
Pressure atmospheres	0.97	0.83	0.67
Radiation cal/sq cm/day	225	240	385
Temperature degrees C			
Jan.	−2	−5	−12
July	19	11	2
Difference	21	16	14
Total year	9	3	−6
Days of frost/year	95	165	292
Days of snowfall/year	30	90	190
Days of snow cover/year	50	170	350
Max. snow depth meters	0.3	1.5	5.4
Precipitation mm/yr	—	750	1400
(North Swiss Alps	1200	2050	2800)
(Inner Swiss Alps	850	1600	2450)

B. Interior E. Alps

	Innsbruck	Davos	Sonnblick
Altitude meters	582	1561	3106
Temperature degrees C average (Veyret 1972)			
Winter	−2.2	−6.2	−12.9
Summer	17.0	11.2	0.2
Difference	19.2	17.4	13.1
Total year	7.9	2.7	−6.5
Precipitation mm average (Veyret 1972)			
Winter	133	178	383
Summer	342	373	459
Difference	209	195	76
Total year	838	959	1734

Exterior W. & N.

	Grenoble	Thones	Santis
Altitude meters	214	625	2500
Temperature degrees C average (Veyret 1972)			
Winter	1.7	−1.7	−8.5
Summer	18.9	16.0	4.1
Difference	20.6	17.7	12.6
Total year	10.4	7.5	−2.6
Precipitation mm average (Veyret 1972)			
Winter	250	473	471
Summer	294	401	853
Difference	44	72	382
Total year	1161	1642	2397

TABLE 3—Continued

Interior E. Alps	Innsbruck	Arosa	Sonnblick
Altitude meters	582	1864	3106
Temperature degrees C (Schneider 1981)			
Jan. average max.	9.0	5.0	−3.9
Jan. average min.	−14.6	−15.9	−25.4
Difference	23.6	20.9	21.5
July average max.	33.0	20.8	9.1
July average min.	7.8	3.0	−6.8
Difference	25.2	17.8	15.9
Wind velocity days (Schneider 1981)			
Calm (< 1 km/hr)	154	—	42
Storm (> 75 km/hr)	16	—	98

the high-altitude plants and animals much adapt. The reason for these swings is that the high-altitude air is thinner (with a pressure of 0.97 atmospheres at 300 meters versus 0.67 atmospheres at 3,000 meters), so that the power of the sun's radiation increases markedly (from 225 to 385 cal/sq cm/day).

At the summit of Mont Blanc (4,807 m), the pressure of the air is only slightly more than half as great as it is at sea level, and the sun's radiation is correspondingly more intense. This indicates the need for special protection from sunburn. The oxygen content also drops in proportion to the pressure, which, at the altitudes of the upper Alps, can interfere with energy and sleep or even cause high-altitude sickness, unless one is adequately acclimatized.

Precipitation

With only partial relationship to temperature, the precipitation in the upper Alps, whether as rain or snow, varies widely, both seasonally and geographically. At high altitude, it is greater in the northern and western parts of the range, because those are the directions from which much of the bad weather arrives. For example, at 3,000 meters in the north-central Swiss Alps, the annual precipitation is 2,800 millimeters per year compared to 2,450 millimeters per year in the inner Swiss Alps. Meanwhile, at Santis, at 2,500 meters in the northeast Swiss Alps, the average precipitation for the three summer months is 853 millimeters compared to 471 millimeters for the three winter months.

This seasonal pattern, with more precipitation in summer than in winter, is typical for most of the Alps. It is a pattern that is favorable for winter climbers and for spring and summer skiers, but less so for winter skiers, who are often disappointed by the lack of snow (as during the Winter Olympic Games at Innsbruck). However, in the north and west French Alps, which are closer to the Atlantic Ocean, the seasonal pattern is more oceanic and more constant. At Thones, at 625 meters in Haute-Savoie, the pattern is even reversed, with somewhat more precipitation in winter (473 mm) than in summer (401 mm).

Since temperature is lower at high altitudes, and with less difference there between summer and winter, it often snows in the mountains in summer when it is raining in the valleys. Summer snowstorms, even long-lasting blizzards, are not unusual in the Alps. The intensity of these blizzards is accentuated by the tendency of average precipitation to increase with altitude over most of the slopes in the Alps (850 mm/yr. at 300 m. in the inner Swiss Alps vs. 2,450 mm/yr. at 3000 m.).

On the Schynige Platte, above Grindelwald, at 2,068 meters (6,785 ft.), we were trapped for two days by a 20-inch snowfall in July (and we saw the grim faces of those who were coming to see the alpine garden at the annual meeting of their botanical society). We were also marooned by a four-day August blizzard at the Mutthorn Hut, at 2,901 meters (9,512 ft.), during a twelve-day Bernese glacier trek. Long-lasting summer blizzards can spell disaster for the most experienced mountaineers (see the Bonnatti story in chap. 12).

In the Alps, the weather can change rapidly and unpredictably, especially at high altitude in summer. A summer snowfall often closely follows fast-moving cigar-shaped or lenticular clouds or an electrical storm. Such a storm is most dangerous on exposed rocky summits, which act like lightning rods. The charged atmosphere, even without lightning or before it strikes, makes one's hair and eyebrows stand on end and tingle while the tips of one's ice ax buzz or give off sparks. One should then get far away from all metal objects, and one should wear clothing with plastic fasteners rather than metal zippers or clasps.

As Julius Kugy wrote: "Heaven help you in a Kanin thunderstorm! It is the worst mountain for lightning in the Julians. Once the sky darkens, be off quickly! The Kanin has no cairn; the lightning destroys them at once. . . . Each time I climbed the peak, I found on the top fresh clefts and hollows in the rock, the work of lightning, revealing ammonites and other marine fossils. One thunderstorm which I experienced on the Kanin ridge, cowering in a cleft, is among the grimmest of my memories" (1934, 152). His comments show how such storms contribute to the erosion of peaks.

The great Kandersteg guide Hans Hari was hit by lightning on the Dent Blanche. Thereafter electrical storms in the mountains were painful for him until he found that a spoonful of powdered coffee would relieve the discomfort or, as he thought, neutralize the charge.

Winds

In the eastern Alps, storms with a wind velocity greater than 75 kilometers per hour occur six times more often at 3,106 meters than at 582 meters (98 vs. 16 days per year). The high-altitude gales add to the windchill factor for trekkers, climbers and skiers. In addition to the prevailing north and west winds, a warm dry south wind often occurs in the Alps, especially in spring and autumn. It is called the foehn and is the Alpine counterpart of the mistral of Provence, the sirocco of Italy, the *mltimi* of Greece and the Santa Ana and chinook of the American West. The foehn is usually benign and helps the grapes to ripen, but sometimes it is so powerful and destructive that it breaks trees and blows the roofs off chalets. It does not come from Africa, as previously thought, but is of more local origin, losing its moisture as it cools while climbing a south slope, and reheating as it compresses, minus its moisture, on its way down the north side.

A writer of macabre Gothic tales found solace, with a mystical touch, in the benign side of the foehn.

> Beyond, reared the immense buttresses of the Dents du Midi, their streaked precipices tilting up at violent angles toward the stars. And while my eyes lifted to sift their way between the darkness and the snow, I became aware that It was already coming down the village street. It ran on feathered feet, pressing close against the enclosing walls, yet at the same time spreading from side to side, brushing the window panes, rustling against the doors. And, as it passed, it touched me—touched me through all skin and flesh upon the naked nerves, loosening, relieving, setting free the congealed sources of life, so that magic currents, flowing and released, washed down all the secret byways of the spirit and flooded again with full tide into a thousand dried-up cisterns of the heart. Far overhead, across those desolate bleak shoulders of the mountains, ran some sudden

softness like the rush of awakening life—and was gone. (Blackwood 1962, 166)

When winds encounter an obstacle in the form of a mountain, the eddies produced may become stationary vortices, which, depending on the shape of the mountain, may be horizontal or vertical. Leonardo da Vinci, in one of his theoretical speculations, described how a vertical vortex can form and how it can become stationary: "When a wind has been divided by mountains [and then reunites] . . . the movement which it makes after this reunion will be of a rotary nature in the shape of a twisted column; and if the winds which are thus reunited should be equal then this column will not change its position" (1938, 1:404). Such vortices, whether horizontal or vertical, affect the formation of snow cornices (discussed in a later section of this chapter).

Snow

Types of Alpine Snow

At 3,000 meters in the eastern Alps, the average days per year of frost, snowfall and snow cover are respectively 292, 190 and 350. Each of these averages is four or more times the corresponding number of days at 300 meters. These data, along with the appearance of snow-peak landscapes, show how snow is a major element of the upper Alpine environment. However, both the data and the landscapes fail to reflect the enormous variety of snow phenomena that are important for safety of travel over the mountains on foot or ski. Seligman (1936), in his classical study of Alpine snowfields and ski fields, describes twenty-four different types of snow, such as sand snow, corn snow, sun crust, spring crust, marble crust, firn snow, spring powder, foam crust, ablation snow, penitent snow and various forms of hoar. Such differences can be rather temporary, since snow that is cold, crisp and crunchy in the morning can become soft like mashed potatoes in the afternoon. LaChapelle (1969) gives a diagram of forty different shapes of snow crystals of ten basic types, but their variety is actually endless. The variables of altitude, temperature, humidity, snow depth and wind velocity during snowfall have infinite combinations affecting the character of snow for driving, walking, skiing and climbing.

At the microscopic level, this is the subject of a famous passage by Thomas Mann.

The little soundless flakes were coming down more quickly . . . tiniest drops of water, which in freezing had darted together in symmetrical variation—parts, then, of the same anorganic substance which was the source of protoplasm, of plant life, of the human body. And among these myriads of enchanting little stars, in their hidden splendour that was too small for man's naked eye to see, there was not one like unto another; an endless inventiveness governed the development and unthinkable differentiation of one and the same basic scheme, the equilateral, equiangled hexagon. Yet each, in itself—this was the uncanny, the anti-organic, the life-denying character of them all—each of them was absolutely symmetrical, icily regular in form. They were too regular, as substance adapted to life never was to this degree—the living principle shuddered at this perfect precision, found it deathly, the very marrow of death. (1927, 480)

The exquisite snow crystals that Mann describes are extremely short-lived. Almost as soon as they fall, they begin to change, losing the structure of their microscopic branches, becoming more rounded, and then joining with each other in a large and changing variety of ways. Supplementing Seligman's work, these changes and their dynamics are actively studied, both in the laboratory and in the field (Brody 1988).

Avalanches

When snow becomes too deep on a steep slope, it often gives way as an avalanche. Probably no other phenomenon in the Alps has occasioned as much study as avalanches. They not only are a hazard to trekkers, climbers and skiers but also damage forests, buildings and even whole villages. They often fall in the same places year after year, but in some years the avalanches grow catastrophically and are then more likely to deviate from their usual channels, which is when they cause the most damage.

Predicting avalanches depends on many factors, including temperature, moisture, time of day, time of year, steepness and direction of the slope, depth and density of the snow and especially any variation and looseness between its layers. Avalanches are of the dust or slab types, mostly wet or dry. Dry dust avalanches happen at lower temperatures, at lower altitudes in winter or higher up all year round. They can be highly destructive because of the blasts of air that they entrain. If trapped by this type, one can swim up through it during the few minutes before it settles and hardens, if one is lucky enough to be alive and uninjured. Dust avalanches usually start rather narrow and widen on the way down. Slab avalanches are more uniformly wide from top to bottom, with a deeper break through the surface of the snow at the top. Slab avalanches, which usually fall from spring to early winter, are often more lethal and destructive than the dust type, because the snow that they bring down is typically more dense and massive and often, though not always, wet. Moreover, like the dust type, slab avalanches entrain destructive blasts of air.

Avalanches can be dangerous even in summer. The Kandersteg guide Hans Hari almost perished in one of these summer avalanches. He had just climbed the Similaun with a female client when, on their way down, a violent blizzard hit them. The nearby Italian Similaun Hut was closed, and they had to reach the Martin Busch Hut farther down the Austrian side. Suddenly, a major avalanche buried Hans. With incredible strength and presence of mind, he literally swam up through the loose snow to the surface several feet above him, before the snow could settle and harden around his body like concrete. He found his client standing in a daze but unhurt at the side of the avalanche, still tied to him with a rope. They then groped their way for 4 kilometers through the dense blizzard, with zero visibility, until Hans, with phenomenal instinct, located the hut and brought his client and himself to safety. They were both badly shaken and exhausted.

Many slopes above alpine valleys have rows of steel fences on them, to prevent avalanches from starting or to arrest them if they do. For the same reason, many villages rigorously protect the forests on the slopes above them. In the avalanche-prone Lötschental, some houses have thick concrete walls on the uphill side as fortification against avalanches. Many villages use explosives to deliberately produce avalanches at precisely known times, preventing larger ones from happening at uncertain times in the future. Avalanches sometimes start from a natural shock, such as the fall of a snow cornice from a ridge above. Undesirable man-made avalanches occur when a skier makes a horizontal traverse across a steep snow slope, and his or her track cuts through the cohesiveness of the snow surface, allowing an avalanche to develop.

Snow Cornices

Overhanging snow cornices typically occur at the crest of a ridge or summit of high snow peaks in the Alps. They are among the most spectacular of mountain phenomena but can be a mortal danger for a climber who is unaware that he or she is walking on one, with nothing beneath him or her except a protruding shelf of snow that may give way from the climber's added weight. In a blizzard, when visibility is poor or zero, this danger can be particularly great. The only safe rule is to walk far enough away from the edge to be sure one is supported by terra firma. The basic cause for the growth of cornices is wind, specifically the rolling action of wind on the leeward side of a ridge, like that which causes stationary lee-wave clouds (clouds on the lee side of the ridge).

Cornices, however, are not a simple phenomenon. Seligman (1936) describes suction and pressure cornices, the sinking and involution of cornices, temporary and permanent cornices, alternating and double cornices, the lines of fracture of cornices, the development of firn-snow ridges and cornices over crevasses. Among the most unusual are those cornices that point in opposite directions along the same ridge, as they do between the Blümlisalphorn and the Weissefrau, apparently because of a stationary vortex.

Glaciers

Great Ice Ages

In 1837, Louis Agassiz, at the age of thirty, was president of the Swiss Society of Natural Sciences. He startled his colleagues, and even shocked the biblically minded ones, by demonstrating that the "erratic" granite boulders on the limestone hills near his home in Neuchatel had originated in the Bernese Alps, from which immense glaciers had brought them many thousands of years ago (Lunn 1914). This idea had been put forth earlier by his friend Charpentier, by the engineer Venetz, by the chamois hunter Perraudin and even by an anonymous woodcutter on the Brünig Pass. Both Venetz and Charpentier presented lectures about it to natural history societies, which were published in 1833 and 1841. In 1787 and 1802, B. F. Kuhn and J. Playfair published papers on the subject. However, all were ignored except Agassiz, who became known as the father of the ice-age concept, even though he fully acknowledged the work of others.

Since then, geologists and glaciologists have worked out the chronology of the major ice ages, as shown in table 4. In addition to the erratic boulders, the ice ages have left other evidence of their passage. This includes the *roches moutonées,* rocks whose surfaces have been gouged and polished by the movement of the ancient glaciers over them. Some of these can be seen above the trail north of the Gemmi Pass and on the slopes above Lech in Austria.

More important evidence is the terraced structure of major glacial valleys, such as the upper Rhone and the Inn Valley near Innsbruck. The terraces resulted from the alternation between the ice ages, when erosion occurred, and the warm interglacial periods, when erosion stopped. Thus the older glacial terraces (Gunz and Mindel) are nearest the top of the slopes, while the more recent (Riss II and Würm), whose defining erosion started out of the previous ones, are near the valley bottom (Heierli 1983).

Glaciologists and paleoclimatologists estimate the characteristics of climate that existed in ages past by cutting out vertical cores from within a glacier to identify the corresponding ages of its different layers. Their studies include measurements of oxygen-18, which is slightly less concentrated in snow that falls at lower temperatures. Analyses of encapsulated

TABLE 4.   Chronology of the Major Ice Ages

Years Ago	Condition
30,000	
	Würm glaciation
120,000	
	Riss/Würm interglacial
180,000	
	Riss II glaciation
190,000	
	Riss I/Riss II interglacial
220,000	
	Riss I glaciation
240,000	
	Mindel/Riss I interglacial
420,000	
	Mindel glaciation
480,000	
	Gunz/Mindel interglacial
530,000	
	Gunz glaciation
590,000	
	Danube glaciations (several?)
2,000,000	

air—that is, literally, samples of ancient air—from the deep layers of glaciers and mountain snow provide a means for studying the long-term history of the Alpine environment. This in turn helps scientists to understand current trends and perhaps better predict the near future.

Not only the ice ages themselves but also the interglacial periods are important for the natural history of the Alps. They give clues to the evolution and ancient migrations of Alpine plants, animals and peoples of the Old Stone Age (see chaps. 5, 6 and 7). In ages past as well as now, both glaciers and avalanches, despite their occasional destructiveness, have been important in the natural ecology of the Alps, bringing snow and ice down from the peaks into the valleys. There the avalanche snow may last for months or even years, while the glaciers may last for thousands of years. By thereby moderating the local climate, these deposits of snow and ice promote the growth of locally specialized alpine plants.

Glacier Formation

At high elevations where the snow melts little or not at all, it accumulates until some escapes in the form of either avalanches or glaciers, though some is also lost by evaporation. Glaciers descend from upper snowfields through crags, screes, meadows, moors and sometimes even forests, until they end at a stream or pond or just melt into the earth, thus often forming a physical link between the upper and lower parts of a mountain slope.

The process of glacier formation takes place in a series of stages. In mountain glaciers, the first stage is usually an upper snowfield, high on the slopes of a mountain. In the snowfield stage, the amount of snow that accumulates in the course of a year exceeds the amount that moves downward by the force of gravity. The downward movement slowly accelerates within the snowfield until it equals the amount that accumulates above. This occurs at an invisible line across the snowfield, called the equilibrium line. If this line itself moves downward, the glacier is growing, but if the line moves upward, the glacier is shrinking. In either case, the snowfield is the main source of material that feeds a glacier, but whether it is increasing or decreasing is not easy to measure.

In the course of its downward movement within the snowfield, the character of the snow gradually changes, initially below the surface, from its original fine or powdery structure into small granular crystals called corn snow. This is the beginning of the second stage of glacier formation, which is intermediate between snow and ice, and is called firn in German and English, névé in French. At the surface, the point where the fine white snow ends and the firn appears is often marked by a sharp visible line across the glacier, which is called the firn line. This is not the same as the equilibrium line. With further downward movement, the air between the grains is slowly expelled and the grains coalesce, gradually forming larger crystals up to 8 or 10 inches across. The large crystals then freeze together and become solid ice.

This is the beginning of a glacier's third and last stage, during which it is a true river of ice, which gradually melts as it moves into the lower and warmer altitudes. At a point where the ice melts faster than it flows down, the glacier comes to an end. The end has various anatomically inconsistent names: tongue, snout, bottom, foot, toe or terminus. Some end in a smooth well-rounded tongue with little or no water flowing out, while others plunge into a glacial lake, but most end in streams of water, with or without an ice cave from which it flows.

In the Alps, glaciers occur in many shapes and sizes. The classical types flow down from a snow peak at the end of a valley and, if large enough, may continue along the valley floor. They can flow straight down or in a spectacular sweeping curve. On the way down, they may be joined by smaller glaciers descending from the sides. Some glaciers are steep and others are nearly flat, depending on the terrain. Some, called piedmont glaciers, flare out into a spatulate form on a wide slope when they emerge from the bottom of a gully. Others, called hanging glaciers, rest on a shelf above a slope or are merely patches of ice plastered against a near-vertical crag, apparently frozen to its surface. Some glaciers seem to tumble down the side of a mountain in spectacular disarray. Some fall over a cliff in an icefall, breaking up into a wild jumble of cracks and blocks of ice called seracs, but may again form a solid glacier at the bottom. Others flow around one or both sides of the cliff and may or may not come back together at the bottom. Still others simply end at the top of the cliff, from which blocks of ice occasionally fall.

One glacier in the Alps even flows both ways, like a miniature arctic ice cap. It is perched at the top of the Jungfraujoch, a saddle between the peaks of the Jungfrau and the Mönch. In the interior of that glacier, scientists have established a laboratory of paleoglaciology, where its history and the mechanics of its movement are being studied.

Some visible existing glaciers flow on top of older ones that are darker and densely filled with crushed rocks. This occurs on the Austrian side of the Similaun peak, where both glaciers end abruptly in a sharp, vertical break near the Martin Busch Hut. There one can clearly see how the beautiful younger glacier has been riding on top of the dark ancient one, which ends a bit farther down.

Erosion by Glaciers

Almost all glaciers carry rocks that they have picked up along their way. Some of these rocks scrape the ground over which the glaciers flow and are the means by which glaciers gouge out the troughs and valleys that contain them. Most glaciers flow in such a trough, which they have carved. With rising global temperatures, some glaciers have pulled back, leaving part or all of their troughs empty. On a larger scale, many of the existing major Alpine valleys and lakes were formed by the huge former glaciers of ages past, providing the habitats for natural and human life.

Many glaciers have picked up rocks from the sides of their trough, carried them along for a while and later deposited them into continuous piles on the sides of the trough to form lateral moraines. The lateral moraines may or may not be symmetrical, and some are left high and dry when a glacier shrinks. At the point where two glaciers join, their adjacent lateral moraines usually merge and form a single line of rocks that is called a medial moraine. Large glaciers that result from several tributary glaciers may carry two or more medial moraines and thereby acquire a picturesque striped pattern on the surface. This is evident on the Great Aletsch Glacier, the largest of all the Alpine glaciers, and is a familiar sight on the great glaciers of Alaska. A medial moraine is free from crevasses and is usually the safest place to walk.

Some glaciers are beautifully white in winter and spring but not in summer, when rock debris that has fallen on them from the slopes above is exposed. These glaciers become dark in summer, often with a thick layer of rocks that completely covers their surface. Meanwhile, as the glacier slowly melts in the course of its downward travel, large and small rocks that had been invisible inside the glacier often emerge at the surface and join the debris that is already there. There have been many reports of glaciers regurgitating objects that had fallen into deep crevasses. Our Grindelwald guide, Hans Burgener, thus found his father's watch on the surface of the Aletsch Glacier, downstream from where his father had fallen into a crevasse and perished some years earlier.

Some large glaciers, such as the Glacier du Mont Miné in the Pennine

Alps, form natural ice caves at their bottom, from which accumulated meltwater gushes out in a powerful stream. One can see that the ice inside the cave of this glacier is pure pristine blue, while its surface above is dark with a thick layer of debris. More accessible large glaciers such as the Rhone Glacier have artificial ice caves cut into their lower ends each year as an attraction for tourists. The ice inside the cave of the Rhone Glacier is likewise pure blue. In these two glaciers, in contrast to the ancient Similaun Glacier, one does not see a significant accumulation of rocks or debris inside the ice at the lower end. When all glaciers finally end, they deposit the rocks and debris that they have carried along into piles called terminal moraines. When a glacier shrinks, identifying the locations of its earlier, stranded terminal moraines are one means for reconstructing the glacier's history (Messerli et al. 1978).

Glacier Movement

In 1841, on the great Unteraar Glacier in the Bernese Alps, three campers received a distinguished visitor. The campers were Louis Agassiz of Neuchatel; his German wife, Cäcilia; and Edouard Desor, a French political refugee who became a doctor of science from Heidelberg (Lunn 1914). The visitor was Professor James D. Forbes from Scotland. The camp, ironically called the Hotel des Neuchatelois, was at first an overhanging boulder and later a canvas-covered frame with a wooden floor, at the site of the present Lauteraar Hut, which was previously called the Pavillon Dollfuss. Mme. Agassiz did the cooking and complained about the lack of privacy, but she and her husband spent five summers there in the company of various assistants and visitors, after which Agassiz wrote a book about glaciers (1847).

Agassiz mapped the Unteraar Glacier. Using stakes, as suggested by Forbes, to measure its movement, he found that its average speed was 100 meters per year but it was moving faster in the middle than at the edges. Agassiz promptly announced his findings to the scientific world—so promptly that it ended his friendship with Forbes. The following year, in 1842, Forbes made such measurements on the glaciers above Chamonix with similar results, which were the basis for his theory that glaciers flow like a viscous liquid, such as honey.

This theory involves, among other things, the observation of crevasses. Early observers were puzzled by crevasses that mostly run across a glacier but point forward at the edges, giving the appearance that they are being dragged forward. This gives the false impression that the edges are moving faster. Actually, in the manner of viscous liquids, these outer edges of a glacier are moving slower (as Agassiz and Forbes observed), because of drag from contact with the earth. Here, however, a critical difference between ice and a viscous liquid comes into play. Ice can be deformed only by compression, not by tension—that is, by pushing, but not by pulling, which causes the ice to crack. The drag at the edges of a glacier has the effect of pulling back from the faster-moving center, which results in cracks. The cracks, moreover, being tension failures, are at right angles to the direction of pull. This is why the cracks point forward at the edges.

The faster movement of a glacier's center can sometimes be observed directly. Wide glaciers, such as the Glacier du Géant (as seen from above), may have surface waves that are farther forward in the middle, resembling the flow of a liquid film, contrary to the pattern of the forward-pointing outer crevasses. Another way that one can be aware that a glacier is moving is from the noises it makes when it cracks. When the sound reverberates between surrounding peaks, as on the Great Aletsch Glacier near the Concordia Hut, the noise that accompanies the formation of crevasses resembles the roar of artillery. Such roars may be one reason why Alpine people formerly thought that the mountains were inhabited by dragons.

In 1856, another major player, John Tyndall (who made the first ascent of the majestic Weisshorn five years later), entered the scene. He too measured the Chamonix glaciers and made experiments with ice, forcing it into molds to deform it, and causing it to melt from pressure—also showing what every server of drinks now knows: that ice cubes stick together when they melt. After heated arguments with Forbes, Tyndall put forth a new and now widely accepted theory that a glacier moves because of pressure from its own weight upstream, acting against various forms of resistance from the bed in which it moves. From Tyndall's experiments, scientists know that the movement is a combination of deformation, melting, sliding and refreezing. The meltwater, caused by the pressure and by the heat of the sun, partly refreezes inside the glacier but partly trickles down to its underside, where it lubricates its movement. Thus some movement occurs by deformation of the glacier itself, some by slipping at the bottom (Tyndall 1871).

Modern theories have been built up from these basic concepts and typically formalize them into mathematical equations (Hutter 1982).

However, some of the critical variables, which concern the interaction between the bottom of a glacier, its underlying rock and any intervening layer of meltwater, are hard to measure, since glaciers may be hundreds of feet thick. Walking on a glacier, one often hears it gurgling underneath. Such melting at the bottom makes a glacier move faster in the daytime than at night and faster in summer than in winter.

Recent Trends

Despite the difficulties of verifying the theoretical analysis of glacier movement, the actual movement of Alpine glaciers is evident from historical information and from widespread periodic measurement. Alpine prints from the seventeenth and eighteenth centuries which show glaciers reaching into the valleys appear to be exaggerations, but they are not. That period, when the glaciers were larger than they are now, is called the Little Ice Age—being little in comparison with the great ice ages of the distant past. Messerli et al. (1978) have charted the relevant chronology from the elevations of the Lower Grindelwald Glacier's tongue, obtained from pictorial evidence and positions of its terminal moraines, correlated with records of air temperature at Basel. They found that the Little Ice Age lasted from 1540 to 1820, with an interruption between 1750 and 1790.

In the seventeenth and eighteenth centuries, when many glaciers advanced and spread out into the valleys, some families lost their hereditary lands, and some villages were even destroyed. Two centuries later, when the glaciers retreated, they uncovered lands whose ownership became a legal problem. In most cases they became state or cantonal property rather than the property of local communes or individuals.

The glaciers that remain, of which there are several hundred in the Alps, vary in length from a fraction of a mile in Slovenia to the 25 kilometers (15 mi.) of the Great Aletsch Glacier in the Bernese Alps. Alpine countries have elaborate programs for measuring changes in their glaciers, mostly by the position of the end of each glacier. Switzerland has 117 glaciers, of which all but 8 or 10 are measured by this method annually. In 1900, 90 percent of these glaciers were retreating; in 1920, 70 percent were advancing; in 1950, 99 percent were retreating; in 1980, 75 percent were advancing. These changes can be quite rapid. From 1976 to 1977, the Lavaz Glacier in east Switzerland retreated 357 feet, but the following year, it advanced 303 feet. Since 1980, most Swiss glaciers have been rapidly receding, and since 1900, they have retreated more than they have advanced.

A recent global study of 200 glaciers, with data for various periods up to 1993 (Dyurgerov and Meier 1997), included 25 in the Alps and found that 20 of these had retreated based on their total areas, while 20 (not all the same ones) had retreated based on their calculated mass balances, expressed in terms of the equivalent height of water. This study concluded that "the contribution of glaciers to sea-level rise has increased greatly since the middle 1980s and even more steeply since the late 1980s."

Such measurements are important in various ways, mostly as an index of water supply and hydropower resources. Though the trend has not been steady, it forms part of the evidence for the global-warming effect. Another correlated indication is the upward migration of mountain plants on twenty-six Austrian peaks, currently at the rate of between 3 and 12 feet per decade (Yoon 1994). Another result is the marked reduction of available skiing areas.

Glacier Disasters

Keeping track of changes at the lower ends of glaciers is also important to provide warnings of possible glacier breaks, some of which have been disastrous. Early in the twentieth century, a large piece of the Blümlisalp Glacier fell into the Öschinensee and the water it displaced flooded the village of Kandersteg. A similar glacier break from the nearby Altels killed seven men and a number of cows. According to one report, "The wind in front of it carried cows to points 1,000 yards away and 1,000 feet above the spot where they had been lying" (Irving 1938, 76). Eighty-three people working on a hydroelectric project at Mattmark below Monte Rosa were killed when the Allalin Glacier broke off in 1965. The Vernagd Glacier in the Ötztal Alps advanced all the way across its outlet valley and formed a lake by damming up the upper streams. When the glacier retreated, the dam broke and released a destructive flood on the village of Vent (Field 1975).

In March of one year, the six small inns and all cow chalets in the Gasterntal were closed. Snow and ice were still on the ground, and the valley was generally bleak. The road was still blocked by a huge avalanche that falls every year near the Kander gorge. We sat on the porch of the Waldhaus Inn, near the large cow chalet, and enjoyed the remains of our picnic lunch. We thought we were entirely alone in the valley, but we suddenly realized we were not. The Swiss Army had been quietly arranging the equipment for its annual artillery practice, and we were startled when the guns suddenly opened fire. The roar of the guns was deafening in the deep canyon. That evening, while at dinner in Kandersteg, we learned from one of the soldiers that the noise had caused a glacier break that brought down the body of a young British climber who had perished on the Balmhorn in the 1920s, probably from a fall into a crevasse.

A widely known example of a fatal fall into a crevasse is that of the outstanding young French climber Louis Lachenal, who, with Maurice Herzog, had made the first ascent of Annapurna in the Himalayas, the first successful climb of an 8,000-meter peak. Later, while skiing on the Mer de Glace, he fell into a crevasse, where his warm body became tightly wedged in the narrowing space between the crevasse's ice walls, so tightly that, when his colleagues found him, they were unable to pull him out—even with the aid of a winch—before he died.

Crevasses are probably the most prevalent cause of climbing accidents in the Alps, because the crevasses are so numerous on almost every Alpine glacier. To exacerbate the danger, the crevasses are often hidden from view by snow bridges, especially after a snowfall. Experienced climbers constantly probe the terrain ahead of them with an ice ax.

When we, our two sons and the Swiss guide Hans Rubi were climbing the Lang (Long) Glacier at the upper end of the Lötschental after a four-day August blizzard, everyone in our party except coauthor Nina, including the guide, fell into one or more crevasses, though luckily not major ones. Later on that day, an English group followed us, led by the Austrian guide Steinlöcher (whose name means "one who makes holes in rocks"). Supposedly as a point of honor, the Austrian guide refused to follow in the Swiss guide's tracks and deviated too far to the right, where he fell into a rather deep crevasse (his clients did not). A ledge in the crevasse had stopped his fall, and he climbed out with the aid of his ice ax only. He then noticed that his sunglasses were still lying on the shelf below, whereupon he went back down, retrieved the glasses, climbed out again and nonchalantly led his group as though nothing had happened.

Another, less frequent hazard in the mountains are seracs, which are towers of snow or ice that can topple over unexpectedly, because of movement of their underlying snow or ice. Most often they occur on major glacier icefalls. They were named seracs by Horace-Bénédict de Saussure, using a French word that means "a chunk of cheese."

Precautions, experience and knowledge of the local terrain can go far in promoting safety of travel by foot or ski on snow peaks and glaciers. However, the hazards, especially of avalanches and crevasses, are always present and have caused many accidents and fatalities, even among the best mountaineers.

Chapter 5

Vegetable Kingdom

Ecology

Ecological Variability

Average temperature, atmospheric pressure and oxygen content decrease with altitude while solar radiation rises (see chap. 4). This combination of variables shortens the Alpine growing season six or seven days, on the average, for each 100 meters or 304.8 feet of altitude (Faverger 1972). It has the charming effect that the springtime gradually moves upward, so that one can see spring flowers from February or March in the valleys to as late as August or even September high above. From a distance, a more obvious effect is the difference in types of vegetation at different heights, from the forests below through the moors and open meadows to the zone of year-round snow.

To reach the level of year-round snow in the Alps requires a change in altitude from sea level to 3,000 meters (9,843 ft.). To reach the same conditions horizontally northward requires a trip of about 3,000 kilometers (1,864 miles), or a thousand times as far. (This is a change in latitude of 27°, and when this is added to the average latitude of the Alps, 46° North, one reaches 73° North. This is well within the land of the midnight sun, which begins at 67.5° North, where arctic conditions prevail.) This means that on the average in the Alps, the gradient of ecological change is about a thousand times greater vertically than it is horizontally on the surrounding plains.

This, however, is only one of several ways that the ecology of the upper Alps is more variable, within short distances, than it is on the plains below. Other factors are the differences in steepness, direction and total height of the slope; more rugged terrain with thinner or nonexistent soil; more intimate exposure (because of erosion) to bedrocks of differing

74

chemical composition (see chap. 3); total and seasonal differences in precipitation as rain or snow; shielding by surrounding mountains; and local effects, such as avalanches and glaciers (see chap. 4).

Forest Belts

The lowest belt of mountain forests, ranging from 600 to 1,600 meters (1,969–5,249 ft.) in altitude, is called the montane zone (Faverger 1972). Its precise upper and lower limits vary in different parts of the Alps and on different sides of individual mountains. After a lower band of oaks, spectacularly blooming chestnuts and occasional stands of maples, this zone is occupied mainly by beech and white fir in most of the Alps, though in the southern French Alps Scotch pine often takes the place of the fir.

Above the montane zone, up to 2,000 meters (6,562 ft.), the sub-alpine zone is the habitat of primarily coniferous forests. In most of the Alps, it begins with a layer of Norway spruce, which is gradually replaced by larch, a lovely deciduous conifer that turns golden yellow in the fall, loses its needles in winter and sprouts light green needles with bright red flowers in the spring. At the upper levels in the central Alps, the much-prized arolla pine *(Pinus cembra)* often mixes with or grows adjacent to the larch. In the eastern Alps, shrub pine *(P. mugo),* which can be almost impenetrable, displaces or mixes with the arolla pine and larch. Larch and shrub pine are thus the prevailing trees at the upper subalpine zone.

The prevalence of conifers at the upper altitudes and latitudes has been the subject of various explanations (Price 1981). Conifers are more primitive than broadleaf trees and have had more time to adapt to severe environments. Their narrow pointed tops more easily shed or withstand the weight of snow and the force of wind. Their tight needle-shaped leaves are less vulnerable to wind, cold and dryness. When the needles freeze, the moisture is squeezed out between cells, so the cells themselves do not burst. Conifers require less organic nutrients and survive more easily on rocky and acid soils. The evergreens begin photosynthesis earlier in spring without having to wait for new leaves to develop. Among the highest conifers, larches shed their leaves to conserve energy in winter. Meanwhile, shrub pine survives by hugging the ground. Near their upper limits, trees become dwarfed and crooked. Their stunted forest is called a krummholz. Some trees, battered by the wind, have a flag shape, with branches on one side only.

Alpine forest trees now grow almost only where the terrain is too steep or rugged to be used for fields and pastures. On such slopes, the original stands are often largely intact, and these are among the few surviving natural forests of Europe. Throughout the Alps, such forests are treasured and for the most part legally protected or regulated. They shield Alpine villages from avalanches, rockfalls and erosion. They also provide the villages with a continuing supply of building materials and fuel for heating and cooking, as long as this resource is not used beyond the limit of its own regeneration. In the past, woodsmen widely exceeded this limit by cutting and selling more lumber than was necessary to meet the needs of the Alpine people and by excessive clearing for hayfields and pastures. Even now, despite restoration of some of the forests by enlightened silviculture, they face a new and serious threat from industrial air pollution and acid rain (Mehr 1989).

Forest Utilization

Of all the Alpine countries, Austria has the largest and most important mountain forests (Würz and Stemberger 1975; Trzesniowski 1976). More than 40 percent of the country's total area is covered by forests, 48 percent of which are in the mountains on slopes steeper than 20°. These forests are 62 percent fir, 19 percent other conifers (including spruce, pine and larch), 10 percent beech and 9 percent other hardwoods (mostly birch, willow and poplar). Some 15 percent of the total is national forest, while the privately owned 85 percent has more than 250,000 owners, the great majority of whom own less than 50 acres. Austrian wood-using industries do not have significant forest properties and buy almost all their wood from individual owners of small woodlots, typically farmers who preserve and tend their woods carefully, regarding them as bank savings accounts from which they withdraw only as needed, for example, to buy a new tractor.

The growth rate of the Austrian forests is 3 percent per year while the amount consumed for all reasons is 2 percent per year, so the standing forest is increasing at the rate of 1 percent per year. Even individual owners must obtain permission from the government when they wish to cut more than 2 percent per year. Of the total wood used in Austria, 47 percent is for lumber, 21 percent is for wood pulp to make paper and synthetic textiles, 14 percent is for firewood, 13 percent is for plywood and other building products, and the remaining 5 percent is for other purposes, such as fences and various exports. These figures do not reflect the use of forests for private hunting preserves by the leading baronial families. These preserves include some of the oldest, finest and largest forest properties. Their owners occasionally sell some trees to finance the expenses of their hobby, but many of their trees are unfit for lumber because stags scrape them with their horns.

In Switzerland, the pattern of forest ownership is markedly different. Local communes own 68 percent; private individuals, 26 percent; and the state, including cantons, only 6 percent. In France, Italy, Germany and Slovenia, the forestry methods are similar, but separate statistics are not available for the mountain areas.

Those who cut trees in the Alps do so more carefully and with more hand labor than is customary in America. For example, instead of using cables to bring logs down from steep slopes, Alpine woodsmen will, if necessary, peel the logs by hand, which makes them slippery enough to slide down when guided by a hook at the end of a stick, like a boat hook. Larger logs are often sawed by hand or hewed into chalet timbers in the mountains. Even thin short logs that are used as firewood or to make newsprint are handled and stacked with remarkable care and neatness.

Upper Forest Limits

When the altitude is too high and the cold too severe for even conifers to endure, the forest ends completely and often abruptly (Tranquillini 1979). The altitude at which this occurs varies in different parts of the Alps, depending partly on latitude and distance from the ocean. It also varies among individual mountains and even between different slopes on the same mountain. Among the causes are the desiccating effect of the sun's radiation, exposure to cold and wind, and variation in the topography of a slope or of surrounding peaks. Where a slope is too steep, soil may never form or may erode away, leaving bare rock or scree. These factors reinforce or counteract each other, producing a rich diversity of tree-line heights, as table 5 shows for the north and south slopes on twenty-eight important Alpine peaks.

One can only speculate about some of these differences. According to the table, the forest of arolla pine with a fringe of larch on the north slope of the Matterhorn has the highest forest limit to be found in the Alps, much higher than on the corresponding slope of nearby Monte Rosa. This probably results from the Matterhorn's protected position south of the Weisshorn and Mischabel, both of which are higher than it. Monte Rosa, in comparison, is not only higher but also more massive and has far more snow than the Matterhorn. The east face of Monte Rosa is too vertical for forest growth, but the snows of its other slopes produce downward blasts of cold ("catabatic") wind that prevent the formation of forests. An identical situation occurs on Mont Blanc, with sheer cliffs on the south and east in Italy, snows and glaciers on the north and west in France (see map 8) and tree lines even lower than Monte Rosa's, especially on the sunbaked Italian side (Shoumatoff and Shoumatoff 1978).

TABLE 5.   Upper Forest Limits

Range	Location Peak	Peak Altitude in Meters	Tree-line Altitude in Meters	
			South Slope	North Slope
Maritime	Argentera	3,257	2,280	2,040
Cottian	Monte Viso	3,841	2,310	2,220
Écrins	Pte. Écrins	4,102	2,000	2,160
Vanoise	Gr. Casse	3,852	2,140	2,160
Gr. Paradiso	Gr. Paradiso	4,061	1,840	2,280
Mt. Blanc	Mt. Blanc	4,807	1,840	1,980
Pennine	Gr. Combin	4,314	2,180	2,040
Pennine	Matterhorn	4,478	2,270	2,490
Pennine	Monte Rosa	4,634	2,200	2,260
Bernese	Diablerets	3,210	1,750	1,840
Bernese	Balmhorn	3,709	2,130	1,980
Bernese	Jungfrau	4,158	2,040	1,950
Bernese	Dammastock	3,630	1,900	1,970
Glarner	Todi	3,614	1,900	1,940
Splugen	Surettahorn	3,027	1,830	1,890
Bernina	Bernina	4,049	2,020	2,260
Ortler	Ortler	3,905	2,320	2,210
Lechtaler	Valluga	2,809	2,130	2,070
Ötztaler	Wildspitse	3,772	2,030	2,100
Karwendel	Grubenkarsp	2,663	2,100	1,820
Dolomites	Marmolada	3,309	2,030	2,280
Zillertal	Hochfeiler	3,510	2,160	2,060
Hoch Tauern	Gr. Venedigr	3,674	1,900	2,000
Hoch Tauern	Gr. Glockner	3,797	2,100	1,760
Berchtsgdn	Watzmann	2,713	1,600	1,780
Dachstein	Dachstein	2,995	1,990	2,100
Julian	Triglav	2,864	2,160	1,590
Rax	Schneeberg	2,076	1,720	1,590

Where a slope above a cliff becomes less steep, herdsmen have usually cleared it from trees to enlarge a natural alpine pasture. However, a nineteenth-century program in the southern French Alps aimed to restore natural tree lines that unwise forestry and overgrazing had severely depressed (Dougedroit 1978). Two hundred years earlier, the aristocratic absentee owners became concerned about the destruction of their forests. Finally, in 1860 and 1882, despite objections from local herders, the French government enacted laws prohibiting deforestation and providing for restoration of the mountain forests. Today, the restored tree lines are essentially at the same height as the local natural ones, of which there are still many in that region. The restoration techniques included the transplantation of seedlings complete with balls of earth and planting of selected seeds (Giono 1985).

Open Slopes

Just above the forests, up to an altitude of 2,200 meters (7,218 ft.), the first part of the open slope is often a belt of shrubs. In the western and central Alps, such moors are usually of the juniper and rhododendron type, while in the eastern Alps, blueberries and their relatives often grow among the shrub pine.

The layer of shrubs, where it exists at all, is a prelude to the completely open arctic-type meadows, whose habitat is called the alpine zone. Nominally, it reaches up to the beginning of the year-round snows, which is also variable, ranging from 2,750 meters (9,022 ft.) in Austria's Hohe Tauern to 3,100 meters (10,171 ft.) in the Pennine Alps of Switzerland. In the alpine zone, the grass is short and the flowers are small, forming carpets in brilliant colors that vary greatly from place to place. The landscapes within this zone vary dramatically, sometimes even more than the peaks above. In addition to upland pastures and flowering meadows, they may include treacherously steep grass slopes, unstable scree, boulder fields, rock walls, snow patches, glaciers, streams, waterfalls and lakes, all of which affect the vegetation (Faverger 1972).

Confined to upper valleys by ridges above and forests below, pockets of local alpine flowers are isolated at the upper ends of many valleys throughout the Alps. On massive mountains, such as Mont Blanc and Monte Rosa, the open slopes are wrapped around the mountain, but more often they are tucked away inside high valleys that glaciers originally formed or that still have glaciers in them. Streams usually water these inside slopes, while the exposed ridges between them are windswept and arid. On the ridges, only lichens and other pioneer types of vegetation can survive. That is the main reason why alpine plants are often confined to upper valleys and differ from one valley to the next, in a process that is equivalent to island evolution.

Adaptation on Open Slopes

The main reasons why alpine plants survive where trees cannot are that they are not as tall and keep close to the ground, which is heated by the sun; there the air is warmer, the wind is weaker, and the winter snow provides insulation. A 30-centimeter (12 in.) blanket of snow can prevent freezing when the air is −32°C (−25°F) and still allow enough light for photosynthesis (Faverger 1972). Many alpine plants thus keep their leaves alive all winter and get a head start on the short growing season, even pushing up flowers through the snow before it melts completely. The snow waters the plants when it melts. At that time, it also makes available to the plants as nutrients those organic and mineral particles that the wind has carried up and deposited on the snow.

However, high-altitude conditions are, on balance, an impediment that all local plants must overcome to survive. Snow retards their growth where it buries them for nine or ten months each year. Also, being close to the ground, the plants have to withstand its heat in summer, with daily swings from below freezing at night to a daytime surface temperature above 38°C (100°F). This is especially trying for plants that grow on bare rock facing south, where they have no protection either night or day.

To keep a low profile with least exposure to the elements, alpine plants adopt one of three main shapes. The shape regarded most typically alpine is the cushion. Many high-altitude plants unrelated to each other, such as moss campion and glacier crowfoot, grow in this shape. Because of its compactness, a cushion plant does not actually shed its leaves. Instead, when they wither, they remain inside, enabling the plant to form its own humus. However, this is a time-consuming process, and in extreme cases a cushion plant, clinging to a crack in bare rock, may have to survive for up to twenty years before it blooms for the first time (Faverger 1972).

A second common shape of alpine plants is the rosette, in which the leaves are grouped tightly around the base. This too makes the plant compact and helps the leaves to stay alive all year. Examples of this shape are spring and stemless gentians, primulas, asters and edelweiss. For plants of the succulent type, such as stonecrops, saxifrages and house-leeks, it is sometimes hard to say whether they are cushions or rosettes.

The third major form of low alpine plants can be described as the espalier type, in which the plant simply spreads itself flat against the ground. Examples are the creeping avens and alpine azaleas.

In some alpines, such as snow gentians, milkworts, azaleas and an-drosaces, the flowers as well as the entire plants are miniatures, but in others the flowers are large in relation to the rest of the plant. Examples of the latter are spring anemones, chrysanthemums and asters. Some ecologists theorize that this is an evolutionary adaptation to attract polli-nating insects (Price 1981), but one could also assume that these plants evolved as they migrated to higher, colder and windier altitudes, merely shortening their stems without shrinking their flowers. Such adaptation also occurs when flowers that are more ancient than the mountains sim-ply rise to higher altitude together with their habitat in the process of mountain uplift.

Pollinating insects are as important in the mountains as they are in the lowlands (see chap. 6). Not all alpines, however, rely on insects entirely. Some depend on pollination by the wind or on other methods of reproduction. A few spread underground, via rootlike stems (rhizomes) that sprout new plants nearby. Others, such as the white *Polygonum viviparum,* drop from their stems small tubers, called bulbils, that take root and produce new plants. Still others, like the alpine hen and chick-ens, produce small spherical satellite rosettes that detach themselves and are rolled by wind or gravity, like miniature tumbleweeds, until they take root somewhere else.

Flora

Lilies to Buttercups

The species of flora in the Alps are fewer than in other regions, such as the tropics, but they exceed 1,200, not including most of the 200 species of grasses and sedges. Huxley (1967) describes, illustrates and classifies these flora into 101 families. Among several others who give detailed information and illustrations of Alpine flowers are Kohlhaupt (1966, with text by Helmut Gams), Barneby (1967), Landolt and Corbaz (1969), Polunin (1969) and Tosco (1974).

Even within families, however, the lack of similarity can be astound-ing. In addition to the pink martagon, orange, and white St. Bruno's lilies, the lily family includes the lovely mauve alpine garlics, dogtooth violets, snakesheads, tulips, scillas, stars of Bethlehem, asphodels, lilies of the valley, Solomon's seals, hyacinths, tiny yellow *Gagea fistulosa,* white *Lloydia serotina,* and the autumn crocus. The "purple" crocus, however, is in the iris family, with its purple and white forms mixed together on high, early spring meadows still covered by patches of snow. The related daffodil family includes spring snowflakes and *Narcissus poeticus.* The orchid family, which is typically tropical, is well represented in the Alps, with thirty-two species, including the lady's slipper, black vanilla, fragrant, butterfly, elder, and early purple orchids. The dock family is small but distinctive in the Alps, including the high-altitude white *Polygonum viviparum* and the dense spikes of pink bistorts in lower alpine fields.

Grasses and sedges are not famous for brilliant flowers. Both are large families that are a subject for specialists. Generically, they include feathergrass, timothy, cattail, mat grass, fescue, *sesleria* and *poa.* Fescue and *sesleria* are especially important as defining species of the upper alpine meadows. Among the sedges, several species of cotton grass, with their fluffy white tops, are conspicuous in high-altitude marshes up to the start of the year-round snows.

In the pink or carnation family, which is large and important, the several species of *Dianthus,* especially the small ones, are spectacular. This family includes other pink or white alpines, such as soapwort, sandwort, mouse-eared chickweed and moss campion, which is a miniature pink or red flower that grows in cushions on rocky slopes throughout the Alps up to 3,600 meters (11,811 ft.) and in the tundras of the Arctic across the Old and New Worlds, thus a true circumpolar species. The pink flowers of alpine pennycress, a representative of the cabbage family, form unusually large cushions on the limestones of the northern Swiss Alps and the Dolomites. This family also includes several alpine miniatures, such as rock cress *(Arabis)* and Whitlow grass *(Draba).*

One of the largest and most surprisingly diversified groups is the Ranunculus or buttercup family, which includes marsh marigolds, anemones, hepaticas, Christmas roses, globeflowers, hellebores, columbines, delphiniums, monkshoods, lousehats, baneberries, meadow rues and clematis, in addition to the rare glacier crowfoot and other high-altitude buttercups. A meadow full of globeflowers above Trient in the Mont Blanc range and one of *Anemone narcissiflora* at Col de Vars in the Cottian Alps are the glory of their mountain landscapes. The white alpine anemone has a yellow form *(Pulsatilla sulphurea),* and both forms are among the beauties of the southern Swiss, French and Italian Alps. The colorful spring and purple anemones are examples of large flowers on single short stems.

Stonecrops to Edelweiss

Among the succulent plants of the Alps, the stonecrop family includes several species of *sedum,* also the attractive red mountain and cobweb houseleeks. The name of the latter derives from the crisscross hairs on their rosettes. The lovely white-flowered grass of Parnassus is closely related to the saxifrage family (in Latin, literally "stone breakers"), which has fifty-nine Alpine species in two genera, some of which grow up to 4,000 meters (13,123 ft.) and are often hard to tell apart. The yellow and red saxifrages flourish in high-altitude stony streambeds, while the pink and white species, several with spectacular plumes of flowers, prefer the crags.

Like the Ranunculaceae, the rose family is startling in its variety. In the Alps, it includes not only numerous wild roses (eglantines) but also such dissimilar cousins as sweet briars, rock brambles, raspberries, cloudberries, strawberries, avens, dryads, cinquefoils, lady's mantles, spiraeas, cotoneasters, pears, cherries marmot plums, mountain ash and the red-topped grasslike great burnet *(Sanguisorba),* which occurs in the upper Bregaglia and Öschinen Valleys. The legume family, also called Papilion-aceae, includes several species at the high alpine zone, such as brown clover, red alpine clover, sorrel and birdsfoot trefoil *(Lotus alpinus),* which grows at the top of the Lötschenpass as well as in the lowlands.

An alpine family important ecologically rather than in number of species is the family of heathers (Ericaceae), which includes rhododendrons (alpenrose), azaleas, andromedas, bearberries and blueberries. The lovely red spring heather *(Erica carnea),* which grows on limestones, is a jewel of many mountain landscapes. The hairy and rusty alpenrose, which grow on alkaline and acid soils, respectively, lend color to the moors with their masses of brilliant red flowers. The creeping azalea is a true miniature flower of the granite massifs and silicate schists, while the pink azalea is limited to the Dolomites.

The primrose family is prominent in the Alps, where it is best known for its common cowslips and oxlips. The red *Primula hirsuta* enhances many slopes in the southern Swiss and northern Italian Alps. Also in this family, the yellow bear's-ear *(P. auricula)* of the northern Alps, *P. minima* and *P. glutinosa* of Austria's East Tirol (Defereggental), *P. daonensis* of the Sexten Dolomites and pedemontana of the Plateau de Nivolet are prized species. Notable members of the primrose family are the tiny cushion-forming androsaces, which are never common, and the mauve or pink snowbells (soldanellas), which are charming alpines of the early spring.

The borage family is represented throughout the Alps, as elsewhere, by lovely forget-me-nots. In the Val Entremont, the common lowland species turns some mountain fields almost completely blue, often with highlights of tall pink *Dianthus*. At higher altitudes, the alpine forget-me-nots are a separate species, growing in well-separated plants, occasionally in the cushion form. This family also includes the rare, high-altitude King of the Alps *(Eritrichium nanum)* at the Lac de Mercantour and a few other special places.

Among familiar lesser families of alpine flowers are the geraniums, violets, daphnes, evening primroses, cow parsleys, bellflowers (campanulas, which include rampions, also called rapunzels) and mints, which include thymes and ajugas. Less familiar but often conspicuous alpines are the valerians, rock roses and ball-shaped globularias. One of the largest groups is the family of the figworts, which includes snapdragons, mulleins, toadflaxes, veronicas, foxgloves *(Digitalis)*, yellow rattles, red rattles, louseworts and one of the great alpine rarities, *Wulfenia carinthiaca*, found only in southeast Austria. Largest of all is the composite, or daisy, family, which in the Alps includes goldenrods, asters, fleabanes, chamomiles, milfoils, chrysanthemums, wormwoods, coltsfoots, arnicas, groundsels, thistles, knapweeds, dandelions, hawkweeds, edelweiss and the rare *Senecio uniflorus* of Monte Rosa. We describe the gentian family separately.

Gentians

The gentian family is named for King Gentius (ca. 180 B.C.) of ancient Adriatic Illyria, who was especially fond of the cordial distilled from the roots of tall yellow gentians. Yellow gentians are common in the northern Alps. Their disheveled flowers are unlike other gentians except for their close cousin, the spotted gentian, *(Gentiana punctata)*, which blooms at the Albigna Glacier in the Bregaglia.

Out of 800 species in the worldwide gentian family, 40 grow in the Alps. Most familiar are the deep blue trumpet-shaped "stemless" gentians whose beauty enriches thousands of rock gardens, window boxes, postcards, prints, textiles, ceramics, murals and furniture. Even sedate botanical books call them the most gorgeous of alpine flowers. To one French botanist, Roger de Vilmorin, who was totally carried away, their "eclat and incomparable beauty" suggest "the nostalgia of distant mountains and the richness of the Thousand and One Nights (1956, 165). On high and steep grassy slopes, they grow in pairs or foursomes, occasionally in clusters of eight or ten flowers, often partly submerged in last year's dead grass. They normally bloom in the spring before the grass turns green, which means between May and August within their altitude range of 1,500 meters (4,921 ft.) to 2,400 meters (7,874 ft.). They have bumpy green throats and little or no stems, because of which the different species are lumped together under the horticultural name *G. acaulis*.

The *acaulis* group includes four species: *G. clusii, G. kochiana, G. angustifolia* and *G. alpina. G. clusii,* which has the widest distribution, is the species of alkaline soils in the northern limestone mountains and in the Dolomites and Julian Alps. It is named for a sixteenth-century French botanist, Charles de l'Écluse. *G. kochiana* is the species of the acid soils in the main-crest mountains from east of Mont Blanc to the Hohe Tauern. It has wider leaves, and its flowers are thinner at the base, with more prominent green bumps in the throat. Its flowers are sometimes pale and occasionally white. The narrow-leaved *G. angustifolia* is the species of the granite massifs in the northern part of the western Alps including the Mont Blanc Range. *G. alpina,* whose name falsely suggests a wider distribution, grows only in the French-Italian limestone mountains southward to the Mediterranean. Since seams of limestone can sometimes be seen in granite rocks, these gentians have transitional forms that are not easy to tell apart.

Smaller and more graceful, the bright blue star-shaped gentians also follow the springtime to even higher altitudes, up to the year-round snow line. The most widely distributed species is the spring gentian, *G. verna*. It likes but does not insist on limestone soil, and it grows throughout the Alps, the Caucasus and much farther east. Two of its cousins prefer acid soils and are less common: the short-leaved *G. brachyphylla* and the Bavarian gentian, *G. bavarica,* which differs from *G. verna* by being darker and having leaves growing up along its stem instead of in a rosette at the base. *G. bavarica* has a rare, high-altitude, dwarf cushion-forming variety called *subacaulis*.

The star-shaped gentians have five blue petals that flatten out into a single plane after emerging from a narrow or slightly inflated throat, with short white points that are vestigial petals between each pair of blue petals; thus they evolved from a ten-petal flower. Like the "stemless" gentians, those of the star-shaped group have only one flower on each stem, but their stems are 4 to 6 inches high. At night or when thick clouds darken the sky, the flowers curl up into a thin tube, as many other gentians do. On the Oberalp Pass, at the source of the Rhine, the spring gentians cover an entire south-facing slope with a dense, intensely blue carpet.

On the north slopes of the Gemmi and Julier Passes in Switzerland, and on the southwest slope of the Wildspitze in Austria, the charming snow gentians *(G. nivalis)* have tiny, pale blue, star-shaped flowers, with several on each stem. The willow gentian *(G. asclepiadea)* has several pairs of trumpet-shaped flowers on each stem, of a pure blue reminiscent of a Fra Angelico painting of the Madonna's robe. The tall closed purple gentian is the species for which the powerful synthetic dye and medication gentian violet is named. They grow, surrounded by glaciers, near the Monte Rosa Hut, also at the upper end of the Lötschental and, in the hundreds, at the Alpe des Baux near the St. Bernard Pass.

Like most high-altitude flowers, true gentians are perennials, which is part of their survival strategy with short growing seasons. Fringed gentians, however, are annual or biennial and usually grow at somewhat lower altitudes. They are classified in a separate genus, *Gentianella*. In the Alps, the common form is the field gentian *(Gentianella campestris),* whose four non-fringed pink petals are separated by fringed white vestigial petals in the throat. They are moderately common in the Bernese Alps, though a rare white form occurs at the Öschinensee. The German gentian, which is similar but with five petals, grows at the top of the Rax and other east Austrian mountains. In the Gran Paradiso Park, the felwort *(Gentianella amarella)* is taller but with smaller, deep purple flowers. Though gentians may be locally numerous, they are seldom actually common, and they usually grow in places that are laborious to reach. They never seem to lose their power as a talisman of the high mountain world.

King of the Alps

Probably no single species among the alpine flowers has produced such effusion of comments by normally staid botanists as the King of the Alps

(Eritrichium nanum), whose German name, Himmelsherold (Herald of Heaven), is even more impressive. The French sometimes call it "mousse d'azure." The Danish botanist Will Ingwersen, who is rarely given to hyperbole, wrote of this species, "As seen high in the European Alps, this is one of the most supremely beautiful of all alpine plants, reflecting in its sheets of azure, yellow-eyed flowers the color of the skies above" (1978, 169). An English horticulturist, Reginald Farrer, who found it near the Petit Mont Cenis, wrote, "I could hardly dare believe my eyes" (1911, 49). An Italian, Uberto Tosco, reported that it is found on "the steepest rocks, within sight of the eagles" (1974, 76). Helmut Gams (Kohlhaupt 1966, 1:174) wrote that it "elected its habitat in the Alps well before the last ice ages, and survived on the summits which were not covered by the ice," growing on rocky lime-free ridges between 2,600 meters (8,530 ft.) and 3,750 meters (12,303 ft.). This means that its habitat begins above where that of many alpine plants has already ended.

On the advice of an alpine-flower enthusiast from Lausanne, we went to the summit of Lagalb, just below 3,000 meters (9,843 ft.), in southeast Switzerland. On our way down, not far from the top, we spotted several cushions of tiny blue flowers on the rocks high above the trail. After scrambling up, we found that they were indeed the King of the Alps, certainly the most prized of all alpine flowers, which had been the object of our search that day and for many previous years. With near views of the Bernina snow peaks and glaciers, this is a suitable habitat for this supreme treasure. The day's last hikers walked down the trail, leaving us with the "mousse d'azure" in our solitude. We lingered and left reluctantly as the daylight began to fade.

Chapter 6

Animal Kingdom

Invertebrates

Underground Denizens

In the upper Alps, in intimate association with the roots of alpine plants, large numbers of living things spend all or most of their lives underground. They do so because that is their way of life or to protect themselves from freezing during the nights and colder seasons of the high-altitude environment while they sleep, hibernate or just live in their burrows. They include viruses, bacteria, protozoa, nematodes, earthworms, arthropods, salamanders, snakes and rodents. Together with the others, the nematodes and earthworms enrich the soil and are the food of other creatures.

Mollusks

Among the treasures of the Alps, from the viewpoint of the French, are the snails. In France, they are such a popular delicacy that official conservation measures are attempting to save these gastropod mollusks from extinction. According to a sign in the Arve Valley south of Lake Geneva, picking snails before the first of July is forbidden. As in the fable of the tortoise and hare, this gives the snails a head start to escape into the mountains near the beginning of their one-year life span, before the aficionados come to clean them out. Only the largest of some three dozen kinds of snails in the Alps are suitable for cuisine. Their smaller and more numerous cousins remain as subjects for the conchologists (Schauer and Caspari 1975).

The wood snail *(escargot des bois, Helicogona arbustorum)* is one of the largest and commonest species. Its domain reaches from the valleys, through the forests and Alpine meadows, all the way to the year-round snow line, where it makes its home in rocky crevices filled with humus. Its well-rounded shape of more than an inch in diameter is ideal for culinary use, but its pattern of vague brown and buff stripes gives it some camouflage protection. On the cold upper slopes, because of slower growth within a shorter growing season, the wood snails are smaller and even have the status of a subspecies.

Some of the smaller mollusks also live up near the permanent snows, where they too become even smaller. Most, but not all, alpine snails limit their habitat to the limestone mountains, because they need calcium carbonate as the material for their shells. To endure the winter, they seal up their openings with a porous calcified membrane and hibernate under dead leaves or other debris. Some snails live in water and some in the air. Among them are vegetarians, carnivores, omnivores and even cannibals. One aquatic species incubates a kidney parasite that afflicts sheep and other mammals, including people. A small (5 mm) alpine clam lives in stagnant or gently flowing water up to 2,500 meters (8,202 ft.) and in ponds that freeze for most of the year.

Arthropods

By far the most numerous of the alpine creatures are the arthropods, so called because of their segmented bodies. They include millipedes, centipedes, crustaceans, insects and arachnids, which include spiders, scorpions and mites. Their numbers are astronomical, and their species and ways of life in the Alps are phenomenal in their variety (Mani 1968). Most of these small creatures have restricted mobility and adapt to narrow ranges of altitude, especially at extreme cold. Some live all of their lives at or above the year-round snow line and may never leave subfreezing temperatures.

The tiniest of all are the mites (Acarina), which are often parasitic on other arthropods or vertebrates. They reach extremely high altitudes, and some live on the highest summits only, even that of Monte Rosa. Scorpions are denizens of the southern Alps. A few species of spiders (Araneae) spin webs on the alpine meadows or between rocks at high altitude, but most do not, because of the wind. Those that live there depend on capturing their prey by jumping. One of these, the black wolf spider *(Lycosa monticola),* lives at heights up to 4,000 meters (13,123 ft.) and is often seen running on the snow or barren screes. For all high-altitude arthropods, black is the most usual color, because it helps to keep them warm by absorbing solar heat but also protects them from harmful ultraviolet radiation.

In the Alps, the most numerous high-altitude arthropods are insects (Mani 1968; Rougeot 1972). They include springtails (Collembola), grasshoppers (Orthoptera), bugs (Hemiptera), beetles (Coleoptera), flies (Diptera) and butterflies and moths (Lepidoptera). Bees, wasps and ants (Hymenoptera) do not thrive in the mountains, and they generally stay in the lower valleys. Although extremely small, the springtails are among the most interesting of the high-altitude insects, because some of them live entirely above the snow line, where they have so sensitively adapted to a narrow microclimate that they rapidly die if brought to lower and warmer places. They make up for their small size by their large numbers of species and individuals, often forming huge dark swarms on the snow, where they feed on pollen and other organic matter brought up by the wind. The most common species are the snow flea *(Entomobrya nivalis)* and the glacier flea *(Isotoma saltans),* which lives under stones and in crevasses at up to 3,800 meters (12,467 ft.). These tiny creatures dominate the animal kingdom on the year-round snows.

Of all the alpine insects, beetles have the largest number of species, fully half of which are in the family of ground beetles (Carabidae). A common and beautiful large species is the gold *Carabus auronitens.* Gereben (1995) collected twenty species of ground beetles in ten genera in the retreat area of the Hornkees Glacier in the Zillertal Alps, at an altitude of 2,100 meters (6,890 ft.). Most beetles do not venture far above the tree line. However, Mani (1968) lists twelve species in seven families that range up to the snow line and above it, on glaciers and moraines.

The large and spectacular beetle *Rosalia alpina,* a denizen of the sparse old maple forests, is so beautiful in its light blue and black design that it has become a collector's treasure and is now rare and legally protected. Among the most attractive of the beetles are the ladybugs (Coccinellidae), whose black dots mark their red wing covers. Different species have two, seven or ten black spots on each side. One has a larger number of spots, each ringed with yellow, while another is entirely black. One of the dark species, the rare *Semiadalia alpina,* lives at up to 2,000 meters (6,562 ft.). Ladybugs are ecologically important in controlling the numbers of smaller creatures on which they feed.

Parnassian Butterflies

Despite their frail beauty, butterflies and moths (Lepidoptera) are among the hardiest inhabitants of the upper Alps, where they are also the most visible of the invertebrates (Higgins and Riley 1970; Spuler 1908). The yellow and black swallowtails are common below the tree line, but rarely above that. The parnassians, which belong to the swallowtail family, are relatively large butterflies, with wings magnificently marked with red, orange, yellow or blue spots within patterns of black or gray stripes on their semitransparent beige wings.

Taxonomists have reserved for these butterflies some of the grandest classical names. *Parnassius apollo* ranges widely in Europe and flies up to 1,800 meters (5,906 ft.) in the Alps. *Apollo* is almost indistinguishable from its higher-altitude cousin, the somewhat smaller *P. phoebus,* which ranges into the American northwest. The main exterior difference between them (which does not always hold) is that the antennae of *P. phoebus* are whitish and ringed with black while those of *P. apollo* are gray and ringed with darker gray. *P. apollo* has 168 named subspecies and more than 200 other named forms (Bryk 1935). This makes it the champion of all insects—indeed, of the entire animal kingdom—in number of names, but this represents excessive zeal in publishing Latin names rather than biological validity in the sense of geographically distinct populations.

The caterpillars of *P. apollo* and *P. phoebus* feed on succulent alpine plants, such as saxifrage, sedum and houseleek. The caterpillars are black with a row of red or orange spots on the side of the body. They spend the winter, sometimes two, in the caterpillar stage. Both *P. apollo* and *P. phoebus* are legally protected in the Alps. Parnassian butterflies have hairy bodies for conservation of heat and moisture and for protection from harmful radiation. Mated parnassian females have a peculiar structure at the tip of their abdomen, called a *sphragis,* which is a solidified mold of shellac formed by the male at the time of mating. Like a permanent chastity belt, it prevents further mating and thus preserves the integrity of the original male's genes. Its shape is useful for species identification.

Fritillary Butterflies

The nymphalids are one of the larger families of alpine butterflies, whose sizes are large, medium and small. They include the tortoiseshells and the world-ranging painted ladies, both of which fly up to the highest altitudes, often well above the snow line. Another conspicuous, related species is the red admiral. The nymphalids include a large group called the fritillaries, which are typically orange brown with rows of dark spots above and silver, green or brown spots below. Thirty-five fritillary species, including large ones in several genera, fly in the Alps, but most are not exclusively Alpine. Two smaller species, often hard to tell apart, are the shepherd's and mountain fritillaries, *Boloria pales* and *B. napaea*. They are both high-altitude butterflies, and *B. napaea* reaches to Alaska and the Rocky Mountains.

The marsh fritillary *(Euphydryas aurinia),* which flies up to 2,300 meters (7,546 ft.) at Sorebois, in the Val d'Anniviers, has been the subject of important studies of migration into the Alps (Verity 1940) and of evolution in action. From 1881 to 1935, Ford found that its variability increased and new forms appeared only when the population was growing. This supports Darwin's concept of variability as the source of evolution and also the view that in equilibrium, variability is constant, while "evolution is essentially a modification of this equilibrium" (Dobzhansky 1937, 124).

The Glanville fritillary, one of five small butterflies of the genus *Melitaea* that fly in the Alps, also is present in much of Europe and northern Asia (Higgins 1941). It is associated with a landmark lawsuit.

This Fly took its Name from the ingenious Lady Glanvil, whose Memory had like to have suffered for her Curiosity. Some Relations that was disappointed by her Will, attempted to set it aside by Acts of Lunacy, for they suggested that none but those who were deprived of their sense would go in Pursuit of Butterflies. Her Relations and Legatees subpoenaed Dr. Sloan [Hans Sloan, founder of the British Museum] and Mr. Ray to support her Character. The last Gentleman went to Exeter, and on the Tryal satisfied the Judge and Jury of the Lady's laudable Inquiry into the wonderful Works of the Creation, and established her Will. (Harris 1766)

Satyr Butterflies

In the satyr family (Satyridae), the alpine grayling *(Oeneis glacialis)* flies only in the Alps and only above 1,800 meters (5,906 ft.). It has a habit of leaning far to one side when at rest, so as not to be blown away by the wind or, as some say, the better to bask in the sun. At other times, it may conceal itself deep in the vegetation. The genus *Erebia* is a high-altitude group of satyrs that has evolved into a large number of species (Warren 1936). They are slow-flying medium-sized dark brown butterflies that are mostly hard to identify from their wing markings. They are confusingly called "alpines" in America but "ringlets" in England, while those of the related genus *Coenonympha* are called "ringlets" in America and "heaths" in England. Thirty-four species of *Erebia* make their home in the Alps, sixteen of which are restricted to those mountains, a few to small parts thereof.

Many *Erebia* butterflies are defined mainly by the genitalia of the males, which are easier to identify than those of the females. They have not only a dark pigment, like many high-altitude creatures, but also often a long life cycle. Because of the short growing season and low ambient temperature, their hibernating caterpillars need two or more years to complete their development. The *Erebia* caterpillars feed on alpine grasses that are also not easy to identify. Some are not choosy about which grasses they eat, but for many the food plant is still unknown. Only two *Erebia* butterflies in the Alps (*E. flavofasciata* and *E. christi*) are known to be restricted to the range of a single food plant *(Festuca ovina),* which grows only in a small area of southeast Switzerland and nearby Italy.

In the same region, two confusingly similar *Erebia* species have confusingly similar names: the Styrian and Stygian ringlets. Their habitats are respectively on the west and east sides of the 2,150-meter (7,054 ft.) Ofen Pass in the Swiss National Park. They were defined as different species in 1952, based on their different chromosome count. Their caterpillars feed on various *poa* and sesleria grasses. Owing to their preference for grassy slopes, they were confined, after surviving the ice ages, to the upper valleys, by forests that rose when the glaciers receded. The valleys on either side of the pass are flanked by ridges that are seldom lower than 2,700 meters (8,858 ft.), so these butterflies, which do not fly above 2,300 meters (7,546 ft.), are bottled up by forests that rise to 1,900 meters (6,234 ft.). They can, however, fly over the pass and hybridize when they meet. Their evolution is thus a combined process of isolation and limited contact.

Other Lepidoptera

Several lovely species of the white (pierid) and blue (lycaenid) families reside in the Alps. In the green-veined white, which flies up to 1,800 meters (5,906 ft.), the spring brood has dark veins while the summer brood is almost pure white, an example of seasonal variation. The tiny Glandon blues often congregate to drink from moist earth, where they may be joined by an alpine moth of the tineid family, *Melasina lugubris,* which mimics their white-fringed, dark blue wings (Spuler 1908). Occasionally, two or more species of blues congregate together, in close contact within deep vegetation, as we observed on the Oberalp Pass. The scarce copper (*Heodes virgaurea,* also a lycaenid), whose caterpillars feed on alpine goldenrod *(Solidago virgaurea)* which is also a favorite food of the adults, are local but not uncommon in the lower Lötschental.

The skipper family is large in North America and the tropics but extremely small in the Alps, where they fly up to the alpine zone. The mature dingy skippers sometimes congregate to feed on horse manure, while their caterpillars have the more elegant food of *Lotus alpinus.*

Because of freezing nights, most alpine moths, like other high-altitude insects, fly only in the daytime. At night they hide under rocks or freeze until the sun comes out. Some moths, however, have been attracted by lanterns high in the mountains at night, even when snow was falling. Alpine moths can be as colorful as butterflies. The species *Zygaena exulans* has bright red spots on its narrow blue black wings and can be seen feeding on moss campion interspersed with dwarf Bavarian gentians at 2,400 meters (7,874 ft.) in the Turtmanntal.

Most of the butterflies and moths in the Alps are thought to have migrated from older parts of Eurasia, mainly in the north and east (Verity 1940). Based on primitive fossils, the first butterflies and moths are believed to have evolved 120 million years ago, 55 million years before the Alps first emerged from the sea. Since then, the processes of upheaval, glaciation and erosion have produced the rigorous highland environment to which these insects have adapted themselves, often when their habitat was being lifted along with the mountains. More than most high-altitude creatures, they have been studied intensely, along with other insects, in their ecology, taxonomy, genital anatomy, molecular biology and neurobiology (Dyar 1997).

Close-up photography of butterflies and moths in the field can be a challenging and rewarding activity, much safer than the chase over the mountains with a net. Identification through binoculars is an increasingly popular skill (Glassberg 1993). Capturing a live female and rearing a new generation on-site from her eggs and local food plant, which has been done for centuries (Harris 1766), still yields the most new information—

now especially for the moths—about how these insects live and relate to their environment. Because of their remarkable transfiguration from creeping larvae to magnificent flying creatures, butterflies have been regarded, since ancient times, as symbols of human immortality—as reflected in the fact that the Greek word for butterfly is *psyche,* which is also the word for the human soul.

Nonmammal Vertebrates

Fish and Amphibians

Out of a dozen kinds of fish that inhabit the Alps, only one, the brown trout, ranges almost up to the snow line, through turbulent streams. Among amphibians, the common frogs *(Rana temporaria)* live up to the top of the alpine zone, in marshes, pools or streams. Their strategy is to lay eggs immediately after they thaw out in early summer. This gives them a head start in their reproductive cycle, though the tadpoles may have to hibernate and mature the following year. Alpine newts, which live up to the same altitudes, get a different head start, by maturing sexually while still in the aquatic larval stage (Schauer and Caspari 1973).

Among the smallest and also most interesting of the Alpine vertebrates are the all-black high-altitude *Salamandra atra* (Häfeli 1970; Gaussen and Barruel 1955). Unlike the yellow-spotted lowland fire salamanders and most other amphibians, the black salamanders are viviparous, giving birth to usually only two and rarely three or four fully developed offspring rather than to numerous eggs or aquatic larvae. No other animals have made such a radical biological adaptation to high altitude. They produce as many eggs as lowland salamanders (usually between ten and forty, with a maximum of seventy) but usually only one becomes fertilized on each side. The embryos then eat the other eggs, after which they sprout large gills that attach to the walls of the uterus, absorbing oxygen and food from their mothers until they complete their development. They then reabsorb the gills and are ready to be born.

This is a slow process, since alpine salamanders are cold-blooded animals who live in a world of frost most of each year and almost every night. Even though they protect themselves by going underground, their temperature drops too low for development of the embryos. Because of this, they have the longest gestation period of any animal in the world, longer even than the elephant's 640 days. At 1,200 meters (3,937 ft.), black salamanders need two years—that is, parts of three summers—to produce their young. At 1,800 meters (5,906 ft.), they require three years, and they probably need longer than that at their upper limit of 3,000 meters (9,843 ft.). They live long enough to produce two or three sets of young.

Their mating is unusual. It requires between two and four hours of the male rubbing the neck and throat of the female, with both facing down. At the start, the male is on top, but later he lifts the female to his back, by gripping her forelegs with his. The female is disinterested until the very end, when her genital opening swallows up the sperm sack that the male finally deposits on the ground. Some observers have erroneously reported that these salamanders mate belly to belly. Occasionally one can find two in this position, but then they are usually both males. The difference between male and female is so nonexistent from the outside that even salamanders get confused. The belly-to-belly contacts probably occur when one male fights off the mistaken advances of another male.

When alpine salamanders see something to eat, such as a worm, they can move like lightning. At other times, they seem to be totally lethargic. When the sun is warm enough, they bask lazily on a warm rock, where their pure black skin helps to absorb the solar heat. They do so at 1,800 meters (5,906 ft.) in the Gasterntal and above the Oschinensee in the Bernese Alps. At such times, they do not mind if someone picks them up by hand. However, if treated roughly, they give off an irritating oily substance that people in earlier centuries thought to be fatally poisonous even to the touch. It is toxic to predators, against which it is an effective protection.

Reptiles

Out of four kinds of vipers in the Alps (Schauer and Caspari 1973), the most common ones are adders *(Vipera berus)* and asps *(V. aspic)*. Being much larger and more rapidly moving than the amphibians, they are more conspicuous when one encounters them. Adders range over most of northern Europe and up to the snow line in the Alps. The males are usually 50 centimeters (20 in.) long, and the females are considerably longer. Both sexes have a dark gray zigzag pattern that forms an X or a V at the top of the head. Asps are a southern species that inhabits the Alps from France through Italy to the Dolomites, up to an altitude of 2,600 meters (8,530 ft.). They are brownish, with a sharp, slightly turned-up snout, and are usually larger than adders. The difference between the sexes is in the opposite direction, the males being up to 75 centimeters (30 in.) long, and the females being somewhat shorter.

Both species hatch their young internally and give birth to fully developed infant snakes. They cannot survive below freezing and must go underground to hibernate and to sleep through the freezing alpine nights. In the morning, before warming up in the sun, they are lethargic, but later in the day, they give vent to their usual activity and irritable temperament. Both species are venomous. They eat small birds, lizards, frogs, rodents or any animal they can swallow, except salamanders, whose poisonous skin oils are lethal to them. Among lizards, the common species *(Lacerta vivipara)* ranges as high as the vipers and likewise produces fully developed young (Schauer and Caspari 1975).

Soaring Birds

The birds of the Alps have been a familiar topic for ornithologists and all naturalists (Peterson et al. 1954; Paccaud 1972). The only predators to have solved the problem of feeding on salamanders are the ravens. These extremely intelligent birds have figured out that they can eat the inside of a salamander but discard its poisonous outer skin. Ravens once ranged over almost all of Europe and across northern Asia and North America. Now their European habitat has effectively shrunk to the northern latitudes and to the Alps, where one often hears their unmistakable hoarse croaking well before seeing the creatures themselves. They are huge black birds with enormous beaks, 64 centimeters (26 in.) from beak to tail. They skillfully soar and glide through the air, with minimum loss of energy in beating their wings—an important advantage in the rarefied air and the cold of the upper altitudes. Their nuptial flight is said to be acrobatic. They nest in trees or crags at up to 2,400 meters (7,874 ft.). Ravens are truly omnivorous, eating grain and berries as well as any live or dead animals they can capture. These intelligent creatures can be domesticated and taught to bark like dogs, laugh like people, or coo like pigeons.

By far the most conspicuous birds in the Alps are alpine choughs. They are about 38 centimeters (15 in.) long from head to tail and are all black except for red feet and straight yellow bills, a distinction from the lower altitude choughs, which have curved red bills. They eat worms, insects, snails and berries and are especially fond of scraps from human food. In summer, they gather around mountain inns and climbers' huts, up to 3,560 meters (11,680 ft.) on the Jungfraujoch, wherever they can find tasty tidbits. In winter, they usually come down each day to lower elevations and flock in villages, such as Kandersteg at 1,200 meters (3,937 ft.), but return each night to the crags where they have their nests, at a maximum altitude of 3,000 meters (9,843 ft.). Even in winter, they follow climbers and skiers up to the snow peaks, such as the 3,709-meter (12,169 ft.) Balmhorn. They occasionally reach the summit of Monte Rosa and parts of the Himalayas above 8,000 meters (26,247 ft.). These birds offer clear evidence that life in the Alps rises above the level of the year-round snow.

Often flying in flocks in unison, but at times in chaotic disarray, the choughs sail and swoop with their wings curled up. One day in July at the Öschinensee, after a two-day Bernese snowfall, we witnessed a large flock of alpine choughs cavorting with more than their usual exuberance above the water. They swooped up and down joyously in crisscross patterns, their screams echoing from the encircling crags. Perhaps they were feeding on flying insects, but they also seemed engrossed in the pure pleasure of their masterful flight and its glorious setting.

Among the most skillful of birds that soar above the Alps are the golden eagles, which the French call *aigles royals*, as distinct from the imperial eagles, which do not fly in the Alps. Like the ravens, golden eagles range over most of the temperate zones of the Old and New Worlds. They are nongregarious birds, typically living in pairs. They measure up to 88 centimeters (35 in.) from beak to tail, with a wingspread of up to 2 meters (80 in.). In Asia, golden eagles are often trained as hunting birds. In Austria, one lived in the Schonbrunn Palace for 80 years and another in the Hofburg Palace in Vienna for 104 years.

In the mountains, the eagles nest on rock ledges, usually below the tree line, to a recorded maximum of 2,460 meters (8,071 ft.). Four pairs normally nest in the Swiss National Park. They alternate nesting sites, so some are unoccupied for several years. It is usually possible, through a telescope, to observe an aerie, with the young in the nest and the parents bringing in food. They feed on infant sheep and goats (wild or domestic), hares, marmots, foxes, grouse and snakes. Some years ago, in the Rote Kumme, near the Gemmi Pass, vipers often basked on rocks in the sun while golden eagles circled above. They became so efficient in capturing the vipers that both eagles and vipers are seldom seen there now. The young eagles need four years to reach maturity. As seen from below, they differ from their parents by elongated white patches on their wings and white at the base of their tails.

In the Dauphiné Alps, at the summit of the difficult 3,970-meter (13,025 ft.) Pic Central of the Meije (also known as the Doigt de Dieu), Julius Kugy was startled when "There was a sudden rushing sound above us. It was a large eagle. The great beast drew near with frightening speed, wings wide-outspread, eyes turned keenly on us, talons stretched forward, bent upon attack. We sprang up and instinctively seized our axes. But just in front of us it turned aside, and soared away in a superb curve. A confused swarm of choughs followed in pursuit, and scattered screaming in its rear. We felt that a royal wing-beat had brushed against us" (1934, 290).

Other Birds

Among all the birds, the snow finches have the record for the highest nests in the Alps, at 3,476 meters (11,404 ft.) (Schauer and Caspari 1973). They normally lay four to seven eggs at a time. They fly and rest on the rocks, probably not far from their nests, on both sides of Monte Rosa's Gorner Glacier, at altitudes well above 3,000 meters (9,843 ft.). Both sexes have similar markings, which are striking, especially in flight. They have reddish brown backs, pale tan breasts, gray heads, black throats, white wings tipped with black, and white tails with a black central stripe. They measure 18 centimeters (7 in.) in length. They inhabit the Alps, Pyrenées, Balkans and Caucasus and the mountains of Central Asia. In winter they come down to lower altitudes, showing how a short flight up or down in the mountains is equivalent to a major north or south migration in the lowlands.

The alpine accentors, which nest at up to 2,830 meters (9,285 ft.), are true alpine birds, confining themselves to the mountains of southern Europe. They are of the same size as the snow finches but are less conspicuous, with brownish bodies and gray heads—an effective camouflage among the rocks. In winter, against the snow, they are easier to spot. One January, we saw one perched at the tip of a fir tree near the Sunnbuhl ski slope, above Kandersteg, at 1,900 meters (6,234 ft.).

Among other alpine birds, the water pipit, also a well-camouflaged brown-striped sparrowlike bird, nests only in the mountains of southern Europe, at up to 2,700 meters (8,858 ft.) in the Alps, but it ranges widely over the lowlands in winter. The redstart is not exclusively Alpine, since it inhabits virtually all of Europe and much of Asia, but it nests at above 3,000 meters (9,843 ft.) in the Alps and higher than that on the Tibetan Plateau. It is easy to identify by its red tail. The wall creeper has a striking appearance, with its long curved bill and broad, crimson-striped black-and-white wings. It nests at up to 2,500 meters (8,202 ft.) in the Alps but also ranges widely throughout most of Europe.

The rock partridge has a conspicuous black necklace between its white throat and its gray breast. It is a southern bird that inhabits only the Balkans, Italy and the Alps, where it nests at up to 2,700 meters (8,858 ft.). The ptarmigan, in comparison, is essentially an arctic grouse, with habitats in Norway, Iceland and Scotland as well as in the Pyrenées and the Alps, where it nests at up to 2,800 meters (9,186 ft.). The Alpine population became isolated from its northern counterparts, having remained in the Alps after the last ice age. It is a fairly large bird, 35 centimeters (14 in.) long. At all seasons, it has white wings and a white belly, but in winter its brown body turns almost entirely white, except for a black tail and black stripes on the sides of its face. At 2,000 meters (6,562 ft.), below the Gemmi Pass, after a snowstorm in May, we saw one that still had most of its winter plumage. Ptarmigans nest on the ground, in the shelter of a rock or bush. The chicks leave their nest the day they hatch and learn to fly within a few days. The white phase provides camouflage in winter, which is typical of arctic animals, such as the arctic fox and northern populations of the ermine and variable hare. (However, in sharp contrast, the large and less vulnerable chamois and ibex turn dark in winter to absorb solar heat.)

One of the most striking but also rarest birds in the Alps is the dotterel plover. With a generally brown back, it has no less than six contrasting segments below: a white throat, a brown upper breast, a white pectoral band, an orange lower breast, a black belly and a white patch beneath its tail. It has prominent white eyebrows that meet at its nape in a characteristic V. It too is mainly an arctic bird that remained in the Alps after the last ice age. It is a bird of high open country, including meadows, tundras and crags, where it nests at up to 2,300 meters (7,546 ft.) in the Alps. Previously known in the Alps only from southeast Austria, it was recently found to nest in east Switzerland too. In the winter, it migrates to the warmth of southern Italy and Greece. Significantly, it is hard to see not only because it is rare but also because it is extremely tame, so that it does not reveal itself in alarm when approached—an effective protection.

Mammals

Forest Mammals

In the mountain forests of the Alps, it is not unusual to see various individual mammals, such as roe deer, fox, ermine and marten, though larger predators, such as lynx, wolf and bear, are now uncommon. In the summer mating season, one can also see herds of the large red deer and hear their weird hymeneal barking and baying. These forest animals rarely venture beyond the tree line into the open slopes above.

The brown bear *(Ursus arctos)* survives in most of its forest habitat of Eurasia, even in remote corners of the eastern Alps, including the Swiss National Park. The bear is the emblem of Bern's flag and seal and is said to be the source of that canton's name, but it no longer lives there in the wild. One of the last bears seen in that canton was above Kleine Scheidegg in 1792, where a huge specimen had been attacking the grazing flocks and terrorizing the neighborhood. Three hunters from Grindelwald wounded it with musket balls, with no immediate effect, and it escaped into the nearby woods. There it ran into a fourth hunter, Hans Kaufmann, who tried to shoot it, but his powder was damp and his gun failed to go off. The bear reared up on its hind legs and was about to envelop Kaufmann when the latter attacked it so vigorously with the butt of his musket that the weapon flew apart and the bear was killed. The government of Bern gave Kaufmann an extra reward of one gold louis and a new musket from the canton armory (Coolidge 1908). Thus did Bern contribute to the local extermination of its emblem.

The European brown bear is a close relative of the American brown bear, which is a color phase of the American black bear *(Ursus americanus)*, definitely not the same or as large as the grizzly or Kodiak bears *(U. horribilis)*. Brown bears are a familiar sight in zoos and at carnivals in European cities, where the trained "dancing bears" move rhythmically with music. In centuries past, bearbaiting was popular, especially in England, where Parliament outlawed this cruel "sport" in 1835.

Rodents

Among the true alpine animals that make their homes in the open spaces above the tree line, the most numerous are the rodents, which are generally small, inconspicuous and often hard to see because they keep to their burrows among the rocks. A typical species are the alpine voles, for which the French have a euphonious name, *compagnols des Alpes* (Schauer and Caspari 1975).

The largest of the rodents are the marmots, also called rockchucks or groundhogs (Müller 1988). They are true alpine animals, rarely going below the tree line. They are common up to 2,700 meters (8,858 ft.) above the Monte Rosa Hut and beyond 2,300 meters (7,546 ft.) on the Engstligenalp and Gran Paradiso. They are vegetarians, typically 60 centimeters (24 in.) long. The Alpine species lives only in Eurasia. In summer, the adults live singly or in pairs among the high rocks, but when one of their warning whistles pierces the air, all marmots on the mountain take cover. In winter, fifteen or more sleep together in a large chamber of a burrow up to thirty feet deep that they dig into the side of the mountain, usually just above the forest. They sleep from October to April or longer. They are intelligent animals that can be domesticated and trained to obey commands and do tricks, such as walking about with a cane.

Chamois

Chamois inhabit all the mountains of Europe and Asia Minor, but they are especially at home in Austria and Bavaria (Schaller 1977; Hutter and Glauser 1974; Schauer and Caspari 1975). An average adult male stands 35 inches high at the shoulders; has 11-inch horns, 5-inch ears and a 3-inch tail; and weighs 82 pounds. An average adult female weighs 50 pounds but otherwise looks much like a male. Their most conspicuous marking is a sharp black stripe from ear to nose, which gives them a purposeful look in profile, while from the front it suggests a quizzical smile. Their horns, before ending in a small backward curve, point forward in line with their neck, which gives the chamois a dynamic look. At rest, they are not notably elegant, but when they run, as they often do, their shapes are transformed into graceful flowing lines.

Chamois horns are largely useless for combat or even for scratching their backs as ibex do. Unlike most wild sheep or goats, chamois males do not joust in spectacular head-on collisions in preparation for the mating season. They limit themselves to threatening gestures, pushing each other, or trying to hook each others' legs with their horns. One of their adversarial gestures is to make the black hairs stand up along the middle of their backs. Hunters collect these hairs as trophies for hats, calling them chamois beards or feathers, though these animals have no beards and certainly no feathers.

Chamois are fairly social animals, though adult chamois males, who are in the minority, live in solitude most of the time, except in the mating season, when they bellow, grunt and compete with each other to assemble a harem. Young males stay with the female herd until they are two or three years old. Chamois live until ten or twelve and occasionally up to fifteen. Those that reside on arid slopes live longer, apparently because they need more time to search for food, leaving less for the rituals and duties of breeding, which can be even more exhausting.

They eat grass in summer, but in winter they have to survive on bark, fir or spruce needles, and lichens. Normally, except in winter, chamois spend their lives on the rugged slopes high above the tree line, where they can, it is said, tell a day or two in advance when an alpine storm is coming. Then they often descend into the forest, where they can occasionally be seen at close range. However, they are vulnerable to avalanches. After the severe winter of 1976–77, the pride of the Gran Paradiso, an albino chamois, was found dead in an avalanche; he was very tame and a mascot of the preserve. Perhaps because chamois are widely hunted, they usually stay far away from humans. It is said that they can distinguish a hunter from an innocuous hiker or woodsman. When alarmed, they whistle through the nose.

They venture high on snow mountains. We saw their tracks prominent in the snow at 3,000 meters (9,843 ft.) on the Wildstrubel. Their ability to ascend steep rock is uncanny. When they climb a rock wall, always diagonally, the lead female finds the way alone while the others wait below, watching where the rocks might be loose. Then they go up one by one. They are especially shy when surprised from above, as when we saw a herd of about thirty plunge without accident down the north face of the Diablerets.

Rambert described the antics of a group of young chamois near the Grand Muveran in the Alpes Vaudoises (where the climber's hut has been named the Cabane Rambert).

The games of the animals resemble those of children. They have the grace, the improvisation, the unimaginable fantasies, the freedom and the joyous abandon. Starting together at the bottom of the snowfield, they climbed it with prodigious speed in short tight jumps, with forelegs curved like the arms of an anchor; then they suddenly turned and challenged each other to race down. When the slope got steep, they slid down with all their weight on their hind legs. When they reached the bottom, they stopped suddenly at the edge of a cliff, where I thought they would crash to the rocks below. But from the sureness of their movements it was clear that they did not even conceive of a possible fall; they had measured their forces precisely, and it must have been a joy for them to rear up at the extreme edge and lean over to examine the precipice below. (1875, 71)

Chamois do not mingle with ibex. They often inhabit the same valleys, but usually on opposite sides or at opposite ends, with the chamois more often, but not always, at the upper end. Among the exceptions is the Gasterntal, where chamois inhabit the slopes above the lower end of the valley.

Ibex

In French the ibex are called *bouquetin;* in German, *Steinbock.* The best-known species is the one found in the Alps, *Capra ibex,* which also inhabits Central Asia (Schaller 1977; Hutter and Glauser 1974). (We have also seen the two types that live in the Caucasus—*Capra caucasica* and *C. cylindricornis.* They are both locally called *tur,* and both are larger than those in Europe.) In human history, the ibex are among the most ancient of animals. They appear in the art of the Scythians and Romans, who brought them to confront the gladiators in the arenas. They are painted in Persian and Indian prints and in Chinese art also. Their first protector was the archbishop of Salzburg, who decreed that they not be hunted in 1584, as they were getting scarce even then. Instead, he would give them as presents to foreign emissaries.

Ibex live in caves on the highest Alps and come down on very steep rocks to eat their fill of grass. Their favorite foods besides grass are wild parsley, thyme, artemisia, alder, birch, roses and dwarf rhododendron, and they love salt. In the winter they have little to eat, scratching the snow to find some lichens or to munch on roots, bark, needles of coniferous trees or windblown leaves. This is why they eat large amounts in the spring, summer and fall. In the winter, their greatest enemies are the cold and lack of food; in the spring, the avalanche; and formerly, the lynx, wolf and bear. Humans are no longer their enemy, since the ibex are protected in almost every nation from being hunted.

The ibex is one of the noblest-looking animals. The male, about twice as heavy as a chamois, walks proudly and gives the impression of great strength and physical endurance. His coat varies from pale brown or palest yellow to gray. His horns can be more than 1 meter (40 in.) long and are saber-shaped, with bumps on the upper edge—one bump for each year of his life. His chest is massive, and his legs, like those of the chamois, are short and stubby, which helps to keep him warm in the fierce alpine winters. The females, more daring than the males, come down to lower altitudes, even into the forests. They resemble the chamois female, the difference being that the chamois has a black stripe on either side of her face while the ibex has one on either side of her tail. The fur of both species becomes thicker and darker in winter to retain body heat and absorb heat from the sun.

The male's eyes are large and beautiful. Perhaps this is because, every day of their lives, they leap from crag to crag, so close to the sky, and see such beauties as the first edelweiss and gentians, sunrises and sunsets, and perhaps mysteries humans have never seen. When in flight, they do not have the grace of the chamois, but they are able to leap farther and more surefootedly in precarious situations, particularly when they fight for the lady of their choice, with the clash of their horns reverberating in the mountains. Like the chamois, they mate in January and give birth in June or the beginning of July. A few hours after birth, the kids can follow their mothers to their stony caves, and in a few days, they can already jump from rock to rock.

In the Bernese Alps, as we descended from the Tschingelochtighorn into the Üschinental one foggy, drizzly morning, eight or nine ibex were standing and lying down on a little plateau, against a background of moving clouds below. At sight of us, the leader, an ancient buck with the largest horns, gave a whistle, which is the only sound ibex usually make, although they also occasionally bay in the mountains. He had trouble getting up and must have had a touch of rheumatism. It was no doubt his future replacement, a much younger buck, who led their flight from us, down over the edge of the cliff. This area is famous for ibex.

The Gran Paradiso is a large Italian park founded by King Victor Emmanuel II to preserve the ibex, which were getting scarce in the 1800s, probably because this tiny king, who was 5'3" tall, was a fierce hunter and had overhunted them himself. It was to the Gran Paradiso, at about the turn of the century, that a group of hardy Swiss came at night to steal some of the ibex, because those in Switzerland had died of eye disease. They stuffed several ibex into bags and carried them on their backs. It was no small task, but they were successful, and that is why the ibex are happily not extinct in Switzerland. Since then they have been protected so well that they have become a problem in some places. Since they eat spruce and fir needles in winter, they were damaging the forests on which villages depend for protection from avalanches and falling rocks. To control their numbers, limited official hunting has been authorized (Grodinsky and Stowe 1987).

One year in June, in the Val Savranche of the Gran Paradiso, we saw at least a hundred ibex. Some wonderful old bucks were sitting in an upper forest, giving one the impression that they were smoking pipes and talking about old times, like old men in pubs and taverns. Meanwhile, a younger group was cavorting in a waterfall nearby. At night, they came down to the valley floor, and one evening, a whole troop of males walked close outside a window at the Gentianella Inn, at an altitude of 1,900 meters (6,234 ft.). The females almost always stay by themselves or with their young—there is no women's liberation in the ibex kingdom!

Another year in July, no ibex were visible in the Val Savranche, perhaps because the August vacation crowds were on their way. An Englishman told us that some ibex had been seen on Col d'Entrelor. After we climbed three hours through steep forests and meadows, past a stone shepherd's hut, to a large snowfield, no animals were in sight, but we saw plenty of exciting flowers and a majestic view of the Gran Paradiso peak across the valley. (With two sunlit streams flowing out of its glacier, over the meadows, and through the forest, it is a classical example of where "young rivers flow rejoicing from the glacial caves" [John Muir].) At the top of the snowfield, which was dusted with red algae, the col was a notch in the rock ridge at 3,007 meters (9,865 ft.), about 200 meters from us.

Suddenly an ibex came through the pass. A few seconds later, another came through. Then a whole herd, about three dozen males, all sauntered down the slope. They crossed the face of a vertical cliff, in the middle of which some younger males paired off and jousted dangerously. A young group heard the click of our camera and came down to investigate, from about 50 feet away. Then an older male whistled and led the herd up the slope to the top of a rock wall directly above us, from which several peered down intently while others crashed against each other's horns with no thought about people. After almost an hour, they all retreated over the pass. Then we too turned back, marveling at what we had seen.

It was also in the Gran Paradiso that we saw our most unforgettable single ibex, a mature male sitting on a rock as we came down from the mountain. We passed directly under him. Then, much to our surprise, he turned all the way around so that he could keep looking at us, which he did for the longest time. We climbed the rock to within a few feet of him, and it was then that we clearly saw his face, so sensitive that it virtually had a spiritual expression in the eyes and mouth. He was anxious to look us human creatures straight in the eyes. It reminded us of a passage by Beston: "We patronize them [the animals] for their incompleteness, for their tragic fate of having taken form so far below ourselves. And therein we err and greatly err. For the animal shall not be measured by man. In a world older and more complete than ours they move, finished and complete, gifted with extensions of the senses we have lost or never attained, living by voices we shall never hear" (1928).

Chapter 7

People Talking

Origins

Stone-Age Tribes

People first came to the Alps during the mild years before the onset of the last great ice age, about 120,000 years ago. They were people of the Old Stone Age. Presumably they were mostly Neanderthals, but a single "Neanderthaloid" tooth is the only direct evidence of Neanderthal presence in the mountains at that time. These early people, who at first were probably seasonal hunters rather than year-round residents, left other evidence of their occupancy in twenty-one caves and rock shelters in several parts of the Alps from Slovenia to France (Sauter 1976).

Two important sites, both in glacial territory of east Switzerland but not submerged by the last ice sheet, are the Wildkirchli cave, at an altitude of 1,477 meters (4,846 ft.) in the Santis range, and the Drachenloch (dragon's hole) cave, which is the highest of all the archaeological sites, at 2,445 meters (8,022 ft.) above Vattis. Its discoverer, Bachler (1940), found seven bear skulls buried in that cave, in what he thought was a crude stone box. He interpreted it as a ritual burial implying the existence of an early bear cult. Despite initial acceptance, this view has become doubtful, because Bachler took no photographs and left none of the evidence in place for others to see, except for coals in the hearth, which radioactive dating has found to be 49,000 years old.

After surviving the 90,000 rigorous years of the Würm glaciation, and just as it was coming to an end 30,000 years ago, the Neanderthals apparently became extinct—in the Alps and in their large habitat elsewhere. Why this happened is unclear. Possibly it was due to competition from the Cro-Magnons, a more advanced people who arrived in Europe about 35,000 years ago from the east and produced the exquisite cave paintings at Lascaux and Altamira. The Cro-Magnons reached their peak about 20,000 years ago, and their descendants are the Indo-European and Caucasoid peoples of Europe, western Asia and North Africa today.

When the Cro-Magnons and their descendants spread out over their large geographical range, they began to split up into physically dissimilar tribes, possibly because of differences in climate or because of decreased mobility following the return of the temperate forests. These groups included the so-called lake dwellers, whose settlements projected over a number of Swiss and Austrian Alpine lakes. Most of these probably were originally built on bogs at the water's edge and became submerged when the water rose, after which the sites were discovered when the water level went down.

Early Metallurgists

The naturally mummified, almost perfectly preserved leather-clad body of a man who lived about 5,500 years ago was found in the Ötztal Alps, partly exposed on the Niederjoch Glacier in 1991 (Fowler 1991, 1992; Roberts 1993). The study of the body and of its artifacts is opening new vistas into the culture of the earliest of the metallurgical periods, called the Copper Age. The man's most significant artifact is a copper ax with a flanged design previously known only from 1,500 years later, from the Bronze Age of 4,000 years ago.

The Austrian village of Halstatt is a still-functioning lake-dwellers' site. Among its ancient artifacts, archaeologists have unearthed Bronze Age and early Iron Age objects. Beginning about 3,000 years ago and for several centuries thereafter, what is known as the Halstatt culture prevailed throughout the Alps and in considerable areas north and south of the mountains. The use of wood for building construction, now familiar in Swiss chalets, was made possible by ax heads forged from Halstatt iron.

Early Historic Peoples

The original builders of Halstatt were Illyrians, who inhabited southeast Austria and the west Balkans north of Greece. Their Adriatic shores became Greek colonies in the seventh century B.C., and since then they fought many battles with Greeks, Macedonians and Romans, the last of whom finally subdued them in the year A.D. 9 and established the province of Illyricum. After that, many Illyrians, who were valiant soldiers, rose high in the Roman hierarchy, mainly through the Praetorian Guard. Their leaders included five sons of Illyrian peasants who became emperors of Rome: Claudius II, Aurelian, Probus, Diocletian and Maximian (Gibbon 1952). Despite later invasions of Illyria by Celts, Slavs and Turks, some Illyrian genes probably have survived.

Also during the first millennium B.C., northeast Italy and most of what is now west Austria and east Switzerland were the realm of the Raetians, the most powerful and warlike of the early Alpine tribes, who were possibly of Etruscan origin. Raetia became a province of the Roman Empire in 15 B.C. and had two chief towns: Curia, which is now Chur in Switzerland, and Tridentum, which is now Trent in Italy. The Roman roads through these towns were those that respectively crossed the Maloja Pass to Switzerland and Germany and the Brenner Pass into Austria. Parts of the Raetian language survive in the Romansh and Ladin dialects of the Grisons and South Tirol, some of whose people probably descend from the original Raetians. In northwest Italy, the contemporaries of the Raetians and Illyrians were the Ligurians, who occupied the Piedmont area from Genoa and Turin to the Maritime Alps. They were a short dark-complexioned Mediterranean people, who made effective soldiers in the Roman army.

Celts

The most widespread mountain people of pre-Roman Europe were the Celts. They originated in the Hercynian forests north of the Alps, where one of their best-known tribes, the Boi, were centered in Bohemia. In the sixth century B.C., the Celts ranged from Spain and France across the northern Alps into Austria. At that time, they were known as Keltoi in Greek and as Celtae in Latin. In the fourth century B.C., they crossed the central passes of the Alps into Italy and then became known as Galli (Gauls) in Latin and as Galatai (Galatians) in Greek. During the years that followed, they colonized parts of Italy, Sicily, the Balkans and even Asia Minor, where they received one of the letters from St. Paul.

In Gallia Cisalpina, which was the region south of the Alps, the Romans conquered the Celts in 225 B.C. Compared to the Greeks and Romans, the Celts were fair-complexioned, taller and physically stronger, though these characteristics were mainly those of their warrior class. They were known for their hospitality, feasting, drinking and carousing, but apparently they often quarreled among themselves and were generally undependable (Caesar). Despite that, they were able to conquer numerous indigenous peoples, using Halstatt iron weapons. They ruled over, rather than replaced, the original inhabitants in the territories that they conquered. Among the Celts, the druids, who were centered in France, were an elite priestly caste selected from members of their warrior class.

Nordics

Soon after the Celts, another group from the north arrived in the Alps. They were the Cimbri, who came from Jutland and marauded the mountainous regions from Spain to the Adriatic, even defeating the Romans in battle. However, their army was finally annihilated by the Romans in 101 B.C., and they apparently left no major trace in the blood of the Alpine folk. The Cimbri were the forerunners of a large assortment of Germanic tribes that overran the Alps from the north in the fourth and fifth centuries A.D. They included the Goths, Franks, Burgundians, Swabians, Alemanns, Lombards and Bavarians.

The Lombards, or Long Beards, established themselves in north central Italy, which is still called Lombardy. The Burgundians, a Baltic tribe that included the protagonists of the Nibelung saga, ruled parts of medieval France, with their capital at Arles, until they retreated into what is now Burgundy, northwest of Switzerland, with its capital at Dijon. The Franks, who came from the region around Frankfurt am Main, became rulers of France and gave that country its name. Under Charlemagne, they also conquered the Alps. The Alemanns are the main bloodline in the German part of Switzerland and in the German-speaking valleys south and east of Monte Rosa in Italy. The Germanic people of Austria and northeast Italy are mostly of Bavarian stock. The rest of the people of the Italian Alps are mostly of Celtic origin, as are those of the French Alps and the southwest Swiss Alps (Suisse Romande).

Easterners

Also in the fourth and fifth centuries A.D., several militant tribes arrived in the Alps from the Ukrainian and north Caucasus steppes, namely, the Alans, Huns and Avars. The most formidable were the Huns, who, under Attila, successively defeated the Roman armies in the eastern and western parts of the empire and fought their way through to western France, where they were defeated by the Romans in 451 A.D. In the following year, however, the Huns invaded Italy and sacked several of the north Italian cities, paving the way for the end of the Western Roman Empire at the hands of the Goths (Gibbon 1952). In the seventh century A.D., the Slavs from the north and east invaded Illyria and other parts of the Balkans in what became Yugoslavia and Bulgaria, where they are now the dominant people, despite centuries of subjection to the Turks. The military campaigns of the past 1,500 years have probably affected the local populations in parts of the Alps, but not to the same degree as the earlier migrations into the mountains from the north, east, south and west. Along with the Slavs of Slovenia, southeast Austria and northeast Italy, people of Celtic and Germanic stock are now the prevailing folk of the Alps.

Inheritance

In alpine villages, ownership of the land is organized according to the different customs of the three prevailing ethnic groups going back to medieval and perhaps to ancient times. In the Celtic group, all of the heirs share equally in the inheritance of the land, except for the lands of communal ownership, where the inheritance of grazing rights is likewise on a kinship basis but is subject to recombination by marriage or purchase. In the Slavic group, the division of the land on inheritance is also equally according to kinship, but with a greater part of the land held in common by brotherhoods or volunteer associations. In the Germanic group, inheritance of the land does not occur by subdivision, at least not below a viable size. Instead, it passes on through the male line, usually through the oldest son.

These different systems of inheritance have major effects on the way of life in alpine communities (Paccaud 1972). For example, the Austrian Alps, where the Germanic tradition prevails and the oldest son inherits all the physical property, have a high rate of illegitimate births, because a woman does not like to marry before her husband takes over the family's holdings, fearing that she will become a maid in his parents' household (Niederer 1972).

Xenophobia

Despite increased mobility in recent times, isolation in the high valleys still results in a low rate of intermarriage between different parts of the

Alps, even between adjacent valleys and villages. One reason for this is opportunity. During the long and sometimes rugged winter evenings, prospective suitors who are close neighbors obviously have a strategic advantage over those who live farther away.

Perhaps partly because of this, xenophobia is still prevalent in parts of the Alps. It is associated with long-standing landed resident families and possibly with ancient tribal taboos. It affects even closely neighboring communities. The most celebrated and extreme example of this was the case of Alexander Seiler (Lunn 1963), the man who put Zermatt on the map by bringing in tourists.

The village elders would not accept Seiler as a burgher, though he came from a nearby village in the upper Rhone Valley and was a member of the same Swiss canton. They rejected his application to become a burgher, even after he made a payment fixed by the canton of Valais and after his burgher status was sustained by the federal parliament, the federal cabinet and the federal court of appeal in Lausanne.

He was finally made a burgher in 1889, when the federal government sent in troops to Zermatt. Even after that, the village elders refused to allow Seiler to have access from the Gornergrat railroad to his nearby Riffelalp Hotel. In the 1960s, this attitude was still strong in Zermatt, where the frontier restaurant was closed at Testa Grigia, disappointing crowds of summer skiers. The Zermatt elders refused to have it run by an Italian or even by a Swiss from Lausanne, who had applied for a permit to do so.

Trends

The growth of tourism in the Alps during the past two centuries has greatly increased the diversity of peoples there. They include not only visitors and temporary residents but also foreign workers in factories, construction and services. Meanwhile, members of the old village families are increasingly occupied with providing food, lodging, transport, guides, instructors, entertainers and all types of retail supplies for the visitors and themselves. Training young people for these professions, especially in languages, starts early. They are sent to special schools and serve as assistants to guides or apprentices in hotels, even in countries other than their own. In addition, many of the local people have moved from the villages of their birth to larger cities in their own countries and abroad, in search of more gainful employment.

To measure the effects of these demographic and economic changes, Bätzing et al. (1996) made an analysis of those parts of the Alps that have had losses or gains of population (see table 6). They concluded, "Only in the western part of the Eastern Alps does tourism account for widespread population growth at higher altitudes; elsewhere the Alps have not been affected by modern development, and the economy and population are declining." Nevertheless, as is shown in table 6, in each of the seven countries involved, the total Alpine population has grown since 1870.

Folk Talk

Dialects

For centuries, people of the Alps have taken their local speech for granted, but many of them now value it as a key to their native identity and cultural heritage. The vocabularies of the local dialects are especially colorful, and often distinctive, where they apply to pastoral and domestic life and to features of high mountain landscapes. Some dialect words differ markedly from the corresponding modern languages and even within the major groups of dialects—French, Italian, Rhaeto-Romanic (Romansh), Germanic and Slavic. These groups have also shared similar words since ancient times, probably from Indo-European origins.

From Provençal

Old Provençal, rather than modern French, is the origin of all French alpine dialects: Savoyard, Dauphinois and modern Provençal in France; Vaudois and Valaisan in southwest Switzerland; and Valdotain in north-

TABLE 6.   Population Changes, Dynamics of Alpine Population in Thousands

Areas	Without Gain		With Gain		Total	
	1870	1990	1870	1990	1870	1990
Italy	1,590	1,010	1,352	2,816	2,943	3,827
Austria	385	332	1,093	2,563	1,479	2,895
France	747	409	458	1,317	1,204	1,726
Switzerland	336	267	603	1,452	938	1,719
Slovenia	143	97	123	275	266	371
Germany	0	0	126	445	126	445
Liechtenstein	0	0	7	29	7	29
Total	3,201	2,115	3,762	8,896	6,963	11,012

west Italy. The term Valdotain is a contraction from Valle d'Aosta, where Aosta, the city's Italian name, is a contraction from the Latin, Civitas Augusti. The Latin name commemorates the founder of the city, Caesar Augustus, the first emperor of Rome, whose aqueduct, theater and triumphal arch are still in place in the city. In Valdotain itself the name Aosta is further contracted to Auta.

Compared to modern French, which came from the dialect of Ile de France, Provençal is an older language with stronger ties to Latin and Celtic. Daudet's charming novel *Tartarin sur les Alpes* (see chap. 8) is laden with Provençal expressions, such as "ques aco" (what's going on?), and expletives, such as *outre, boufre, vai, zou,* and *diou.* Apart from the alpine scene, Valdotain offers numerous distinctive and colorful words, such as *einllia,* which describes how one's teeth feel when eating unripe fruit; *creili,* the word for a tub that leaks; *requi,* the term for a family meal after a wedding; and numerous synonyms for a young girl: *raga, drola, pitetta, meugnotte, mignotta* and *matta.* The last of these is the same in Romansh. France Alpine dialects, such as Savoyard (Guichonnel 1986), have rich literatures of local proverbs and folktales, as do those of the other dialect groups.

Germanic

Bavarian, Tirolean and the many forms of Swiss-German (Schenker and Hedinger 1941), including the archaic Walliser of the Italian valleys, reflect the speech of various Germanic tribes that settled these areas. Many words in these dialects are close to high German (Blüme), but many are not. For example, in Bavarian, *Blimoo* = a featherbed, while in Bernese, *Chaib* = a curse, *luege* = to look (unlike the Germen *schauen*), *Muni* = a bull, *Muntschi* = a kiss, *Warche* = work (unlike the German *Arbeit*), *ume* = backwards, and *Schockli* = a pile of hay.

The German diminutives *-chen* and *-lein* have many contracted local equivalents, especially in Swiss-German: *-li, -el, -i, -u, -tschi* and *-kki.* Thus Likki = Elise; Lukki = Luise; Rikki = Maria; Schukki = Julie; Schaki = Jacques; Jokkel, Jokki or Kchobu = Jakob; Chrigel, Chrigi or Hikki = Christian; Bartschi = Albrecht; Peterli = Peter; *Grütsi* = greetings; *es Mumpfeli* = a mouthful; *es Bitsli* = a little bit; *da Bubi* = the boys; *Jumpfere* = *Jungfrau,* an unmarried young woman.

Common Swiss expressions are "Gruss Gott mit Einander" (greetings with God to each other); "Zyt ha zu" (it's time to go); "auf wieder Luege" ("auf Wiedersehen," good-bye); "mi weiss nid" (I don't know);

and "er isch grusli Chind" (he is a terrible child). The Swiss-Germans borrow many French words, as in "merci vielmal" (thank you very much), *dischiniere* (breakfast, from *dejeuner*), *Spekchtakchel* (a movie), *kchelorli* (a watch, "what time?") and *orlogeli* (a clock). In Austria, police are called Gendarmerie, which is a holdover from Napoleonic times. Austrians make a point of saying "Gruss Gott" to distinguish themselves from Germans, who say "Guten Tag" (good day).

Romanic

Romansh is often used as a generic term for Rhaeto-Romanic dialects, which together are one of the four official Swiss languages (along with German, French and Italian). It is specific to southeast Switzerland and northeast Italy. It includes a few allegedly Etruscan words and place-names, such as the name for the town of Thusis, thought to be an old form for Tuscany. Some scholars, however, question the Etruscan connection and consider that its Latin component comes from the vernacular of Roman soldiers after their conquest of Rhaetia in 15 B.C. Romansh is not so much a common language for this area as a group of local dialects: Surselvian, Sutselvian and Surmenian in the upper Rhine Valley; Ladin in the lower Engadine, Val Mustair, Dolomites and Friuli. The Rhine group is often called Romansh as distinct from Ladin.

Romansh (in this sense) and Ladin include words unrelated to other languages or to each other, such as, respectively, *cazola* and *gluesch* (a light), *uault* and *god* (a forest), *tschitta* and *chueralla* (a butterfly) and *tschale* and *muruetsch* (a cellar). Distinctive words in Engadine (Ladin) dialect include *lindorna* (snail), *sola* (cockroach), *ampa* (strawberry), *uzun* (blueberry), *palu* (swamp), *fop* or *lajet* (pond) and *cotschen* (red). German words in these dialects, such as *giunfra* (= *Jungfrau*), trace to the Gothic and Alleman invasions in the fifth century A.D. Local Ladin dialects intermingle with those of Italian, especially in their application to the Alpine world (as can be seen in the place-names given in atlases).

Slavic

In Slovenia, there are nineteen local dialects, in two groups: Gorensko in the mountains and Doljensko in the lowlands. Some examples of distinctive words from the general Slovene vocabulary are *hsi* (daughter), *grm* (bush) and *god* (bog). Most Slovene words are closely related or even identical to those in other Slavic languages, such as *bel* or *bled* (white); *dan* (day); *dom* (house); *govor* (speech); *grad* (castle); *jagoda* (berry); *jama* (cave); *kniga* (book); *medved* (a bear); *metulj* (butterfly); *mak* (poppy); *oblak* (cloud); *ptic* (bird); *reka* (river); *topol* (poplar); *veter* (wind), from which comes *vetric* (breeze); *vrata* (gate); *vrv* (rope); and *zlato* (gold).

Pastoral Words

The words for a pasture display both striking similarities and differences among dialects. The most basic word, from which the name of the Alps derives, refers not to a mountain but to an upper pasture, with minor variations: *Alp* in German and Slovene, *Alm* in Tirolean, *alpe* or *alpage* in French and *arpa* in Savoyard. They are all thought to come from *al* in Celtic or *alimentum* in Latin, both being early words for food. In Valdotain, however, *arpa* means migration to an upper pasture, not the pasture itself (Cerlogne 1907). Other local dialect words for pasture are contractions from the French *champ* or Latin *campus: Tsan, tsa, tza* or *za.*

Such contractions are typical of local tongues. The Haut Glacier de la Tza de Tzan, hidden behind the Matterhorn, has an impressive sounding name, apparently meaning "pasture of pastures," though *tza,* in this case, may refer to its limestone bedrock (*chaux* in French). In the Walliser dialect of the upper Rhone Valley, *Matt* also means a high pasture, as in Zer*matt* and Ander*matt*. Thus the mighty Matterhorn's name refers to the pasture at its feet. Likewise, the Jungfrau acquired its name because its upland pasture belonged to the convent of Interlaken nuns who were known as the Jungfrauen. These examples show that Alpine people, in earlier times, were more interested in pastures than summits, and many still are. In Italian, the word for a pasture is *pastura* or *pascolo,* while in Slovene it is *pasnik;* thus one of the words with wide interlingual similarity.

The French dialects have special words for a cow that lifts its tail and returns to the stable (*besolla in Vaudois*) or that runs with its tail up (*bedzole in Valdotain*), for one with a spot on its forehead (*motelaye in Valaisan* and *Valdotain*), for one with a white part on the front of its head (*bautsan in Valdotain*) and for one with spots on its snout (*bocharda in Savoyard*). In Valaisan, a cowherd is a *gwarnyo,* while he or she is a *vatseran* (in French *vacheron*) in Valdotain, where *vatse* is a cow (like *vache* in French) and *modzenai* to a cowherd for heifers only. A trench for cows' droppings has no less than three quite different words in Valdotain: *leija, gronda* and *roara*.

In different parts of the Alps, the word for sheep is highly diverse: *Schaf* in German and Swiss-German, *brebis* or *mouton* in French, *fia* in Savoyard, *faya* in Valdotain, *feye* or *bema* in Valaisan, *pecora* or *ovina* in Italian, *nuorsa* in Romansh, *besch* in Ladin and *ovca* in Slovene. Other pastoral words have mostly common Latin origin: *vacca* (cow) in Romansh and Italian, *vacha* in Ladin and *vache* in French, but *Kuh* in German and *krava* in Slovene; also *fein* (hay) in Romansh, *fain* in Ladin, *fieno* in Italian and *foin* in French, but *Heu* in German and *sena* or *mrva* in Slovene.

Distinctive pastoral words in Ladin are *muvel* (livestock), *scossa* (herd), *ui* (stable) and *gial* (rooster). Some Slovene pastoral words are *svisli* (barn), *krvji hlev* (cowshed), *tele* (calf), *telica* (heifer), *vol* (ox), *pastir* (herdsman), *ovcar* (shepherd), *mleko* (milk) and *kura* (hen).

Mountain Words

In the Alps, there are many words for a mountain. In the German part of Switzerland, most peaks are called a *Horn*, often with a descriptive adjective, as in Nadelhorn (Needle Peak); Gspaltenhorn (Split Peak); Schreckhorn (Terrible Peak). Other German words for mountain names are *Kogel* (peak), *Stock* (stick), *Kopf* (head), *Huebel* (hillock), *Huegel* (hill), *Berg* (mountain), *Grat* (ridge), *Kulm* and *First* (summit) and Stein (stone); but *Gipfel* (summit), or *Gipfl* in Tirolean, rarely enters into the name of a peak. Some Alpine peaks have personified names in German, as do Eiger (Ogre), Mönch (Monk), and Wilde Frau (Wild Woman). In Austria the most common term in the names of peaks is *Spitze,* but the suffix *-er* suffices for some, as for Grossglockner and Grossvenediger.

In the French group, the most common prefixes for the name of a peak are *mont* (mount), as in Mont Blanc, and *aiguille* (needle), as in Aiguille du Géant. A small but formidable peak near Grenoble, Mont Aiguille, combines both terms. Other common French words used in mountain names are *pic* (peak), *pointe* (point), *tete* (head), *roc* or *roche* (rock), *pierre* (stone), *pilier* (pillar), *dent* (tooth), *tour* (tower), *pigne* (pine cone), *cime* (summit), and, occasionally, *sommet* (summit). In addition, many peaks have French dialect names, such as *be, bek, bec, becca, brec,* or *bric* (peak); *six, sex,* or *sasse* (rock), from the Latin word *saxum;* or *crep, crap, grap, grep, grip,* or *grepon* (rocky place). In Savoyard, *sonzon* means "summit." Some peaks are named for climbers, as are Les Dames Anglaises (for Mrs. and Miss Campbell) and Pic Coolidge (for W. A. B., not Calvin). Unlike North America, political names for mountains are rare in the Alps. Pic Wilson, a minor spire in the Mont Blanc range named for President Woodrow Wilson, is an exception. In Valaisan, as an example of local irony, Mont des Ritzes, which literally means "mountain of the rich," is a common term for a poor, stony, barren slope, not related to the name of the Ritz family (Guex 1976).

The Dents de Veisivi is a lovely twin-pointed snow peak in the Swiss Val d'Herens. *Dents* (teeth) is a common French name for sharp-pointed peaks, while *veisivi* translates, in local Valaisan, as "a cow that ought to calve but does not" or, more simply, "a cow that does not calve or is empty," that is, a heifer. The meadows below were in fact used for heifers, so this mountain too was named for the pasture on its slope. *Veisivi* (locally pronounced "veijivik") has many variations—*visivi, veisivey* and *vasevey* in the Valais, *veisiva* in Val d'Aosta and *vaxivier* in the Dauphine—all of which come from the Latin *vacivus* (empty)—as does the word *vacuum* (Guex 1976).

French dialect words are also used for parts of mountains. Examples are *balme* or *barme* (overhanging rock) and *eboulis* (scree or talus). Many Vaudois place-names end in *-az*, as in Anzeindaz, but the last two letters are silent. The name Gandegg is used for a moraine in the Bernese Alps but for a rock near Zermatt. *Egg* is a dialect version of the German *Ecke*, which means "a corner or edge." The suffixes *-au* and *-gau* are used in Bavarian and Swiss place-names, such as Murnau, Oberammergau and Aargau, or Argou in dialect. The name of the Swiss village Saas Fee comes from the Latin *saxum* (rock).

Italian names for peaks are prefixed by *monte, cima, torre, punta, rocca, roccia* or *testa,* which are equivalent to the aforementioned French terms. Examples are Monte Viso in the Cottian Alps, Testa Grigia near the Matterhorn, and Torre Venezia and Tre Cime de Lavaredo in the Dolomites. In Romansh and Ladin, most peaks are called *piz*, as is Piz Bernina, while others, as in Italian, are called *monte, pizzo, cima* or *sasso* (rock). One peak, south of Bernina, is called Sassalbo (White Rock). Another, in the Dolomites, called Sassolungo, is also known in its German version as Langkofel. In Ladin, a distinctive word, unrelated to Latin, Italian or Romansh, is *spelm* (rock).

In Slovene, *gora* means "mountain." It is the same in other Slavic languages and distinguishes the Gorensko mountain dialects in Slovenia from the Doljensko dialects of the lowlands. Other mountain words in Slovene are *gorski* or *alpski* (alpine); *pogorje* (mountain range); *gorski greben* (ridge), where *greben* means "crest"; *vrh* or *vrhunec* (peak or summit) and *visek* (summit); *konicast vrh* (spire; i.e., pointed peak); *kamen* (rock); and *skala* (cliff); by coincidence, this resembles the English *scale* in reference to scaling a cliff or a mountain.

Snow and Avalanche Words

The words for snow have much in common throughout the Alps. They are *Schnee* in German and Swiss-German, *sneg* in Slovene, *neige* in French, *neu* in Provençal, *na* in Savoyard, *nai* in Valdotain, *ney* or *na* in Valaisan, *neve* in Italian, *neiv* in Romansh, *naiv* in Ladin, and *nix, nivis* in Latin. The dialect words for an avalanche all appear to relate to the French *aval*, which means "down toward the valley." The words are *valanga* in Italian, *lavanca* in Provençal, *laveintse* in Valdotain, *avetse* in Valaisan, and *valeste* or *lavanche* in Savoyard, as in the name of the hamlet Le Levancher near Chamonix. The German *Lawine* or the Swiss-German *Laui* are clearly in the same pattern. The name of the Bernese village of Rosenlaui literally means "an avalanche from a glacier." In Ladin, the word for avalanche is *lavina,* which is close to the German and to *labina* in medieval Latin. In Slovene, the word is *lavina* as in Ladin, but with an alternative distinctive form, *plaz* (that which creeps or slides).

Glacier Words

In Italian and its dialects there are many words for a glacier: *ghiacciao, vedretta, gelas, veira, verina, byenio, truino, cristallo* and *rosa.* The last of these, as in Monte Rosa, has nothing to do with the rose flower or the color rose. It comes from the Teutonic *hrosa* or *chrosa*, brought into Italy by the Lombards, and means "crust of snow or ice." Virgil (*Georgics* 3.360) described a frozen river with the related Latin word *crusta.* In French dialects, this word has many variations: *reuse, rouise, roese, rouese, ruise, roise, rueze, ruegese* and *roija.* In Dauphinois, *royse* means "a glacial torrent." Related common words are *ruisseau* (brook) in French and *ruscello* in Italian. The Islandic *hrjosa* means "shivering with cold," as do the Savoyard *grevola* and Valdotain *grevole,* as in the name of Grivola, a peak south of Aosta.

In the Dolomites, the name of Monte Cristallo, which means Mt. Glacier, comes from the Greek *crustallos,* meaning "ice" or "rock crystal," which are visually similar, ice being a crystallized form of water. The basic Greek word is *cruos* (cold, as in *cryogenic*), which resembles the origins of *rosa* in Monte Rosa. *Ghiacciao* (glacier) comes from *ghiaccio,* which means "ice" in Italian. It resembles the French word *glacier* from their word *glace,* which has a number of meanings: ice, frost, cold, indifference, glass, mirror, window, flaw, and icing on a cake. The Italian *vedretta* and the Romansh *vadret* are words for glacier in southeast Switzerland and adjacent Italy. They come from the Latin *vitrum* (glass) and are related to the French *verglas* (sheet, or literally glass, of ice).

German dialects have three different words for a glacier. *Gletscher,* resembling the French *glacier,* is used in Switzerland and occasionally in Austria. Two completely different words are commonly used in Austria: *Ferner* in west Tirol and *Kees* east of Innsbruck. *Ferner* is an obvious cousin of the German *Firn* for the upper, transitional part of a glacier, while *Kees* is a Carinthian word that includes the German *eis* (ice). *Biegno,* a dialect word for glacier in Valaisan, resembles the Italian *byenio.* In Slovenia, which has only a few small glaciers, they are often called *zeleni sneg* (green snow), but with an alternative pan-Slavic form, *ledenik,* from *led* (ice).

Adaptations in English

The English word *glacier* comes directly from the French, but the English pronounce it "glass-yer," more like the French than like the American "glay-sher." Many other French mountaineering terms are used in Britain and America: *crevasse,* rather than the German *Spalte,* for a crack in a glacier; *serac* for a large block of ice; *arete* (originally, fish bone) for a ridge; *gendarme* for a tower on a ridge; *moraine* for a pile of stones on or from a glacier; *avalanche* for a torrent of snow; *piton* for an eyebolt; *carabiner* for a snap link; and *piolet,* rather than the German *Pickel,* for an ice ax. *Rappel* is used for "roping down" in America, but the British prefer the German *abseil.* Both the British and Americans use the German *Bergschrund,* rather than the French *rimaye,* for the large crevasse at the base of a snow slope. Anglo-Saxon equivalents of these terms are avoided to enhance the mystique of mountaineering, analogous to the use of French and German words in other specialized English jargons.

Status of Dialects

In 1975, the Swiss, according to their mother tongue, were 75 percent German, 20 percent French, 4 percent Italian and 1 percent Rhaeto-Romanic, the last being clearly an endangered species (Kraas 1992; Mützenberg 1974). Slovenian is locally international, since 44 percent of those who speak it live in Italy or Austria. French Alpine dialects are gradually losing out to modern French except in the higher valleys. They still survive in traditional Catholic areas of the Valais, Aosta and Savoy, but Vaudois is facing extinction in its Protestant Swiss homeland. Religion is not the only factor. Mobility may be even more important. The proportion of Swiss living in communes of their birth was 59 percent in 1860 but only 31 percent in 1947 (see also Bätzing et al. 1996).

In the Alps, differences amont dialects, like the varieties of alpine flowers and butterflies, have evolved through isolation in adjacent valleys. In the story of the Tower of Babel (Genesis 11), diversity of tongues was a punishment for attempting to reach high altitude. In the Alps, people have reached much higher than the Tower of Babel, and their forms of speech have likewise proliferated, but they do not regard it as a punishment. Many of those who speak Valdotain, Romansh, Tirolean and Swiss-German are fighting to save their dialects, which they regard as a gift of God.

Chapter 8

Mountain People's Lives

Pastoral Life

Upland Pastures

Animal husbandry and associated hay making have become less dominant in the Alps during the past century, but raising cows and sheep for dairy products, wool and meat is still a significant activity among many high-valley people (Price 1981). The severe conditions of the Alpine world dictate what they must do. The growing season is short, so they need more land to grow hay for feeding flocks in winter. However, mountains, glaciers, rocky terrain, erosion and avalanche debris restrict the amount of usable land. On north-facing slopes, mountain shadows block out part of the needed sun, while sunny south-facing slopes are more arid, with smaller glaciers, less water and leaner grazing for the flocks. The people must use every bit of usable land without destroying the protective forests above the villages. In most of the mountain areas, the valley land is inadequate, and the pastures above the tree line must be used too. The migration to the upper meadows thus becomes a basic rhythm of Alpine life (Paccaud 1972). This is its main difference from raising livestock in the lowlands.

In most alpine villages, the cows leave for the upper pastures on a day around the middle of June. At Kandersteg, before dawn on that day, a chorus of cowbells echoes on the narrow main street of the village, as several herds of ten to twenty cows start on their annual journey to one of the five contiguous upper valleys. On this important occasion, the cows wear their large, deep-throated ceremonial bells. In each herd, the senior cow leads the rest and proudly wears the largest bell, accompanied by one or two herdsmen with leather rucksacks, carrying steel-pointed staffs. The members of each herd follow the lead cow in descending order of seniority and cowbell size.

After arriving at the upper pastures, the cows wear smaller bells that tinkle day and night during the months that they graze there, while the ceremonial bells form a display in order of size across an outside wall of the herder's summer chalet. About the middle of September, the cows wear the big ceremonial bells again for the march back down to the village. They then also wear garlands of flowers on their foreheads if the summer has passed without accident to any cow in their herd. The same custom applies in Austria and other parts of the Alps.

Two-Stage Migration

In the Alps of Austria and northern Switzerland, the march of the herds to the uplands is a one-day process, but in some south Swiss, French and Italian Alps, where the tree lines are higher (see chap. 5), two stages are customary for the migration in each direction. After grazing in the valleys in April, the cows move in the middle of May to small intermediate pastures cleared halfway up through the forest. Chalets provided there for cows and people, usually under the same roof, often form temporary hamlets that the French call "mayens" (for May). About a month later, the herds complete the journey to the meadows above the trees, where another set of chalets awaits them. These are the true alps. In August, it is already too late to stay above, and the herds come back to the mayens for two or three more weeks. Finally, in September, they return to the villages, where they graze as long as they can before having to be fed hay in their winter stables.

In parts of the southern Alps, the cycle for the people is even more complex. Because of limited economic resources in the mountains, dwellers of high valleys try to supplement their livelihood from richer lands in the lower and larger valleys. In the southern Alps, this often takes the form of vineyards. In the Val d'Anniviers, the villagers have even built lower hamlets in which they stay to harvest the grapes and at other times when the vineyards need attention. They thus work at four different levels during each grazing season: in the vineyards below, in the pastures and hay fields near the villages, in the mayens, and in the pastures above the forest (Paccaud 1972).

Cheese Making

A single cowherd with his family can take care of the cows on the upper meadows for several owners, of whom he may be one. His job is to watch the cows, milk them, make cheese and butter, clean their stalls and spread manure on the pastures. From those pastures that can be reached by jeep, the herdsmen deliver the milk every day to the village cooperative, without having to make cheese in the mountains. Where jeeps cannot go, the herdsmen carry some of the milk down once or twice a week in special cans with shoulder straps, but they convert most of it into cheese or butter on the mountain.

The process for making cheese in the mountains is primitive but basically similar to that in major factories, which produce the most familiar Swiss cheeses in advanced and precisely controlled equipment. After heating the milk to 52°C (125°F), the cheese maker adds rennet (an enzyme obtained from the stomachs of cows) to form the curd, which he lifts from the vat and places into molds. While curing the cheese for three to six months at 22°C (72°F), the characteristic large holes develop by formation of carbon dioxide. Emmental cheeses weigh more than 100 kilos (220 lbs.). Cheeses made on high pastures are about half that size so that the herdsmen can carry them down the mountain in rucksacks. The alpine cheeses have smaller holes because of less prolonged curing at less precisely controlled temperature, and their taste is usually stronger. On remote highlands of the French and Italian Alps, as on the Italian side of the Col d'Agnel near Monte Viso, the cheese-making equipment can be more primitive, mainly a cauldron over an outside bonfire.

Pastoral Arrangements

At the end of summer, if a herd has several owners, each owner receives his share of cheese in proportion to how much milk his cows have produced. In the foothills such as in the Emmental in Switzerland, which do not rise above the tree line, there is no vertical migration, merely rotation between the fields and grazing meadows. Often, however, the local farmers send their heifers to summer pastures in the higher mountains to reduce the strain on local grazing areas. The upland herdsmen in charge of heifers thus do not need to milk or make cheese. In the Alps, there are several breeds of cows that are characteristic of different localities. Most obvious are the large brown Bernese cows, while various smaller gray or brown breeds are typical of other areas. Pure white cows prevail on the Grande Chartreuse and on the south slopes of Monte Viso.

In remote highlands of the French and Italian Alps, the relationship between cows and people can be intimate. A cowherd there may spend the summer in a simple stone hut with an earth floor, in a single room for both his cows and his family, separated only by a waist-high horizontal beam. At the far corner of the people's side, a cauldron suspended over a fire provides both cooking and cheese making. For cold nights, this is a choice of warmth over aroma. Most isolated chalets on alpine slopes tend to be simple, if not extremely so. In the Bernese Alps, at the Bundalp chalet in the upper Kiental, cows occupy the ground floor. There is no running water, and people bathe in a basin on the kitchen floor. In larger pastoral establishments, even on the upper slopes (such as on the Hahnemoos, above Adelboden), the animals occupy a separate stable adjacent to the house, which is also the typical arrangement in most villages.

Hay Making

After walking down the Swiss side of the St. Bernard Pass, with a detour to the enchanting Combe de l'A sanctuary, we found the village of Liddes to be a beehive of activity. The entire population seemed to be mobilized for harvesting hay from the surrounding slopes. Older women raked or tossed hay in the upper fields, while men carried it in huge, rope-tied bundles on their backs to small trucks. Animated young people, loudly calling to each other and wielding rakes, brought hay in the trucks to the village, where they stacked it into several upper haylofts. The girls wore bright bandannas and were clearly enjoying the arduous work.

Making hay in the valleys requires more work than does tending the flocks on the upper pastures. Most cattle owners and their families work full-time on the lower slopes making hay to feed the cows through the winter. Hay making differs locally but is always laborious, often exhilarating and especially picturesque. The first step, if needed, is to pick up stones that have been pushed up through the ground by winter frost. The next steps are harrowing and spring planting, where planting is needed. Harvest is the time, once or twice a year, when the whole village turns out for cutting, raking, drying, transporting and loading hay into local storage sheds or central barns. All of these steps may be manual or partly mechanical, depending on the terrain, but much hand labor always takes place. Mechanical devices are useful where the slope is not too steep. They include small gasoline mowers and blowers, small trucks, jeep-drawn or horse-drawn wagons and occasionally mechanical rakes. Otherwise, on steeper slopes, the tools are scythes, rakes and pitchforks. The men use rope to tie large bundles of hay that can weigh up to 100 kilos (220 lbs.) and carry them to the wagons. Both walking in the hay before it is cut and flattening it while photographing flowers are serious violations of owners' rights.

The largest local differences are in the methods of drying hay. If there is little or no rain and the sun is bright, as in the southern Alps, it may dry on the ground for several days, tossed periodically into the air with pitchforks. Otherwise it dries on racks. In the Bernese Alps, in most of Austria, and farther north, in the Polish Tatras, the racks are posts with crossbars to support the hay, forming rows of ghoulish-looking ricks. In East Tirol and in the Dolomites, the hay dries on long fencelike racks that usually run downhill. In the Julian Alps it is dried on vertical frames with crossbars and small gable roofs at the top. Crossbars also line the sides of haylofts above the living quarters of houses in the Italian Alps. The open walls of barns in Slovenia may have diagonal bars with diamond-shaped openings in which the hay hangs to dry.

Where weather is unpredictable, as in most of the Alps, drying the hay can be precarious. This is especially so for drying it on the ground, which is the prevailing method in the French Alps south of Lake Geneve: "In making hay there is always a wager. The quicker the hay is in, the better it is. Yet the hay must be dry, otherwise it ferments. At the worst, tradition had it, damp hay could eventually set a house on fire [by spontaneous combustion]. If you don't take any risks, you'll never get your hay in early. At the best, you will be left with hay like straw. So, impatient, you bet on the sun lasting and the storm holding off. It's not us making hay, it's sun that makes hay" (Marzorati 1987).

In most alpine valleys, the usable land spreads out in a number of small patches. Owners of cows often have several temporary dwellings, cow barns, and hay-storage sheds in different parts of a valley. Most of these buildings are small and serve only a short time each year, often grouped in hamlets where the avalanche danger is low. The privately owned land is mainly on the lower slopes, while the high pastures are community property where grazing rights are inherited and can be sold within the village like land. However, selling either land or rights to outsiders is rarely allowed.

Limits to Hay and Pastures

Avalanches can be a menace for hay making, burying the land under thick snow and rock debris that require much labor to remove. Avalanche snow, which may have the consistency of concrete, can last all summer, and a second year may pass before the owners clear the land from rocks and trees that the snow brings down. In such places it is useful to have one's land in several parcels in different parts of the valley. This is the typical arrangement in the Lötschental, which is notorious for its avalanches. The average landowner there has 4 hectares (10 acres) divided into fifty parcels. The effect of this arrangement is to limit the avalanche damage to a part of one's land and to spread the disaster among several landowners, rather than preventing a single family from feeding its herds with hay and grass for a whole year or more.

Even with the best of arrangements, it is not always possible to produce enough hay to provide winter fodder for the entire herd, including calves and heifers. It is then necessary to obtain hay from elsewhere or to thin out the herd. This is a calculation that needs to be made in the fall, when grazing ends and feeding begins in the stalls. Annual fairs are a traditional method of selling cows, horses and other livestock for this purpose (Price 1981), or the owners may sell them directly to an abattoir.

Grazing in the high Alps, as in other semidesert environments, is in many places ecologically harmful if not carefully planned and controlled. The widespread aridity and denudation of the southern French Alps and other Mediterranean mountains is the result of centuries of excessive grazing and woodcutting. Sheep are especially harmful to the fragile alpine meadows, because they crop close to the ground and even disturb the roots of the grass. Cows can also be harmful on slopes, by stamping out closely spaced horizontal paths that destroy the vegetation. The solution to most such problems is limiting and rotating the use of pastoral lands. Limits to grazing on the upper pastures are effected through ownership of grazing rights, which controls the size of a herd to correspond with the size of a pasture. In the Bernese Alps and perhaps elsewhere, the measure of a pasture is in "cows," a unit of measure that varies with the local terrain.

In the southern French Alps, there are large herds of cows and especially of sheep. In years past, this resulted in spectacular annual transhumance after a summer in the mountains, with vast herds of sheep driven for the winter to grazing grounds near the Mediterranean, where they do not need shelter. This practice is rapidly declining because of resort development along the coast. Sheep produce mainly wool and meat but also milk for cheeses, such as Roquefort. Various types of goat cheese are also products of the Alps. Goat herds tend to be small throughout the Alps (Spyri 1958). They belong mainly either to those who are less affluent and do not own land or grazing rights or to those who do it as a sideline. In addition to cows, sheep and goats, the pastoral animals include pigs and horses. Herds of yellow-maned reddish brown Haflinger horses are a spectacular sight in Austria and Bavaria.

Pastoral Celebration

About the middle of August, in the Bernese Alps, people gather between the white summits of the Wildstrubel and the Balmhorn for the annual Gemmi Pass Schaeferfest (sheep festival). Dozens of sheep and several hundred people crowd the boulder-strewn slope beside the trail, just above the Daubensee at 2,240 meters (7,350 ft.). Most of the sheep come over the pass from Leukerbad early that morning, having climbed the trail cut into a near-vertical cliff 900 meters (3,000 ft.) high. After a blessing by a priest, the sheep run free to the area of salt licks prepared for them on the ground. Then they run up to their usual grazing slopes, where on hot days they cool themselves by lying on patches of late-melting snow. This is also an occasion for a traditional Alpine sport, in which wrestlers try to upend each other by grabbing the backs of their special leather pants on a sawdust-covered patch of earth. Alphorns playing centuries-old pastoral tunes provide an episode of musical entertainment. A cloud descends on the landscape and blots out everything except the yodeling and dissonant warbling of groups of revelers from the tops of several large boulders.

The sheep festival is a celebration of an entire way of life, steeped in ancient traditions. These, like the sheep festival itself, are related to particular days or seasons of the pastoral and agricultural year, nominally of the Christian year but going back to pre-Christian times. They typically involve fertility rites for crops, domestic animals and human beings, with rituals for exorcizing harmful entities: "The growth of crops, the mainstay of life, is furthered by invoking benevolent powers and warding off spirits of destruction. The orgiastic festivals often attending these rites also serve the propagation of the race" (Leach 1984, 277). Here are a few examples.

In Central Europe, the favorite time for expelling witches is or was Walpurgis Night, the eve of May Day. . . . At Brunnen on the Lake of Lucerne, boys go about in procession at Twelfth Night [of the Christmas season] carrying torches and making a great noise with horns, bells, whips and so forth, to frighten off two female spirits of the wood, Strudeli and Stratteli. The people think that if they do not make enough noise, there will be little fruit that year. (Fraser 1996, 649–50)

Shaggy creatures abound in mountain regions: the Hutterslaufer of Tyrol and the Swiss Rautschegetten with black sheepskin. . . . On Twelfth Night they frighten naughty children and add to the fructification of the crops. . . . These "wild men" are associated with fire, black magic, weather control [with] powers to promote rain, cure, and fertility. . . . Animal bells, though now largely thought of as utilitarian devices for finding strayed animals, were also first used to drive off harmful spirits. . . . Tyrolean farmers insured a good harvest by ringing bells while circling their fields, and at Brunnen on Lake Lucerne, a Twelfth Night ceremony for ringing out witches also carried a potency for making a full fruit crop. (Leach 1984, 133, 281, 856)

Carnival—in Latin, *carne vale,* or "farewell to meat"—is a season of merriment in the days just before the Lenten fast. In French it is called Mardi Gras, "fat Tuesday." In German, Carnival is called Fasching, while Shrove Tuesday itself is called Fastnacht, referring to the night when Carnival ends and Lent begins. It derives from the *kologheroi* of Thrace and dates back to Dionysian *orgia* and Roman bacchanalia: "Carnival is identified with primitive ceremonies for expulsion of death, winter and demons harmful to the coming crops. . . . In modern Carnival celebrations, the din and masquerade persist, but not the ritual purpose" (Leach 1984, 192, 605).

Bätzing et al. (1996) found that out of 122 regions in four Alpine countries, 51 had an "agricultural character" in the 1980s. Even in prosperous Alpine villages that thrive on summer tourism and winter sports, pastoral activity is still a significant part of people's lives. Despite commercial pressures, Alpine people know that in the pastoral life, they have a precious cultural heritage that they will not allow to die, nor can they afford to do so.

Home Life

Beginnings

Early peoples migrating into the Alps brought with them skills and traditions many thousands of years old. They used these abilities to make their homes and to celebrate their lives. In western Europe as early as 32,000 years ago, according to carbon dating, Cro-Magnon foragers ingeniously used mammoth bones as structural members for their dome-shaped dwellings and food-storage buildings, the original yurts, and carved attractive grooved beads from mammoth tusks with flint tools.

At Halstatt in the Austrian Alps, Illyrian graves from 4,500 to 1,500 years ago contained bronze, gold, ceramic, and wrought-iron artifacts, including animal sculptures, collars with pendants, necklaces, bracelets, rings, beads, brooches, pins, girdle clasps, axes, razors, daggers, swords, masks, bowls, urns, pitchers and other household objects, many of them decorated in geometric patterns (Morton 1953). The Halstatt culture, taken over by the Celts, provided iron tools for effective use of stone and wood in the construction of dwellings. Celtic jewelry, weapons and utensils from the fifth to first centuries B.C., found at La Tène near Neuchatel (Sauter 1976) and later at other Alpine sites, utilized bronze or wrought iron with graceful decorations of birds, goats, human figures and Grecian-style floral clusters. A set of tiny human figures and a miniature four-wheel wagon drawn by ten oxen, all made of lead in the seventh century B.C., were a remarkable find at Frogg in Carinthia.

Medieval Homes

More than a thousand years later, a typical Alpine farmhouse of the medieval Gothic period exhibited a way of life that mostly survives today (Niederer-Nelken 1982; Zeller 1976). The main feature was separation of the living room from the kitchen at the rear. Food passed through a hatch in the kitchen wall. A separate stove heated the living room and also served as a baking oven. Such a room, in German, is called a Stube, which etymologically relates to *stove*.

The key furniture in the living room was a dining table with chairs. A removable wooden or metal plate protected the center of the table from damage by a common dish of hot food. All family members ate from the central dish with spoons, which were the only eating utensils. Each member owned a personal spoon carved from animal bone and always carried it in a special pocket or pouch. The spoon was often finely engraved on both sides. Individual plates made of wood or ceramic were a later development. In the evenings and in winter, the table was also the center of indoor activities, such as wood carving, sewing and playing cards. The living room included a sacred corner with votive images or statuettes.

This was the focus of religious observances for births, weddings, festivals and funerals. At Christmas, it included a crèche.

The custom of eating from a communal dish, though using forks, still prevails for traditional group meals. When eating cheese fondue, one spears a small piece of bread from a basket and dips it into a common bowl of melted Gruyère cheese mixed with white wine, kept boiling over an alcohol flame. At an inn, whoever drops a piece of bread into the molten cheese must pay for the next round of wine. Likewise, with *fondue Bourgignonne,* one dips small pieces of raw beef into a communal bowl of boiling oil and then into béarnaise and other sauces. Wooden plates still widely prevail for *Bernerplatte,* which is a hot dish of ham, sausage, potatoes and sauerkraut; and for *Bündnerteller,* a specialty of the Grisons (*Graubünden*) that features paper-thin slices of raw smoked beef. Austria and other parts of the Alps have similar dishes for *Jaussen* (folk-type meals).

In larger farmhouses of Gothic times, the bedroom was a separate room, sometimes directly above the living room with a hatch in the floor that, when open, allowed heat to rise. The beds were Procrustean, shorter than the people, because they slept sitting up, leaning against pillows that were propped against the headboards. Trundle beds, with one fitting under another when not in use, are still fairly common, especially in remote cowherd's chalets. The furniture in both living room and bedroom, including chests, cupboards and wardrobes, traditionally came from the bride's dowry. It featured intricate carving or painting with typical local designs, which also decorated the living-room ceiling beams and the doors between rooms, also fitted with ornamental hardware. The cradle, according to custom, was a gift from the godfather. Its design was especially artistic, with pious religious themes carved or painted on its panels, and it was richly fitted with lace. The inside, however, was also often carved (just in case) with a pagan "Druid's foot" (a hand with the thumb between the first and second fingers) to ward off evil spirits.

A metal hood above the hearth in the kitchen served as a shield against sparks. The cooking pot hung from a metal arm that could be swiveled off to the side. Before matches were available, lighting the fire was laborious, and if possible it was kept from ever going out. A depression at the center of the hearth confined the glowing embers for safety at night. Bread was baked twice a year and normally had to be chopped with an ax and softened in a hot soup to be edible. Wooden molds, made by "reverse carving," were the pride of a kitchen and used for serving butter or for making gingerbread on festive occasions. There were special molds for New Year's Eve, Epiphany, Easter, St. Nicholas Day and Christmas, the last of these often in the shape of an infant in swaddling clothes. "Chain pastry" in the form of fish or swaddled infants joined together were a symbol of fertility and were eaten on New Year's Eve by a couple wishing to have children. These are still available in pastry shops.

Arrangements Today

Probably the earliest Alpine houses were simple, one-room stone huts, freestanding or leaning against a cliff, with stone slab roofs supported by timbers, such as those still widely used by French and Italian shepherds in the Alps. Cowherds also lived in one-room houses, of similar construction but larger size, with the cattle and cowherd's family separated by a waist-high wooden beam.

As noted earlier, in many farmhouses in the Alps today, the cattle and the cowherd's family still live under the same roof, with a wall or a floor to separate them physically, if not olfactorily. In villages with limited space, the cattle often occupy the ground floor, with the family on an upper floor and, above that, an open hayloft below the roof. This arrangement is typical in the Engadine and in most of the Italian Alps. The huge farmhouses of Bavaria combine the same sections horizontally under a single gable roof, with the family rooms at one end and the rest divided between a cow stable, a hay-storage area, and a garage for farm equipment. In Upper Austria, these sections, though still connected by a common roof, are at right angles to each other, forming the sides of a square courtyard in a style called a *Vierkanthof.* In Tirolean and other Alpine areas where the terrain is rough, the farms are spread out into two or more separate buildings, which reduces the fire hazard.

In southern Switzerland, Italy and parts of France, the roofs of the houses are similar to those of the simplest early huts, being covered with flat slabs of schist, gneiss or slate supported by wooden beams. Many have a ground floor of masonry or stucco with wooden walls above, while some, especially in the southern Swiss valleys, are wooden in front with masonry in the back. This facilitates having two or more apartments on separate floors in a single house, each with its own kitchen, located in the masonry part of the building to reduce fire hazard. Throughout the Alps, especially in eastern Switzerland and France, many houses have walls built of masonry only, sometimes with a courtyard entered through an archway leading to the livestock and hay-storage spaces.

Local House Styles

The traditional chalet of the Bernese Alps, now widely imitated elsewhere (Paccaud 1972), has a gable roof covered with wood shingles, with a low slope and wide overhanging eaves for protection against snow sliding off. The walls are of solid wood, with the timbers placed one above the other, often crossed at the corners in the manner of American log cabins. Outside stairs to balconies under the eaves at the side walls give access to the upper rooms in place of hallways inside. The balconies are often enclosed in glass to retain heat and provide space for potted plants in winter. In Lauenen and other Bernese villages, the facades are elaborately carved and painted, typically including pious or poetic mottos. Flower boxes below the windows in summer add much to the decor of chalets throughout the Alps, most magnificently at Grimenz in the Valais.

In an outlying chalet, its main facade, which is a gable end, almost always faces downhill and preferably south. In villages, the chalets face the street, but in high hamlets on sloping ground, they all face downhill rather than facing each other across the street, which may be just a narrow walkway. For a small hay-storage chalet, the length of the timbers determines its size, and the timbers are rough for ventilation. In the Lötschental and elsewhere in the southern Alps, such chalets rest on four stone pedestals, each with a flat, round, mushroom-like stone top that provides a barrier against rats.

In northeast Switzerland, beginning at Schwyz, the wooden houses are architecturally distinct (Paccaud 1972), being tall with several floors, and with each row of windows shielded by its own narrow sloping roof extending across the facade. Such houses typically have a different family or generation on each floor. In the Rhine Valley section of the Grisons, the chalet facades have a central wooden panel, with the remaining walls, including both corners of the facade, built of masonry. In some of the outlying areas of the northern and western Alps, such as the Emmental and the Grande Chartreuse, the chalets and farms have hip roofs sloping in all four directions, with a sloping section replacing all or part of an otherwise sharp gable end. In the southern French Alps, in Styria and in Slovenia, the farmhouse roofs are often covered with long, overlapping wooden slats pointing down, rather than with shingles or stone slabs. In parts of Austria and east Switzerland, the newer house walls are built of hollow tile covered with stucco, even for hay-storage buildings that are ventilated by open lattices made of tiles. Tile roofs are also common there.

Domestic Crafts

During the Middle Ages, the useful and artistic skills that helped the herdsmen and their families to survive and celebrate the severe conditions of life in the Alps were practiced mainly at home (Friedl 1976; Menardi 1990; Wildhaber 1971). They included working with wood, paint, textiles, leather, glass and stone, as well as milling flour, baking bread and pastry and making wine, cheese, bacon and sausage. Woodworking included turning, carving and carpentry. In Tirol, it was an unwritten law that a prospective bridegroom had to learn the carpenter's trade so that he would be able to take care of his house. In the sixteenth century, when a branch of carpentry grew into the joiner's trade, the Austrian emperor decreed that a carpenter could make joints with wooden pegs only, while a joiner had the right to make joints with glue. These trades became organized in the form of guilds.

The products of wood turning were furniture legs, plates, bowls, candlesticks, rolling pins, tool handles, chess men and parts for wooden machinery, such as spinning wheels and looms. A tabletop wood-lathe was convenient to use at home, being no more complex than a spinning wheel and usually smaller. The turning and carving of wood were elements of carpentry in making furniture and doors with carved ornamental panels, such as the intricate rosettes of the Queyras (Guillaume 1986).

Wood carving developed into a traditional artistic activity for creative and lucrative work at home. Like other forms of folk art, it enjoyed a wide and informal practice but also flourished as a specialty in a few well-known places in the Alps, such as Oberammergau in Bavaria, Brienz in Switzerland and Val Gardena in the Dolomites. Among the salable products of wood carving were small and large models of animals, such as bears, ibex, chamois, cows, sheep and horses; dolls and doll heads; floral and other ornamental objects; frames; clock cases; crèches; and statuettes of gnomes and religious figures, such as the Madonna, or worldly ones, such as William Tell. Nativity scenes were a favorite theme.

In Switzerland, the production of elaborately carved cuckoo clocks and music boxes became a major commercial industry combining skills in working with wood, metals and fine machinery. It was customary for skilled wood-carvers to take on apprentices. In Brienz they founded a school, now operated by the canton of Bern, which offers a four-year course in all branches of wood carving. (For part of her year between secondary school and college in Westchester, New York, our daughter was an apprentice to a wood-carver at Graz in Austria.)

Painted Objects

A branch of wood carving that is special to the Alps is the production of grotesque masks for carnivals. The masks require not only skilled carvers but also skilled painters. A leading Tirolean crib painter also specialized in coloring the masks made at Imst. The purpose of such masks, when worn at religious festivals, was to frighten off evil spirits. The making of carnival masks is a major home activity in the Lötschental, where the masked processions are famous. The Lötschental masks are characterized by gigantic size, crooked eyes, distorted noses and irregular teeth. Other important centers for carving such masks are Sargans in east Switzerland and Imst in Tirol. The Sargans masks are more colorful and less frightening, often being caricatures of red-cheeked girls or ruddy double-chinned older women. At St. Gallen, the masks represent St. Nicholas and are worn between Christmas and New Year's Eve.

The painting of furniture and other household objects is also an important domestic industry. In addition to religious, floral and ornamental subjects, much of folk-art painting celebrates scenes from pastoral life. Major centers for primitive peasant painting are Gruyère and Appenzell. An outstanding example of the latter from 1823 is a scene painted on the bottom of a wooden milk pail, showing a cowherd wearing a black hat, white shirt, red vest, tan knickers and white socks, with a black Appenzeller dog, two white goats, and a brown cow wearing a huge bell with an ornamental leather strap. Such bells with embroidered straps are also an important folk-art form. Among favorite subjects for outdoor murals are images of St. Christopher or other saints and designs featuring edelweiss, alpenrose and gentians. Oberammergau in Bavaria and Ardez in the Lower Engadine have outstanding examples of the stucco facades richly decorated by talented mural painters. The Ardez "graffiti" of Adam and Eve is exceptionally fine and famous.

Textile Arts

A large branch of Alpine domestic art includes everything to do with textiles: spinning, weaving, dying, embroidery, lace making and the sewing of traditional local costumes, called *Trachten* in German (De la Harpe 1910). Women make the costumes worn by their men in carnival processions, though the women are not (or were not) allowed to take part. Austrian dirndls and hunting jackets are popular Alpine costumes for dances and other occasions. The designs of these outfits are special for each province.

The traditional local costumes are far more diverse in Switzerland. At the Gemmi Sheep Festival, the men from the Valais wore short black velvet jackets with lapels edged in white and embroidered with edelweiss. In the Lötschental, a young girl going to church wore a black dress embroidered with red flowers above the hem and a long white kerchief on her head. At a Lötschental wedding, the women wore embroidered black dresses and gold-embroidered black hats with wide vertical boards in back, resembling three-cornered hats. An Appenzell lady had a black silk dress with white sleeves and closely spaced red cords crisscrossing the front of the bodice, in a panel between two rows of lace tapering downward. The most extraordinary festive costumes are those of Walliser women in the German-speaking valleys of Italy (Aiby 1986), with embroidered black vests over red blouses and extremely intricate gold embroidery on black hats flairing upward like inverted cones.

From the skills of early herdsmen and their families in high Alpine valleys (Friedl 1976), building homes and working within them, the world has been enriched by treasures of domestic architecture and art.

Chapter 9

Literature

Legends

Myths Familiar and Unfamiliar

The story of William Tell, the Swiss national hero, first became generally known from the Schiller-Rossini nineteenth-century opera, with its familiar galloping theme. How Tell shot the apple from the head of his son and later killed the Austrian oppressor is a tale too long and well known to be repeated here (Cuvelier 1965; Riedler 1989). It lives on along the eastern shores of Lake Lucerne; in Burglen, Altdorf and Kussnacht; in the Tell Museum and two Tell chapels; in statues, murals, books and children's stories; in the minds of thousands of tourists; and in the hearts of millions of Swiss. It is the best-loved legend of the Alps, despite the Swiss government's official finding that William Tell did not in fact exist.

The Alps are a fertile ground for legends. These are stories about real and imaginary people, animals, fanciful creatures, mountains and pastoral life. One book contains 540 legends from the Valle d'Aosta alone (Chanu 1988), so the total for the Alps must be in the thousands. Obviously only a tiny sample can be considered here. The first three involve reptilian creatures, two being of actual types and the last one imaginary. Oddly, all three identify benign aspects in them, at least briefly. All three also deal with historic people.

Charlemagne and the Serpent

The first one concerns Charlemagne, who was one of the four or five most famous people who ever trod the Alps. He was also the last person who ever ruled the entire region. He often traveled through it, dispensing his wise justice; and that is how the legend begins (Müller-Guggenbühl 1958).

It is said that during one of his visits to Zurich (where he is entombed), he let it be known that those who had a complaint should ring the bell outside his palace gate when he was having dinner, and he would personally see that justice was done. Once, when the bell rang, his servant went out but came back saying that no one was at the gate. Still the bell kept ringing. The servant went out again and returned with the same report, after which Charlemagne went to see for himself. According to the story, what he saw was a snake that was ringing the bell by dangling on the chain.

When she (it was a female) saw the great monarch, she dropped to the ground and began moving away but kept looking back, signaling for him to follow, which he did, along with his servant. Soon they came to a nest, where a toad was sitting on the snake's eggs. The snake was afraid to remove the toad without damaging the eggs. Charlemagne ordered his servant to remove the toad and thus saved the eggs. The snake then returned to the palace with Charlemagne, climbed the dining table, and deposited a rare jewel into his wine glass. The monarch was extremely pleased with the gift and had it set in a ring for his queen. The snake had found justice as though it were a human being. For lovers of nature, this is surely one of the most delightful of all snake stories ever told.

St. Eldrade and the Vipers

Another legend is about snakes in their traditional antagonistic relationship to people, going back to the story of the Garden of Eden and perhaps even to earlier sources on human and reptilian genes. It was not St. Patrick but St. Eldrade who banished the snakes from at least one part of the Alps (Sentis 1982). He did it in the brotherly manner of St. Francis speaking to the wolf of Gubbio, but three centuries earlier. In the year A.D. 860, according to records in Turin, Dom Eldrade was abbot of the Benedictine monastery at Susa. He sent a group of monks across the Briançonnais to build a priory for travelers on the Roman road over the Col de Lautaret, which was difficult in winter. It was to be built at a hot spring above the village of Monétier, where Roman legionnaires had often come to nurse their wounds. The monks came and returned in dismay, because masses of vipers, enjoying the warmth of the spring, were rearing up, hissing, and menacing them.

A few days later, the eighty-year-old abbot arrived with a few monks and was ecstatic (which the monks were not) at the grandeur of the glaciers and the peaks, one of which he said was the "finger of God," blessing his project. To this day that towering summit, the central spire of the Meije (3,973 m., 13,035 ft.), bears the name of Doigt de Dieu. Dom Eldrade said mass and spoke to the vipers, who then followed him, as did the terrified monks, around the village on a wide circle that he marked with his abbot's staff. He then led them to a rocky slope, far across the valley, and spoke again, "My sisters, the vipers, I wish you no harm, but you must hold your place in the Creation and leave men in peace. Here is your new home, but even here you must not attack people." The vipers promptly disappeared among the rocks, and at the hot spring the priory was built. Today at that spot, there are an oratory and a chalybeate (ferrous) health spa, but the masses of vipers are gone.

St. Beat and the Dragon

Much larger reptilians, the dragons, were among the least charming creatures who were thought to inhabit the Alps. Four different forms of dragons were precisely described by Johann Jakob Scheuchser in his book on the natural history of Switzerland (1723). There is, however, one relatively charming dragon story. It begins in Rome with a man named Suetonius—not the famous Suetonius, writer of the second century A.D., but an earlier one who was a bon vivant among the patricians at the time of the first emperor Claudius (Cuvelier 1965). Like an early St. Francis, Suetonius was converted to Christianity and changed his name to Beat; he was later known as St. Beat (patron saint of Jack Kerouac?). He was assigned by St. Peter to preach to the mountain Helvetians, who at first received him with traditional Celtic hospitality but turned against him when he preached the Gospel and challenged their pagan gods.

The Helvetians decided that St. Beat was an evil magician who caused accidents and illnesses to their flocks, and they banished him from all their villages. One day, during a terrible snowstorm, St. Beat was walking along the shore of the Lake of Thun looking for shelter, when he came to a cave and went inside. It was the home of a dragon, who rushed at him with open mouth and with fire coming out of its nostrils. St. Beat calmly said, "Brother Dragon, please let me have your cave, because I need it." The dragon then meekly licked St. Beat's feet and slunk out of the cave, where he plunged into the lake and has not been seen since (though it is rumored that, like a local Loch Ness Monster, it still lives in the adjacent Lake of Brienz).

The Helvetians at first were thrilled to be freed from the terrible dragon but reverted to their fear of St. Beat as an even more terrible magician and set out in a flotilla across the lake to attack him. When St. Beat prayed for help, a violent electric storm came up that set the lake on fire and threatened the Helvetians until he prayed again, whereupon the storm stopped and the fire went out. The grateful Helvetians then begged for his forgiveness and allowed him to live among them in peace. According to a mid–seventh century account by the historian Fredegarius (Frigidair?) Scholasticus, the Lake of Thun did catch fire in A.D. 598, because of seepage from petroleum springs, apparently ignited by lightning. (The amount was too small for the Swiss to join the OPEC cartel.)

Devil's Bridge

Even less charming than the dragons was the creature that was thought to have built the bridge over the Schöllenberg Gorge between Lake Lucerne and the St. Gotthard Pass (Cuvelier 1965). In that deep and narrow defile with vertical sides, the Swiss did not know how to build a bridge but they wanted it badly for access to the attractions of Italy. According to legend, they made a contract with the Devil to build the bridge. His price was the body and soul of whoever crossed it first. After he built the bridge and waited to collect his pay, the Swiss arrived with a goat, which rushed across and lunged at the Devil, thinking that he was a rival goat because of his horns and cloven hoofs. The Devil, enraged to be outwitted, threw the goat into the gorge but retreated in defeat. The Swiss were delighted to have their bridge at such low cost. Since then it has been called the Devil's Bridge, and it remains an ominous-looking place.

The first bridge across the gorge, a narrow one about a hundred feet long, was made of wooden planks that often had to be replaced. It was built about A.D. 1290 and enabled the Swiss to conquer what is now the Italian part of Switzerland, in the Ticino lake district. The bridge was then suspended by chains from iron rings driven into the rock, the remains of which are still there—an early suspension bridge. It was rebuilt as a stone arch, still not wide enough for carriages. In 1707 a tunnel was cut through the solid rock, which made the bridge easier to approach from the north.

In 1799 the bridge was destroyed by a division of Napoleon's army that was fleeing from General Suvorov's Russians and Austrians who had defeated the French at the top of the St. Gotthard Pass. The Russians rebuilt the bridge out of wood, but the first one to cross it, Major Mestchersky, was mortally wounded by the French and perished like the goat that had rushed across at the Devil (de Beer 1945). The major's dying words were "Don't forget to mention me in the dispatches." The bridge was rebuilt in stone wide enough for carriages in 1830 but fell in 1888, after which it was rebuilt as the stone arch that still stands. It is no longer in use, being replaced by a modern steel and concrete bridge beside it. Travelers who do not know the history are startled to see a memorial to "Generalissimo Suvorov" with a Russian Orthodox cross carved into the rock above the bridge.

Blümlisalp

The next three legends have to do with the origins of well-known mountain names. According to the first, the upper slope of the Blümlisalp (flowering pasture) peak was once covered with beautiful flowers, hence its name (Müller-Guggenbühl 1958). A young cowherd, who owned that part of it, brought his cows up there each summer, where they were so productive that they gave milk three times a day. However, he married a selfish woman who led him astray. She would not walk on the stones and built steps out of cheese into their hut, washing them each day with milk. When the cowherd's mother heard of this, she climbed up from the valley to warn her son. She arrived tired and thirsty and asked for milk, but her son's wife gave her spoiled milk and laughed about it.

The mother was furious and foretold that ice from the mountain would bury the son with his wife and his cows. Departing down the steep trail, she had hardly left the meadow when a large piece of a glacier fell and covered the slope with a deep layer of ice. To this day at that spot, it is said one can hear the cry of her son and the mournful bellow of his prized lead cow. (What really happened when the glacier broke was even worse; see chap. 4.) Today, just beneath the snout of the Blümlisalp Glacier, a small cow pasture called Oberbergli remains active, and special flowers, notably *Primula auricula,* still bloom on the sheer rocks below.

Mt. Pilatus

A famous peak whose name engendered a legend because of an error in spelling is Mt. Pilatus, west of Lake Lucerne (Cuvelier 1965). In 1307, six men were jailed in Lucerne because they attempted to climb its summit.

This was forbidden because of a local belief that Pontius Pilate had drowned or been thrown into a pond near the top of the mountain and caused fierce storms when he was disturbed. In 1585 Johann Müller, a clergyman, led a group of brave men to the summit of Pilatus, threw stones into the pond and loudly challenged Pilate to come out and cause a storm, but nothing happened. Nevertheless, according to Victor Hugo (1898), the law against the climb was still nominally in force when he visited Lucerne in 1838.

The legend apparently started because the pious people of Lucerne confused the name of Pontius Pilate with the old Latin name of the mountain, Mons Pileatus, which meant "wearing a felt skullcap," a sign of free status. In English, *pileate* means having a cap or a crest, like the pileated woodpecker of North America. The Romans gave the mountain that name because, when the weather was fair, there was always a cloud at its summit. That happened because when the sun was shining, it caused vapor to rise from the pond at the top. The cave above the pond is called the Moon Hole because, as related by Victor Hugo, a white liquid said to be "moon milk" was found inside.

Mont Cervin

As might be expected, the Matterhorn (in local Swiss-German dialect, *matt* = pasture, is thus analogous to the name of the Blümlisalp) has been the subject of numerous tales, mostly concerning its French or Italian name, Cervin or Cervino. Some have suggested that it comes from the French word *cerf* (deer), because in Celtic mythology, mountain nymphs, also called dames or demons, liked to take the form of deer. Another version is based on the Latin phrase *cerna vin* (Chanu 1988). It was said that, in Roman times, when traders often trekked southward across the Theodule Pass beside the Matterhorn to reach the markets at Aosta and Chatillon, a woman ran a trailside inn at the foot of the mountain in Breuil (which twentieth-century Italians have renamed Cervinia), where she served her customers wine that she had diluted with water. After her death, as an atonement for her sin, her ghost was condemned to climb the Matterhorn every night and (presumably not while climbing) to separate the wine from the water, hence *cerna vin* (as in the word *discern*).

The truth about the name Cervin seems to be another misspelling, a careless one by the great Alpine explorer Horace-Bénédict de Saussure (see chaps. 12 and 13). The spelling Cervin first appeared in a book of his

Alpine travels, published in the 1790s. Before that, in books and maps, the name of the mountain was always spelled Servin, but such was the prestige of de Saussure that every one has copied his mistake, including all the official maps of today, as well as the Italian village and a leading Zermatt hotel. Actually, in the western Alps, four lesser peaks are named Servin. In the Valdotain dialect, *serva* means "forest" and derives from the Latin *silva*. De Saussure's error was comparable to writing Cylvia instead of Sylvia (Guex 1976). This seems to be the most plausible explanation. If it is true, the Italian gnomes, who are locally called Salvans, have as much or more claim to the Matterhorn's name as the Celtic mountain nymphs.

Gnomes

The gnomes of the Alps are the local representatives of the "little people" who, to this day, inhabit all ancient Celtic lands. Almost all Swiss gardens have statues of one or more gnomes sitting on a rock or pushing a little wheelbarrow. They are usually dressed in red and are often smaller than their natural size, which is about two feet high. They all have long or longish beards. We have a little one at home named Trummelbach (after a torrent from the Jungfrau), who is carved out of wood. He wears black shoes, yellow stockings, brown knee breeches, and a brown jacket or jerkin, tied around his waist. He also has a floppy pointed cap, as all gnomes do. He reclines on one elbow, smoking a pipe. It is obvious from his crinkly eyes that he knows things that we do not. It was rumored that various gnomes emigrated to North America, where Rip van Winkle encountered some in the Catskills, as described by Washington Irving in *The Sketch Book* (1820).

Gnomes usually do not talk very much—more often, not at all. On a pasture above Grindelwald in the Bernese Oberland, a cowherd stubbed his foot against a rock and, before he knew it, a blasphemous curse word escaped from his lips. He knew the gnomes would make him pay for that (Müller-Guggenbühl 1958). One night, hearing a noise in his cows' stable, he got up just in time to see his seven beautiful cows disappear into a solid rock wall below a mountain, led by a yodeling gnome like an Alpine Pied Piper. All that summer, the cowherd kept working, making hay and pretending to milk the cows, calling each one by name as usual and singing his special songs to them. One day, when he came out of the stable, he saw all his cows grazing on the steep meadow, looking more healthy and more beautiful than ever. Near them stood the smiling gnome, who pointed to the lead cow's udder, put his finger in his mouth, then pointed to the sky and again to the cow. The herdsman then saw that one of the cow's four nipples was missing and understood that this was the punishment for his blasphemy.

Some gnomes do poetic things. In the Dolomites of South Tirol, the gnomes are also called Salvans, or "people of the forest." According to one legend, they wove moonbeams and draped them over the dark mountains to make possible the marriage of a princess of the moon to a prince of the earth (Wolff 1927). That was the only way to cure her homesickness for the mountains of the moon, and that is why the Dolomites are now light gray instead of black. The princess loved the bright colors of flowers in the Alps, but she brought with her one of her native flowers from the moon, where all flowers and mountains are white. That was how the edelweiss came to the Alps.

Fiction

Rousseau

Out of the tens of thousands of books that concern the Alps, none has had such an impact as Rousseau's 1761 novel *Julie, ou La Nouvelle Heloise,* which is a tragic love story in the fashionable worlds of Switzerland and other countries (Durant and Durant 1967). Only 2 of its 610 pages concern the mountains in an unidentified part of the Valais, from which we quote.

> Immense rocks in ruins hung above my head. High and noisy waterfalls engulfed me with their mist. An eternal torrent opened at my side an abyss into whose depth my eyes dared not penetrate. . . . A long range of inaccessible rocks separated us from that part of the Alps named the Glacières, because huge ice summits, which are constantly increasing in height, have covered them since the beginning of the world. . . . Nature united all seasons at the same instant, all climates in the same place, contrasting terrains on the same ground. . . . As one approaches the ethereal regions, the soul acquires something of their unalterable purity. (1783, 44)

It is because of such passages that "Rousseau is usually credited with the discovery that mountains are not intrinsically hideous" (Lunn 1914, 1).

Even more significant for Rousseau's social theories is his idealized view of mountain people (Durant and Durant 1967). He describes "their customs, their simplicity, their equality of soul, . . . their disinterested humanity and their zeal for hospitality," for which, without exception, they refused to be paid, so that, although "money was scarce in the High-Valais, . . . work was their pleasure. . . . If ever they had more money, they would be infallibly poorer: they have the wisdom to understand it." (For a more realistic view, see the section on Daudet later in this chapter.)

Dumas

After Rousseau, tragedy ruled a long series of fictional works about the Alps. Ten years before writing *The Three Musketeers*, Alexandre Dumas visited Schwarenbach, then a tiny mountain inn on the Gemmi Pass trail, to verify a story made into a play entitled *The Twenty-Fourth of February* by Zacharias Werner. As told by Dumas, it reads like a Greek tragedy: three homicides happened at Schwarenbach within the same family, always on the twenty-fourth day of February, inflicted by the same knife. First, during an argument, a grown son accidentally killed his aged father. The father's grandson later killed his sister while playing with the knife, after which the boy was banished. But he grew up and returned with money much needed by the family, only to be killed by his father, who mistook him for a burglar. Dumas (1834) was disappointed to learn that the story was pure fiction.

Maupassant

Another gruesome Schwarenbach tale is Guy de Maupassant's "L'Auberge" (1886). When the owners of the inn closed it for the winter and went down to their house at Leukerbad across the Gemmi Pass, an old guide, Gaspard Hari, remained to guard it with his dog, Sam, and the young Ulrich Künzi. From time to time, Gaspard hunted chamois near the Wildstrubel to get fresh meat. One day, after a blizzard, he did not return. Ulrich and Sam searched the mountain for two days without success. Back at the Inn, Ulrich heard a weird cry outside, perhaps a chough, but he imagined it was Gaspard calling his name. He called out but got no answer and was convinced Gaspard was dead and had come to haunt him.

Hearing the cry each day, he consumed the inn's supply of wine and spirits. One day, completely drunk, he opened the door not noticing that Sam ran out, and when the dog whined and scratched to be let in, Ulrich thought it was Gaspard's ghost and barricaded the door with furniture. When the family returned in the spring, they found the dog's skeleton outside, picked clean by eagles, while inside was a man whom they hardly recognized as Ulrich, with a long beard, snow-white hair, shining eyes and tattered clothes, his mind destroyed by the fear of Gaspard's ghost.

Spyri

At the opposite extreme of fictional drama, Johanna Spyri's perennial classic *Heidi* (1958) has introduced five young generations to the Alpine world. It starts when Heidi, a six-year-old orphan, came to live with her grandfather in an isolated cottage high above a village near Mayenfeld in eastern Switzerland. She was thrilled by the flowering pastures to which she climbed every day with the young goatherd Peter and the goats, two of which belonged to her grandfather while the rest belonged to other people in the village. When she asked why the mountains were "on fire" at sunset, her grandfather explained that the sun "throws his most beautiful colors over them, so that they may not forget him before he comes again" (Spyri 1958).

After two years, Heidi went to Frankfurt as a companion to the crippled girl Clara but was homesick for the mountains and returned after a year. She inspired her grandfather to give up his hermitlike way of life and move to the village for the winter, so that she could go to school. Clara spent the next summer with them in the cottage and was cured by the grandfather's special care, by Heidi's exuberance and by the healthful life in the beautiful mountains.

Today, along the superhighway not far from Mayenfeld, a large amusement establishment called Heidiland is a Swiss counterpart of Disneyland.

Daudet

In Alphonse Daudet's novel *Tartarin sur les Alpes* (1885), the caricatures of climbers, guides, hoteliers, tourists and terrorists are devastatingly accurate, and its descriptions of mountain climbing (except for the final accident) are authentic. The realism it introduced into mountaineering fiction was a breath of fresh air.

Tartarin de Tarascon, approaching fifty, was president of a small-town Alpine club in southern France. When a rival challenged his position, he secretly left to climb a major snow peak, which he had not done before. At the hotel on the summit of the Rigi, Tartarin fell for Sonia, an exquisite but sinister twenty-year-old Russian blonde who, unknown to him, was the leader of a band of anti-tsarist terrorists. When he left the hotel, everything was itemized on his bill in the Swiss manner, even a special charge for the panorama of the Bernese Oberland at sunrise, which he had not seen because of thick clouds that day.

Tartarin then climbed the Jungfrau, after falling into a deep crevasse from which he was extracted by one of his two guides. At Montreux, he again ran into Sonia, who was just leaving for St. Petersburg to liberate her country by assassinating the tsar (Alexander II, who was killed by an anarchist in 1881). Tartarin was thought to be one of the Russian terrorists and was imprisoned in the Castle of Chillon on Lake Geneva. Later, he climbed Mont Blanc with a young Swede who wanted to commit suicide upon reading Schopenhauer. After emerging from another crevasse, Tartarin fell to the Glacier du Miage and was thought to have perished. However, he got home just in time to take his presidential chair at the Alpine club meeting that had been called in his memory.

Doyle

When Arthur Conan Doyle no longer wished to write about Sherlock Holmes, he decided that Holmes and his archenemy Professor Moriarty, while grappling with each other, would fall and die together in the Reichenbach Falls of the Bernese Alps. Holmes is considered to be the best-known fictional character of all time, and his demise, in a story called "The Final Problem" (1891), became the best-known fictional occurrence in the Alps.

Doyle described the falls as "indeed, a fearful place. The torrent, swollen by the melting snow, plunges into a tremendous abyss, from which the spray rolls up like the smoke from a burning house. The shaft into which the river hurls itself is an immense chasm, lined by glistening coal-black rock, and narrowing into a creaming, boiling pit of incalculable depth, which brims over and shoots the stream onward over its jagged lip." Perhaps he was inspired to choose this site by J. M. W. Turner's terrifying watercolor *The Upper Fall of the Reichenbach* (ca. 1810).

Unable to resist the clamor from his readers, Doyle resurrected Sherlock Holmes by way of a miraculous escape at the waterfall and a two-year trip to Tibet and Lhasa, "spending some days with the head lama" before returning to London for further detective adventures. Below the falls, at Meiringen, there is now a Sherlock Holmes shrine and museum.

Nietzsche

The Alps are the principal setting for Friedrich Nietzsche's so-called "novel," *Thus Spoke Zarathustra,* inspired by its author's years in Switzerland, where he was professor of philology and became a Swiss subject. A few of the book's passages are relatively intelligible, such as:

> Whence come the highest mountains? I once asked. Then I learned that they came out of the sea. The evidence is written in their rocks and in the walls of their peaks. It is out of the deepest depth that the highest must come to its height. Thus spoke Zarathustra on the peak of the mountain, where it was cold. . . . When Zarathustra had left the ugliest man [who had just killed God], he felt frozen and lonely: for much that was cold and lonely passed through his mind and made his limbs too feel colder. But as he climbed on and on, up and down, now past green pastures, then again over wild stony places where an impatient brook might once have made its bed, all at once he felt warmer and more cheerful again. What happened to me? he asked himself. Something warm and alive refreshes me. Even now I am less alone; unknown companions and brothers roam about me; their warm breath touches my soul. But when he looked around to find those who had comforted his loneliness, behold, they were cows, standing together on a knoll; their proximity and smell had warmed his heart. (Nietzsche 1954, 277)

Mann

The most widely acclaimed major work of Alpine fiction is Thomas Mann's powerful German novel *The Magic Mountain* (Der Zauberberg) set in a tuberculosis sanatorium at Davos Platz. The author started out to write it as a "humorous" short story but ended up with a long novel intended as a microcosm of the entire European bourgeoisie just before World War I. Its plot is about the morbid love of a German engineer for a fellow patient. The narrative is interspersed with lengthy philosophical disputations between an Italian humanist and a cynical Jesuit who was the son of a Polish rabbi. In Mann's comments about the novel, he wrote that it was really about "a searcher after the Holy Grail. . . . You will find it in the chapter called "Snow" [see our chap. 4] where Hans Castorp, lost on the perilous heights, dreams his dream of humanity. . . . The Grail is a mystery, but humanity is a mystery too . . . and all humanity rests upon reverence before the mystery that is man" (1927, 726).

Ramuz

Charles-Ferdinand Ramuz was a Swiss writer whose 1925 novel *La grande peur dans la montagne* (Terror on the Mountain) concerned a pasture that had not been used for years because a glacier had fallen there and it was thought to be jinxed. A young cowherd, defying superstition, took his herd to the evil place. The cows gradually became afflicted by a mysterious disease and had to be killed. He himself was prevented by armed guards from returning to the village. Evading the guards, he arrived in time to see the funeral of his fiancée, who, unknown to him, drowned in a torrent on her way up to see him.

Ramuz's later novel *Derborence* is about the actual disaster of a mountain that had collapsed near the village of that name high on the north slope of the Rhone Valley above Sion. Ramuz was a master of suspense, and his books have the force of biblical tragedy.

Hemingway

Ernest Hemingway's *A Farewell to Arms* (1929) is a romantic novel about the bloody Austro-Italian campaign at Caporetto in World War I. It includes several descriptive passages about the Alps, such as:

> The road climbed steeply going up and back and forth through chestnut woods to level finally along a ridge. I could look down through the woods and see, far below, with the sun on it, the river that separated the two armies. We went along the rough new military road that followed the crest of the ridge and I looked to the north at two ranges of mountains, green and dark to the snow-line and then white and lovely in the sun. Then, as the road mounted along the ridge, I saw a third range of mountains, higher snow mountains, that looked chalky white and furrowed, and then there were mountains

far beyond all these that you could hardly tell if you really saw. These were all the Austrians' mountains and we had nothing like them.

Frison-Roche

Roger Frison-Roche, a former guide, wrote a novel, *Premier de Cordée* (1941). It is the drama of Pierre, a young climber whose father, one of the leading Chamonix guides, died from lightning near the summit of the Petit Dru, on a route considered to be the most challenging ascent in the Mont Blanc range. After skillful climbing over icy rock at the head of a party to retrieve his father's body, Pierre fell and fractured his skull. When he recovered, he suffered from fear of heights, which caused him to fall again when he tested himself on a solo climb of the Brevent. However, he overcame the vertigo by climbing the Aiguillettes de Montets and finally the north face of the Aiguille Verte with a colleague who had lost most of his feet from frostbite after the climb in which Pierre's father died. With renewed confidence, Pierre decided to become a guide and married his childhood sweetheart.

In one of the pastoral episodes, a cow became the queen of a herd by defeating the reigning queen in battle, while the villagers placed bets on one or the other of the combatants. In this novel, the mountains themselves are major characters, described almost inch by inch. The guides often use a Savoyard expression, "Ça fait me pi pas pi" [Things could be worse].

Troyat

Henri Troyat of the Academie Française, the Russian-born author of massive biographies of Dostoyevsky, Pushkin, Tolstoy and Turgenev, was inspired by the crash of an Air India plane in a blizzard near the summit of Mont Blanc to write a novel called *The Mountain* (1952). It is a deeply moving story of a retired guide, Isaiah, who tended his fifteen sheep while living in his ancestral home, in a hamlet whose other three small houses had been abandoned.

A skull fracture in a climbing accident had affected his mind. His much younger brother, Marcellin, living with him, had lost his job in town and failed to persuade Isaiah to sell the house so that they could split the proceeds. Unwilling to refuse his brother twice and also challenged by the chance to repeat a climb he knew so well, Isaiah led

Marcellin up the mountain by a hazardous icy route to the Air India airplane.

When they reached the wreck, Isaiah was horrified to see Marcellin plundering money and valuables from the dead. They found an Indian woman still slightly alive inside the fuselage, the only survivor. When Marcellin proposed to leave her, Isaiah disowned him and carried the woman down through a fog over invisible snow bridges on a glacier, but Marcellin, with his loot, perished in a crevasse. When Isaiah reached his house, the woman was dead—an occurrence reminiscent of Goethe's poem "Der Erlkönig," in which a father gallops through a forest at night to save a delirious child who dies in his arms.

This novel is about a drama between a mountain and a man who had been mentally damaged by it but who retained both his skill and his inherent integrity. The story is rich in details of an Alpine shepherd's life.

Chapter 10

Art and Music

Visual Arts

Pre-Renaissance

Petroglyphs of artifacts, animals and human subjects from 2,000 to 1,000 B.C. survive at forty-two sites in the French, Swiss, Italian, Slovenian and Austrian Alps (Priuli 1984). Splendid cave paintings of red-horned stags still exist at Bessans in Savoy. Paintings remaining from Roman times are much fewer than sculptures but show that both art forms were highly developed then. Murals at Pompeii and the Palatine include views of mountains that display skillful but subdued realism, compatible with the Roman dislike of natural grandeur.

Magnificent fifth-century Byzantine mosaics show stylized steplike mountains at San Vitale in Ravenna and climbing sheep at nearby San Apollinare in Clase. As Whitehead characterizes them: "The first phase of medieval art has a haunting charm beyond compare . . . energized in nature as its medium, but pointed to another world" (1925, 20). Steplike portrayal of mountains lasted until the thirteenth century and can be seen in Duccio's *The Three Marys at the Tomb* in Sienna and in Giotto's *The Miracle of the Water* in Padua.

Early Renaissance

With the onset of the Renaissance, realism began to reappear in the painting of mountains, with the steplike slopes evolving into glaciers with icefalls, crevasses and seracs. In the fourteenth century, Andrea Mantegna surpassed the Roman realism in his *Jesus in the Garden of Olives*, with two authentic-looking Dolomite spires. In 1444, Konrad Witz painted *Jesus Recruiting Fishermen on Lake Galilee*, but the view is of Lake

Geneva with Mont Blanc on the horizon, making this perhaps the earliest painting of a specific mountain in the Alps.

Albrecht Altdorfer of the fifteenth-century Danube school, a pupil of Dürer, was a keen student of nature. In his masterpiece of the battle between Alexander and Darius (Christoffel 1963), a dark central mountain divides the painting into two distinct themes. In the foreground, hundreds of armed and armored cavalry and infantry, with each individual painted in exquisite detail, surge against each other in dramatic swirling waves. The upper half, beyond the mountain, belongs to an elemental world in which a vast landscape of blue lakes, rivers, islands and clearly Alpine mountains stretches to infinity. The sky is a dark mass of swirling clouds that mimic the onrush of the battle. Through a large clearing off to the right, a red blaze envelopes the sun and is reflected in the water while it bathes the foreground in an eerie light. This treatment of light and clouds has influenced later artists right up to the nineteenth and twentieth centuries.

Leonardo da Vinci

At the end of the fifteenth century, Leonardo da Vinci began a tradition that flowered 300 years later, for painters to climb and make intimate contact with the mountains, crags and glaciers that they painted. He wrote of the Mera Valley crags above Chiavenna, "One cannot make ascents there without using hands and feet" (1938, 1:379). Among his drawings (at Windsor) is a panoramic view of the Alps with a dominant peak resembling the Italian side of Mont Blanc. Another view looks into a valley with two villages between mountains partly hidden by clouds, resembling Val Sesia. A third is a dramatic close-up of inclined stratified rocks, and a fourth shows sharp spires and slabs like those of Mont Blanc and the Bregaglia. These were studies for his paintings of the Madonna of the Rocks, St. Anne and Mona Lisa.

Leonardo gave explicit advice to mountain artists: "When you represent mountains, see that from hill to hill the bases are always paler than the summits" (1938, 2:242) and that "the shadows of mountains at a greater distance take a more beautiful and purer blue than those parts that are in the light" (1938, 2:315)

In a famous series of drawings, Leonardo made studies of the dimensions and details of an immense apocalyptic deluge. In these drawings, he showed hierarchies of turbulent vortices, the smallest of which are enveloped by larger ones and so on until the largest of all rise to the heights of mighty peaks. These studies have been regarded as examples of fractal geometry in the modern theory of chaos, which has been highly influential in recent years. As part of his description of the deluge, he wrote in his notebook:

> The waves of the sea, that beats against the shelving base of the mountains which confine it, rush foaming in speed up to the ridge of these same hills. . . . A great number of the inhabitants, men and different animals, may be seen driven by the rising of the deluge up towards the summits of the hills which border on the said waters. . . . Again there might be seen huddled together on the tops of many of the mountains many different sorts of animals, terrified and subdued at last to a state of tameness, in company with men and women who have fled there with their children . . . among them being wolves, foxes, snakes and creatures of every kind, fugitives from death. (1938, 2:288)

Seventeenth to Early Nineteenth Centuries

After Leonardo and Altdorfer, artists began to paint mountains and glaciers as main subjects, not just as backgrounds. Examples from the seventeenth and eighteenth century are Joos Momper's *St. Gotthard Massif,* Felix Meyer's *Rhone Glacier* and Caspar Wolf's Lauterbrunnen Valley in Winter (Christoffel 1963). Notable early nineteenth-century paintings, with a more romantic aura, are Caspar David Friedrich's *Watzmann,* Maximilian de Meuron's *Eiger* and Isaak Fürstenberg's *Devil's Bridge.*

A dramatic approach also appeared in the early nineteenth century. Peter Birmann introduced an element of terror, especially in his painting of the Schreckhorn, with its vast pinnacles contrasting with a foreground of boulders, crevasses with corniced edges, a glacier table and tiny human figures. Elijah Walton's *Mer de Glace* shows crevasses and ice pinnacles on an undulating glacier surface of a terrifying sort. A disturbing version of the Devil's Bridge by Arnold Böcklin shows travelers and pack mules racing across the bridge while a sinister, snakelike dragon peers out from a cave above (Christoffel 1963).

Turner

In the early nineteenth century, the English painter J. M. W. Turner specialized in dense atmospheric effects that tended to obliterate the landscape contours. Reminiscent of Altdorfer, Turner "sought to dissolve reality in an explosion of lights and fluctuating colors" (Christoffel 1963). This vision, perhaps influenced by London fog, dominated Turner's many paintings of the Alps, including those of the Reichenbach Fall, Mt. St. Gotthard and Faido Pass and three versions of the Dent d'Oche seen from across Lake Geneva. Describing a Turner painting, John Ruskin wrote: "One of Goldau shows the Lake of Zug appearing through the chasm of a thunder-cloud under a sunset, its whole surface one blaze of fire and the promontories of the hills thrown out against it like spectres" (1860).

Ruskin praised Turner as "the first poet who has, in all their range, understood the grounds of noble emotion which exist in landscape. . . . I believe myself that [Turner's] works are at the time of their first appearing as perfect as those of Phidias or Leonardo; that is to say, incapable, in their way, of any improvement conceivable by human mind" (1860). Ruskin's five-volume treatise *Modern Painters* (1860) was illustrated with several of his own drawings, some of which were based on paintings by Turner, who was the main subject of this monumental work. In the chapter called "Mountain Glory," Ruskin described his own love for mountains, which he did not climb, even though he became a member of the Alpine Club in London. His drawing of the Matterhorn viewed from the northwest is a sensitive work of mountain art.

Late Nineteenth and Twentieth Centuries

In the second half of the nineteenth century, the leading painter of the Alps was Giovanni Segantini (Christoffel 1963). His palette was similar to Turner's, but his feeling for the mountains was more dreamy, like that of Goustave Courbet, who also painted in the Alps. Several of Segantini's large panoramas of the Engadine Alps, such as the Sciora-Cengalo-Badile group, occupy the upper floor of the Segantini Museum at St. Moritz. He is also known for his pastoral scenes, such as one of a woman pulling a sled of firewood with a wintry view of Engadine peaks in the background.

Several prominent Impressionist and Postimpressionist painters produced Alpine landscapes, including Cézanne, van Gogh, Signac, Braque, Klee, Picasso, Alberto Giacommetti and Kokoschka. At least four by Kokoschka: the Matterhorn, Chamonix-Mont Blanc, the Dolomites and Pontresina. His elongated Matterhorn is reminiscent of early medieval art. Picasso's *Les Maures* (1967), painted mostly in blue from the terrace of his home when he was at the age of eighty-six and newly married, is more realistic than his typical work at that time, but with liberties both in the skyline and in the vortices of the clouds. As he explained, he painted "not what I see but what I think." Most magnificent in this group is van Gogh's *Mountains of St. Remy,* a work of 1889, one year before he died, painted a few miles from his haunts at Arles, Les Baux, and Daudet's Tarascon. The entire landscape is rendered in his most turbulent style.

The museum at Stampa in the Bregaglia Valley is dedicated to works by the talented, resident Giacometti family, including mountain paintings by the world-famous sculptor Alberto and by his uncle Giovanni, a pupil of Segantini. Large paintings of the Alps by Giovanni Giacometti hang at several urban railroad stations in Switzerland. Alberto Giacometti's landscapes of his local Piz Duan and Piz Corvatsch are dramatic, with the mountains almost entirely in brilliant scarlet.

Ferdinand Hodler (1853–1918), a native of Bern, was an exceptionally prolific painter of the Alps in Impressionist and Postimpressionist styles. Most of his paintings have been compared with Cézanne's, while his 1912 painting of the Alpes Vaudoises is in a style more like Rouault. Hodler painted large panoramas of the Engadine Alps and portraits of individual peaks. Edmund Wunderlich's powerful, rather cubistic portraits of snow peaks and rock spires, shown by the Swiss Alpine Museum at Bern, celebrate the 453 major ascents in the Alps by this great mountaineering artist.

Return to Realism

Among those who both painted and climbed mountains, Edward Theodore Compton (1849–1921) and his son Edward Harrison Compton (1881–1960) were outstanding. The elder Compton was born near London, but when he was fourteen his family moved to Germany, where he spent the rest of his life. He painted 1,700 large oils and watercolors of the Alps and Tatras, of which 1,000 were reproduced as illustrations in books and alpine journals. He was also a mountaineer of the first rank, having made 300 major ascents in the Alps, of which 27 were first ascents in the eastern Alps. Both father and son painted mountain landscapes in a similar realistic style, though the younger Compton's paintings are more dramatic. Their work combined heroic compositions with an intimate knowledge of detail, based on their own mountaineering experiences.

Their paintings combined beauty, power and authenticity in a way that made them much prized by mountaineers.

Flemwell's *Alpine Flowers and Gardens* (1910) and his books on Chamonix and Villars reproduce in color his meticulous oil paintings, likewise realistic and attractively colorful, each featuring a portrait of a specific Swiss or French snow peak, mostly with a flowering meadow foreground. Also of the twentieth century, the Austrian painter Anton Filkuka produced large oils of Alpine flowers and mountains in a sunny, unpretentious style, working from his studio on the "Street of Artists" at Alt Aussee in the Salzkammergut, with views of the Totes Gebirge from his windows.

Modern Primitives

Painted on a rock above a sheep meadow, high in the Bernese Alps, a mile north of the Gemmi Pass, we saw a portrait (or self-portrait) of a shepherd, standing beside a small, white, sad-looking sheep. In the painting, he had round black eyes, brushy eyebrows, red cheeks, a scraggly beard, long black hair, a blue shirt, gray knee-length pants, red stockings, brown boots, and a long staff curved at the upper end. There was no need to paint either foreground or background, which nature had already provided in the meadow below the rock and in the Rinderhorn peak above. Four years later, its pigments, exposed to the weather, had completely disappeared, and our photo may be the only record that this painting ever existed. It was, however, authentically Alpine, in the tradition of prehistoric painting and engraving on or within the mountains themselves.

An authentic native Alpine painter who worked in several styles in the 1960s was innkeeper Joseph Georges of Les Haudères in the Val d'Hérens. One of his attractive paintings shows his village's ancient dark chalets in distorted perspectives, dominated by the towering Dent Blanche, whose snow shadows of greens and blues are highlighted in red on the ridges, like jewels in the setting sun. A more realistic painting shows a snow slope with scattered boulders and the Dent Blanche in the distance, which somehow captures a powerful feeling of high-altitude Alpine solitude. Its impact is enhanced by a sinewy white band rising from the snow to the clouds, which the artist explained to us was "a connection between earth and heaven." One of his paintings in a primitive style is a pastoral scene of a woman wearing a long black dress with a black hat and embroidered scarf, riding sidesaddle on a roan horse over a meadow of green, yellow and orange stripes, with three white sheep and a dark gray cow wearing a huge bell. The background includes a tall arolla pine and a hill with a cross at the top, all dominated by the magnificent snow peak Mont Collon. This painting combines most of the components of the artist's home environment. A contemporary colony of Alpine landscape painters works in a primitive style like Grandma Moses at Appenzell in east Switzerland.

Alpine Prints

Prints have been produced by numerous artists, known and unknown. In the seventeenth century, Matthaeus Merian produced a print of an elongated Grossglockner. In the early nineteenth century, Jean DuBois of Geneva engraved prints in a similar exaggerated style, showing numerous popular views of the Swiss and French Alps. Similar prints by several artists were published by George Virtue in London (1836). Gabriel Lory, father and son, produced numerous early nineteenth-century Alpine prints in an attractive realistic style (Lunn 1963), including a scene of Alpine wrestling being watched by a group of women at Rosenlaui with the Wetterhorn in the background.

The most famous and valuable of all Alpine prints are those by Marquart Wocher as illustrations for de Saussure's book on his ascent of Mont Blanc in 1787. They reveal a subtle flattery: the first edition showed the 47-year-old professor as his normal corpulent self, but in the second and third editions, both his waistline and the amount of assistance he was receiving from his guides were successively reduced (Rébuffat 1962).

Edward Whymper, a nineteenth-century artist who led the first ascent of the Matterhorn, followed Leonardo da Vinci's precedent of intimate contact with mountains as subjects of his art. His book *Scrambles amongst the Alps* (1871) is profusely illustrated by himself and his brother J. W. Whymper with twenty-three full-page engravings and ninety-two in the text. The full-page subjects include an electrical storm, an avalanche, a bergschrund and the fogbow seen after the famous fatal accident. Two large colored prints, now quite rare, of the first ascent of the Matterhorn, are by the best-known nineteenth-century illustrator, Gustave Dore, a frequent mountain traveler and keen observer of the Alps. His print of the arrival at the summit is an embellishment of Whymper's version, while his print *La Chute,* showing snow-draped rocks and the despairing gestures of falling climbers, is a remarkable expression of both realism and drama.

Poster art is well developed in the Alps, the best-known example showing a lady dressed in the style of the 1890s, skiing down a precipitous slope above Chamonix with the poise and nonchalance of arriving for tea in a drawing room. A humorous, or perhaps unintentionally humorous, series of prints by Eugene Guerard (1849) shows elegantly dressed and amorous young ladies and gentlemen as alpinists at the Faulhorn above Grindelwald, negotiating torrents, snow slopes, cliffs and ladders with almost audible shrieks of delight. One of the Alpine cartoons by Samivel (1965) shows a thin-necked middle-aged man in a baggy business suit with a furled umbrella, looking up at the Matterhorn and asking, "A quoi ça sert?" [What use is it?].

Photography

Among the earliest published photographs of the Alps are the twenty-eight by Ernest Edwards in H. B. George's *The Oberland and Its Glaciers* (1866). Of these, only a few (notably of the Aletsch Glacier and the Nesthorn) are still in good shape, while most others are partly faded or were overexposed. By the 1880s, Vittorio Sella was producing excellent Alpine photographs of the Matterhorn, Écrins and Ortler (Audisio 1992), and of the Caucasus (Freshfield 1895). In Mummery 1895, the nine photographs of the Alps by Holmes, Miss Bristow and Mummery are even better than those by Sella. Miss Bristow's photo of Mummery with his knee wedged into the vertical "Mummery Crack" during his repeat climb of the Grepon, on which he also led Miss Bristow to the top, is one of the all-time most famous photos ever taken in the mountains. Guido Rey published eleven of his own excellent photographs of the Matterhorn (1907).

In the first half of the twentieth century, the works of various photographers in books by Lunn (1925) and Guiton (1929) are not up to the standards of the 1890s, but those by Smythe (1947), including a color photo of the Matterhorn, are excellent in every way. In the second half of the twentieth century, the use of color in books, articles, calendars and travel brochures has further raised the standards of Alpine photography, as in works by Rébuffat (1959), especially his famous photos featured at the Telluride festival and printed in gold for the space capsule.

This trend has continued in the work of Kammet (Knight 1978; Bersezio and Tirone 1995) and Thompson (Lieberman 1991). The Kammet photos are attractive, with trees and flowering meadows in the foreground of mountain landscapes. The Thompson photos are selected from 800 rolls of film, a luxury not available to Edwards in 1866. Of all the Alpine photographs we have seen, we would give first prize, by technical, artistic and documentary criteria, to those of Löbl (1968), covering all the Alps from the Gesäuse in eastern Austria to the Gorges of the Verdon in southern Provence. Alpine photos by many other photographers, early and recent, are in the archives of the Alpine museums at Turin and Courmayeur and in other collections, including our own.

Films

The first film about the Alps was made in 1900 for the training of mountain guides (Audisio and Natta-Soleri 1995). In 1910, the Societa Anonima Ambrosio di Torino produced a documentary, *Excursions to the Chain of Mont Blanc, from Courmayeur to the Dent du Géant*. The 1913 French feature film *L'Escarpolette Tragique,* produced by Films Valetta and edited by Pathé Frères, was set at the foot of the Matterhorn.

The many Alpine films (in German) starring or directed by Luis Trenker began with *The Wonder of Skis* in 1922, for promotion of St. Moritz, and *The Battle for the Matterhorn* in 1928, which reenacted the original climbs by Whymper and Carrel (remade by Trenker in 1937). Trenker's later films included *The Son of the White Mountain* (1930, about Zermatt), *Love Letters from the Engadin* (1938), *The Fire Devil* (1940, about Napoleon's occupation of Carinthia), *Under the Spell of Miracle Mountain* (1943, an Austrian film about the Valle d'Aosta with music by the Vienna Symphony and the Vienna Choirboys), *Duel in the Mountains* (1950, about French-Italian smugglers) and *In the Shadow of the Dolomites* (1955).

Trenker also collaborated with the well-known dancer and film-maker Leni Riefenstahl. They costarred under the direction of Arnold Fanck in *The Sacred Mountain* (UFA, 1926) with skiing, climbing and dance sequences on location in the Dolomites, Bernina group, Zermatt, Lechtaler Alps and Helgoland. The three collaborated again in *The Great Leap* (UFA, 1927), set in the Dolomites and featuring Hans Schneeberger, known as the Snowflea because of his acrobatic skiing. She, Trenker and Fanck worked together again in 1929 on *White Hell of Piz Palu,* on location at Diavolezza, Piz Palü and the Morteratsch Glacier in the Bernina group (released in 1938).

An early Hollywood film of the Alps was *Lost Patrol* (1930) starring

Victor Varconi, about the Austro-Italian front in World War I. In it a skier races to the top of a snow peak and saves an Italian patrol holding the peak, just before it is blown up by the Austrians. Riefenstahl and Fanck were about to film the same story, to be called *The Black Cat*, but with the Austrians holding the peak until the Italians blew it up. However, Trenker beat them to it with a film called *Mountains in Flames* (Kopp-Verleih 1931). In 1932, Riefenstahl made a film called *Blue Light*, set at the Brenta group in the Dolomites and featuring unsecured barefoot climbing by herself and churchgoing and revelry scenes involving the local peasants. Her film *Storms over Mont Blanc* (1932), including climbs of the peak by the Grands Mulets route with return on skis, was never released because of technical difficulties with the simultaneous advent of talkie films.

Shirley Temple was the star of *Heidi*, the well-known story about a little Swiss girl (Darryl Zanuck, Twentieth Century Fox, 1937). The same story was made into an animated cartoon in 1976 by Isao Takanata of Japan. *The Mountain* (Vista Vision, 1956), starring Spencer Tracy and directed by Edward Dmytryk, is the Hollywood film version of the novel (The Snow in Mourning) by Henri Troyat (see chap. 9), based on the crash of the Air India plane *Malabar Princess* almost at the summit of Mont Blanc in 1950. The novel was a success, but the film was not until its recent (1998) resurrection for frequent television reruns. Troyat thought Tracy, a "robust American," to be a poor choice for the part of his reclusive shepherd hero, while Marcel Ichac (1960, 9) derided Tracy's "rock-climbing" scenes on "cardboard" constructions in the California studio.

The film *Les Etoiles du Midi* (The Stars at Noon), produced by Marcel Ichac and featuring Lional Terray's ascent of the Grand Capucin in the Mont Blanc range, was awarded the Grand Prix du Cinema Francais in 1959. It is probably the most authentic film about a major rock climb up to that time. Ichac put forth an extraordinarily detailed and profusely illustrated account of the making of the film (1960), in which he noted that Terray's terrifying fall at an overhang, when his upper piton gave way, had to be repeated six times for the film.

Hannibal, starring Victor Mature and produced in Eastmancolor in 1959, is the story of the Carthaginian crossing of the Alps with the elephants in 218 B.C. *Third Man on the Mountain*, a 1959 Disney film starring Michael Rennie, is based on J. R. Ullman's novel *Banner in the Sky*, a realistic but unnecessarily modified retelling of the first ascent of the Matterhorn. Totally absurd is Ullman's earlier book turned film *The White*

Tower, about the World War II ascent of an unclimbed peak in Switzerland requiring six days of climbing (therefore as high as Mt. Everest).

The Sound of Music, a film with music by Richard Rodgers and lyrics by Oscar Hammerstein II, starring Julie Andrews and Christopher Plummer, is based on the true story of the escape of Baron von Trapp and his family from the Nazis in Austria, on foot over the Alps to Switzerland, then on to America, where, in Vermont, they established a successful musical and skiing mountain inn. This film won Hollywood's Academy Award for best picture in 1965. *The Eiger Sanction,* Clint Eastwood's film as actor and director, a spy story based on a novel by Trevanian (1972), was released in Technicolor by Universal Pictures in 1975. It shows outdated multiple bivouacs on the Eiger north face. *Avalanche,* starring Rock Hudson and Mia Farrow and directed by Corey Allen, was released by New World Pictures in 1978. *Chronique Paysanne en Gruyère,* a film by Jacqueline Veuve produced in 1991 by Aquarius Films and Television Suisse Romande, is the story of one year in the lives of a pastoral family in the highlands of western Switzerland.

Music and Dance

Mountain Song

Singing is inseparable from life in the Alps. There, "when people relax, get together, they drink, play cards and sing—sit in a room and sing" (John Berger, quoted in Marzorati 1987). Alpine singing often includes yodeling, as described by Murray: "These national melodies are particularly wild in their character, yet full of melody; the choruses consist of a few remarkably shrill notes, uttered with a peculiar falsetto intonation in the throat" (1838, xxxvi). In his great novel *David Copperfield* (1850), Charles Dickens wrote: "I had come out of Italy over one of the great passes of the Alps . . . . I came into the valley, as the evening sun was shining on the remote heights of snow. In the quiet air, there was a sound of distant singing—shepherd voices; but, as one bright evening cloud floated midway along the mountain's-side, I could almost have believed it came from there, and was not earthly music."

In the fifteenth century, Leonardo da Vinci was famous as a singer of songs for which he improvised both words and music and accompanied himself with a lute. This talent attracted him to the attention of the duke of Sforza, who employed him in Milan, which became the base for his exploration of the Alps.

A famous Alpine singing group, mentioned in the preceding section of this chapter, was the Austrian family of Baron von Trapp, who made their home near Salzburg until, during World War II, they escaped on foot to Switzerland and from there moved to America, where they continue their singing tradition, in the world of New England skiing. Their story was made into a musical play, *The Sound of Music* by Richard Rodgers and Oscar Hammerstein II, which had long stage runs in America and England, and was also made into a film, as mentioned earlier. One of its moving songs is "Edelweiss," which epitomizes the beauty and purity of the Alps.

Ranz des Vaches

Rousseau wrote in his *Dictionary of Music* (1767) that for Swiss mercenaries in France, "it was forbidden on pain of death to play the *ranz des vaches* among the troops because it caused those who heard it to burst into tears, to desert, or to die [by suicide]—so much did it arouse in them the longing to see their country again." Boswell (1791) described a *ranz des vaches* as "that air which instantly and irresistibly excites in the Swiss, when in a foreign land, the maladie du pays." Murray wrote of the *ranz des vaches:* "Almost every valley has an air of its own, but the original air is said to be that of Appenzell. Their effect in producing homesickness in the heart of the Swiss mountaineer, when heard in a distant land, and the prohibition of this music in the Swiss regiments in the service of France, on account of the number of desertions occasioned by it, are stories often repeated, and probably founded in fact" (1838, xxxvi). Longfellow wrote of Agassiz, "at times he hears in his dreams the Ranz des Vaches of old" (1893, 199). The Swiss mountaineer Eugene Rambert wondered: "From where does it come, this old refrain / That makes us weep, that makes us smile? / From where does it come, what does it mean, / This ranz naive, grave, and serene? Lioba, lioba" (Club Alpin Suisse, 1909).

Lioba and *ranz* are words of controversial meaning in the dialects of French-speaking Switzerland. As Nidegger (1984) explains, *lioba* is a generic term of endearment when calling cows, like "pussy" for a cat. *Kuhreihen,* the German name for the *ranz des vaches*, (*du bist nach der Reihe*), means "calling cows in turn to be milked," not physically lining them up, though they might do so on their own. *Reihe* in this sense translates to *rintse* in Fribourgeois, and Nidegger suggests this became *ranz* in France, where mercenaries from all parts of Switzerland were thrown together and developed a common vernacular. The origin of the term is not the French *rang* (row).

The classical *ranz des vaches* of Gruyère starts with a "pastoral" of seventeen narrative couplets (Nidegger 1984): Piero, a herdsman, asks a priest to say a mass so that he and his cows can cross a flooded river. The priest agrees on the condition that he be given a nice creamy cheese. Piero says, "Send your servant," and the priest replies, "She is too pretty." Piero chides the suspicious priest, saying that taking anything from him could not be forgiven, but the priest sends Piero away without the mass, telling him to say the Ave Maria twice. When Piero returns, the whole herd crosses safely. The refrain after each couplet is "Come all, white, black, brown, mottled, young, old, under the oak where I will milk you, under the poplar where I make cheese." This "pastoral" dates from before the sixteenth century, when Gruyère became Protestant. The wildness, mentioned by Murray, comes out in the *ranz* from the Jura: "C'est tot pre de elliau bossons [Everything is ready for milking the cows], hi! hou! hai!"

The earliest publications of *ranz* tunes were by Georg Rhaw (Wittemberg, 1545) and Theodore Zwinger (pseudonym Jean Hoffer, Basel, 1710). Eight of the tunes were published as *Kuhreihen mit Musik und Text* for the first Festival of Alpine Herdsmen, at Unspunnen near Interlaken in 1805. Ten, out of a total of fifty, were published in France by Tarènne (1818), and their text by J. R. Wyss (Bern, 1826). A *ranz des vaches* is used in Rossini's popular *William Tell* Overture (1829), in the overture of an earlier William Tell opera by André Grétry, and in the tone poem *Don Quixote* by Richard Strauss, whose home was in the Bavarian Alps.

One of the best-known *ranz des vaches* tunes is the main fourth-movement theme in Beethoven's Sixth (*Pastoral*) Symphony (1808). It is identical to the alphorn tune of the Rigi Kulm, played when the guests stream out of the hotel to see the sunrise over the Alps (see chap. 9, on Daudet). Beethoven's program note is paraphrased by Philip Hale: "The shepherds reappear; they answer each other on the mountain, recalling their scattered flocks; the sky is serene; the torrents soon cease to flow; calmness returns, and with it the rustic songs, whose gentle melodies bring repose to the soul." Berlioz, in his program note for the third movement of his *Fantastic Symphony* (1830), is even more explicit about the source of the theme: "He hears two shepherds who play, back and forth, a pastoral tune, the ranz des vaches. . . . One of the shepherds resumes his naive tune. The other fails to answer. The sun slowly sets—

distant thunder—solitude—silence" (1986). This *ranz* tune is more haunting than Beethoven's.

Minnesingers and Troubadors

Church singing is an important part of music throughout the Alps together with folk songs, and the two traditions go hand in hand. The
Minnesingers were a group of German, Swiss and Austrian singers of
noble knightly rank who flourished from the eleventh to the thirteenth
centuries and took part in the Crusades. One of their prominent Swiss
members was Johannes Hadlaub, who was a pupil of Conrad von Mure,
the great cantor of the Zurich Grossmünster whose compositions for the
year 1260 have been preserved. Hadlaub's songs also survive in manuscript form, but unfortunately without musical notation.

The Minnesingers were counterparts and contemporaries of the troubadors of southern France and adjacent parts of Italy and Spain. Both
Minnesingers and troubadors sang of their love for inaccessible ladies,
but the Minnesingers are said to have been more sincere about it. Daudet
quotes an authentic troubador lyric in old Provençal: "O coumtessa
gento, estelo dou nord, que la neu argento, qu'amour friso en or" [Oh
gentle countess, star of the north, whom snow turns to silver and love
curls up in gold] (1885, 9).

The most famous troubador was Richard the Lion-Hearted, who was
Provençal on the side of his mother, Eleanor of Aquitaine. A crucial
episode of his life concerned a song in the foothills of the Austrian Alps
on his way home from his Crusade. In 1192, hearing of the intrigues of
his brother John, Richard started home from the Holy Land incognito but
was captured by Leopold, duke of Austria, and imprisoned in the castle
of Dürnstein, which is now in ruins, 40 miles up the Danube from Vienna. Not knowing his master's whereabouts, his faithful minstrel
Blondel traveled through Europe singing a song that Richard knew.
When he came to Dürnstein, Richard answered the song. His release was
arranged for 150,000 marks, which almost broke the English treasury
and which required a new system of taxation.

Instrumental Accompaniment

The alphorn, now used mainly for *ranz des vaches* tunes, was also a
means of communication between herdsmen:

This instrument is about eight feet long, and its farther extremity rests on the ground. It is used among these mountains not merely for the herdsmen's call, but as invocation for the solemnities of religion. As soon as the sun has shed his last ray on the snowy summit of the loftiest range, the Alpine shepherd from some elevated point, trumpets forth, Praise God the Lord, while the echoes in the caves of the everlasting hills, roused from their slumbers at the sacred name of God, repeat, Praise God the Lord. Distant horns on lower plains now catch the watch-word, and distant mountains ring again with the solemn sound, Praise God the Lord, and other echoes bounding from other rocks reply, God the Lord. A solemn pause succeeds; with uncovered head and on bended knee, the shepherd's prayer ascends on high. At the close of this evening sacrifice, offered in the temple not made with hands, the Alpine horn sounds long and loud and shrill, Good Night, repeated by other horns; while a thousand Good Nights are reverberated around, and the curtain of Heaven closes on the shepherds and their flocks. (Murray 1829)

Murray also wrote: "The traveller among the Alps will have frequent opportunities of hearing both the music of the horn and the songs of the cow-herds and dairy-maids; the latter being thus described by Mr. Southey:—'Surely the wildest chorus that was ever heard by human ears: a song, not of articulate sounds, but in which the voice is used as a mere instrument of music, more flexible than any which art could produce, sweet, powerful, and thrilling beyond description'" (1838, xxxvi).

At the Gemmi Pass Sheep Festival we attended in the Bernese Alps (see chap. 8), the program ended with a concert of the *ranz des vaches* by an alphorn trio. In the eastern Alps, alphorns are not turned up at the outer end as in Switzerland but are straight, like a trumpet and like the long horns of Romania, Russia and Scandinavia, where it is called a *lur*, and of Tibet and Central Asia, where it is called a *zurna*. It is generally supposed that the alphorn came to the Alps from Central Asia, perhaps during early migrations, which would indicate an early origin for music in the Alps.

In Austria, shin-slapping Schuhplattler dances are accompanied by energetic brass bands, which also parade on festive occasions, such as for children going to their first communion. In Tirol and east Switzerland, folk songs are accompanied by a zither, an ancient instrument with thirty to forty-five strings, made famous in the film of Grahame Green's *The*

Third Man. Mittendorf, in the Tirolean Alps, is well known for its tradition of manufacturing fine violins.

The Alps in Classical Music

Major composers have been inspired by the *ranz des vaches* or by the Alps themselves. In 1835, Franz Liszt toured Switzerland with Countess Marie d'Agoult and wrote piano pieces about the William Tell Chapel, the Lake of Wallenstadt, and the "Valley of Obermann" (at Bex, referring to a novel by Sénancour). Brahms wrote his great Double Concerto while staying at Thun in the Bernese Alps. It is not program music, but de Beer (1945) suggested (with diagrams) that the patterns of the themes in its last two movements correspond to the skylines of the mountains. Works by nineteenth-century Swiss composers are the *Tell Symphony* of Hans Huber and the *Swiss Symphony* of Hermann Suter. Richard Strauss wrote his *Alpine Symphony* from his home in the Bavarian Alps. Some of the music of other composers, including Chopin and Weber, is said to have been inspired by the Alps.

Wagner

Among the great composers who lived in the Alps, Richard Wagner spent more years there and was more deeply influenced by these mountains. In 1845, while still living in Germany, he composed *Tannhaeuser,* an opera about a Minnesinger knight who, accordng to a German legend, spent a year of profane love with the goddess Venus at the top of her mountain, after which he crossed the Alps on a pilgrimage to Rome and was redeemed by the Virgin Mary. A *ranz des vaches* tune appears halfway through the song of the Wartburg shepherd. In 1849, Wagner had to flee from Germany with a price on his head because of his involvement in the unsuccessful German Revolution of 1848. He lived in Zurich for ten years, working on the early phases of his Siegfried cycle, which became *The Ring of the Nibelungen.*

In 1859, he finished his opera *Tristan and Isolde,* based on a legend but also on his own affair with Mathilde Wesendonk, the wife of his friend and patron. Again in this opera, a *ranz des vaches* appears in the herdsman's song. Life in Zurich became too embarrassing and he moved to Lucerne, where he stayed for a year, after which he left for Paris. In 1864, he was able to return to Germany, where he was befriended by the newly ascended ("Mad") King Ludwig II. After Wagner lived and worked for a year in Munich and in Ludwig's Linderhof castle, the king put him up in a villa at Triebschen on Lake Lucerne, where he lived for nine years and finished his work on *The Ring*.

Wagner lived in the Swiss and Bavarian Alps for a total of twenty-one years. An indication of the influence of the Alps on his work can be seen in the four *Ring* operas: two of the scenes take place at Valhalla, the mountaintop home of the gods, two at "the summit of a rocky mountain," two at "Brunnhilde's rock" and one at "a wild rocky place," all of which were clearly in the Alps, being upstream on the Rhine. As Nietzsche wrote: "There is a musician who, more than any other musician, is a master at finding the tones in the realm of suffering, depressed and tortured souls. . . . None can equal him in the colors of late fall, in the indescribably moving happiness of the last, truly last, truly shortest joy. . . . Some things have been added to the realm of art by him alone, things that had hitherto seemed inexpressible. . . . Wagner is one who has suffered deeply" (1954, 2).

Music for Mountains

Great music, like that of the spheres, seems to fill the Alps without even being heard. The tunes go round and round in one's head when one is climbing a mountain. Julius Kugy (1934) wrote about climbing the Julian Alps.

> The glittering triad passes at heaven's height above mountain and valley: Bach, Beethoven, Palestrina. One of Johann Sebastian's mightiest pedal points rang within me when I wrote of the diapason of the Trenta. Duo Seraphim clamabant alter ad alterum: Sanctus, Sanctus, Sanctus! So runs a hymn from the old glorious days of Palestrina, and in the immortal hours of winter upon the Montasch, I heard the tones of Palestrina's angel-choirs. Who does not know Beethoven's splendid sacred song, The Glory of God: To God eternal the heavens utter glory. It filled me with a joyful reverence as I stood upon the wintry summit of Triglav. (xvi)

> As I trod the summit, still panting from the heavy toil of the last hours, and thrust my axe into the sharp snow-crest, I seemed to catch the silver notes of angel choirs in solemn sacred harmony. . . . It

seemed that seraphic companies called in antiphon from peak to peak, and above the horizon rang the Gloria in Excelsis of their clear voices. (199)

Dancing

In virtually all parts of the Alps, dancing is an integral part of popular expression and enjoyment. On various occasions throughout the year, individual couples or groups get together and dance to the accompaniment of music provided by bands or orchestras, depending on the size and type of the gathering, whether it is informal or formal, and whether it is intended for local people or tourists. Semiprofessional individuals or groups, with suitable skills, also perform characteristic dances as a form of entertainment, which usually reflect local folklore traditions. In Austria, at such popular centers as Innsbruck and Mayrhofen, the Tyrolean folk dances are often energetic, in the shin-slapping Schuhplattler style, with brass bands and people dressed in traditional embroidered *Trachten* (folk outfits). These exuberant folk dances often celebrate May Day or a solstice.

In central and eastern Austria, at more elegant Alpine locations, such as Bad Ischl in the Salzkammergut and Graz in Styria, dances with orchestral music often occur on a *Jagerabend,* a hunters' evening, with a menu offering venison and grouse. The ladies wear graceful dirndls whose details are special for their localities, while the men wear hunting jackets that, in most places, are green or gray with red trim, though in Styria they are brown. On such occasions, the dances are mostly of the familiar types, such as Viennese waltzes and polkas. In a few places, one can also dance to the delicate accompaniment of a zither.

We have also taken part in less-formal types of popular dancing. We were in the Bernese village of Lauenen, at the foot of the snowcapped Wildhorn, in the month of October. No tourists were in sight, either there or in nearby Gstaad. The summer crowds had departed, and the winter skiers had not yet arrived. During this breathing spell, on a Saturday evening, the villagers convened for a dance at one of the large decorated chalets for which Lauenen is famous. Now they could enjoy themselves without thinking about tourists. The dancers included slightly aromatic cowherds and cowherdesses who had come down from upper chalets for the occasion. A local oompah band churned out energetic tunes on instruments that included an accordion, a fiddle, a trombone and a bent saw. One of the cowherds, sporting a wide black mustache, invited coauthor Nina to dance by twirling his index finger in the air. That was exactly the way he danced for a long time, going round and round in one direction only.

Forms of various folk dances have classical or semiclassical names. The chaconne is a stately old French dance that reached into the Alps in feudal times. The Chaconne by Johann Sebastian Bach, which he wrote for a solo unaccompanied violin, is probably one of his greatest works. Some years ago, a mountaineering violinist, in complete solitude, played Bach's Chaconne at the summit of the Matterhorn. Many folk dances have inspired classical music, as in the Slavic dances of Smetana and Dvorak and the numerous gavottes, minuets, and so on.

The Weggis is a Swiss couple dance featuring two parallel circles moving in opposite directions. It is "performed holding hands lightly . . . a carefree round expressive of the Swiss temperament." The Lauterbach is "a Swiss couple dance, a waltz of the Central European type," which "shares the gracious smoothness of the Neubayrische rather than the robust vigor of the Ländler and Schuhplattler." In the Austrian Schemen-laufer, "the running and leaping of maskers in a serpentine course, at Carnival time," is "a pagan vegetation rite which has survived through the Middle Ages until now." The Siebenschritt, or Seven Step, is "a German-Austrian couple dance, which originated in Tyrol. In a counter-clockwise circle, the couples, man on left, inner hands joined, run seven steps forward, and seven steps back, following the musical phrases, then apart for three steps, and together for three; then pivot with joined hands for seven runs." This dance "resembles the Swiss Schottishche or Chang-ing Dance" (Leach 1984, 291, 609, 610, 1010, 1169).

In the eastern Alps of Friuli, Carinthia and Slovenia and on the nearby borders of Croatia, Bosnia and Serbia, the folk dances tend to have a Slavic flavor. Typically, the dancers hold hands in a circle and go round and round. Rosa Bailey (see chap. 14) refers to similar dancing by children in the Haute-Savoie. The Slavic dances often involve stamping of the feet and raising or swinging of the arms, also leaping, as in the Yugoslav Soskako Kolo.

In most parts of the Alps, some of the dances are more expressive of local folklore or mythology. In Slovenia and other parts of the former Yugoslavia, the most locally representative mythical creatures are called *vilas.* They are "nymphs of the forests, fields, streams and lakes, said to be spirits of virgins and children, who must leave their graves to dance at night, in typical fairy rings" (Leach 1984, 1157).

> In German-speaking parts of Central Europe including Austria and Switzerland, the Fastnachtsbär (Shrovetide bear) is a man or boy clothed in straw wound with ropes, led from house to house with music. . . . He enters every dwelling and dances with all the girls and women of the household. . . . There exists a fairly general belief in Central Europe one must dance on Shrove Tuesday to insure fertility and growth of all the crops. In some districts the women pluck bits of straw from the Fastnachtsbär to put in their poultry nests and thus insure a plentiful supply of eggs. (Leach 1984, 370)

> In Switzerland it is or used to be customary to kindle bonfires on high places on the evening of the first Sunday in Lent . . . for example, throughout the canton of Lucerne. Boys piled the fuel [wood and straw] on a conspicuous mountain about a pole which bore a straw effigy called "the witch." At nightfall, the pile was set on fire and the young people danced around it wildly. . . . The more bonfires could be seen sparkling or flaring in the darkness, the more fruitful the year was expected to be; and the higher the dancers leaped beside or over the fire, the higher, it was thought, would grow the flax. (Fraser 1996, 710)

In the earlier decades of the twentieth century, the world of the arts became aware of a connection between dance and the Alps when the troupes of Diaghileff, Nijinsky and their successors in the Ballets Russes made their home in Monte Carlo, at the feet of the Maritime Alps. Soon after World War II, this venue for dance became widely known in the charming, romantic film *Red Shoes,* featuring the talents of Balanchine and his troupe under a shifting panorama of the Maritime Alps.

Schafhausen, an old Swiss town overlooking the Rhine, is proud of its medieval Munot Fortress, which is shaped like a large round tower. One July, the senior class of a local military school, dressed in formal regalia, held their graduation ball on the Munot's upper rampart, lit by flaming torches attached to the outer walls. Our dear friend Anni Stadler invited us and all three of our children to attend this dance, and we joyfully accepted. An orchestra played romantic dance music, including

Viennese waltzes. Having just come down from our twelve-day Bernese glacier trek, this elegant occasion on the Munot Fortress combined for us the thrill of the Alps with a rare flavor of the Middle Ages. It was good to know that the young military school graduates, who would be serving their stint in the redoubtable Swiss army, would be unlikely to face the real armed combat that has characterized so much of Alpine history.

Chapter 11

Warfare

Early Campaigns

Prehistoric Combat

For thousands of years before Alpine history began, metallurgists manufactured combat-type weapons that archaeologists have discovered in the Alps. A finely made, flanged copper ax from 3500 B.C., useful mainly for battle, emerged from a glacier in the Austro-Italian Alps (see chap. 7). Swords dating from aproximately 1300 B.C. that are up to 70 centimeters (28 in.) long, also Celtic weapons from the Halstat period (750–450 B.C.) and the La Tène period (450–58 B.C.), have turned up in the Alpine valleys and foothills, but not helmets or shields, which must have been made, if at all, from leather (Sauter 1976). These weapons testify that the early Alpine people were active in combat during prehistoric times.

Celtic Episode

In the course of their conquests throughout the Alps, the Celts crossed the high passes and defeated the Romans at Allia near Rome in 390 B.C. They then ransacked the capital city and burned patrician houses and official buildings, including all the precious historical archives. A few days later, following a disagreement about the ransom they demanded, the Celts retreated in defeat, because the Romans meanwhile had regrouped while the Celts, it is said, celebrated with too much wine. The Celts then went back to their previous positions on the Italian side of the Alps, which became known as Cis-Alpine Gaul.

174

Hannibal

Probably no military operation in the Alps has aroused the world's imagination as keenly as Hannibal's crossing of the main crest with his army, horses and elephants in 218 B.C., for his Italian campaign. The earliest known description of the crossing was by the Greek historian Polybius (ca. 205–125 B.C.) based on personal exploration and interviews with survivors. However, neither he nor the other classical writers for whom he was the main source (Timagenes, Coelius, Varro, Strabo, Livy, Servius and Silius) identified the pass that Hannibal crossed. This remains a mystery that has frustrated scholars (de Beer 1955).

The best-known description is by the Roman historian Livy (Titus Livius, 59 B.C.–A.D. 17), especially the following excerpt.

> Since they [Hannibal's troops] had to cut through the rock, they felled some huge trees that grew near at hand, and lopping off their branches, made an enormous pile of logs. This they set on fire, as soon as the wind blew fresh enough to make it burn, and pouring vinegar over the glowing rocks, caused them to crumble. After thus heating the crag with fire, they opened a way into it with iron tools, and relieved the steepness of the slope with zigzags of an easy gradient, so that not only the baggage animals but even the elephants could be let down. (Spectorsky 1955, 343)

Early Romans

By far the most enduring activities of conquest, rule and construction over all of the Alps were those of the Romans from the third century B.C. through the fifth century A.D. In the Alpine region, they occupied Milan (Mediolanum) in 222 B.C., Como (Comum) in 196 B.C. and proclaimed their dominion over all of Cis-Alpine Gaul in 183 B.C. (Sauter 1976). In 121 B.C., the Romans conquered Trans-Alpine Gaul (Provincia) from the Mediterranean to Lake Geneva, thus ruling both slopes of the French-Italian Alps.

Caesar and Successors

The most warlike of the Celts were the Helvetians, who were living in what is now Switzerland. As their numbers increased, they found that land too small. In 58 B.C., in the tradition of their earlier migrations, their entire population of some 260,000 men, women and children set off, with animals and chariots, for larger spaces in southwest France, having burned their Swiss villages as an act of finality. Julius Caesar, who was in command of both Cis-Alpine and Trans-Alpine Gaul, saw danger to the latter from the Helvetians.

Caesar crossed the Alps with his legions from Ocelum west of Turin, pursued the Helvetians and crushed them at Bibrace near Autun, Saone-et-Loire. He then forced them to return to Switzerland and to rebuild their villages, where they live to this day, in the country whose official name is Confederatio Helvetica. Following this victory and after further crossings of the Alps during the next five years, Caesar conquered all of Gaul, crossed the Rhine and the English Channel and finally defeated the rebellion of Vercingetorix in Gaul in 53 B.C.

Caesar's great literary work, *De Bello Gallico* (51 B.C.), describes the customs of the Celts and Germans of that time. It has little, however, to say about the Alps as mountains, which were not a favorable subject of the Romans. In Caesar's only account of an Alpine battle, in 57 B.C. he sent Servius Galba and the 12th legion to open the crossing of the Great St. Bernard Pass, which the Romans called Mons Jovis. Galba was unsuccessful, barely escaping disaster for his troops at Octodurus, in a narrow rocky gorge on the Swiss side of the pass, not far above Martigny in the valley of the Rhone.

Following the assassination of Caesar in 44 B.C., Roman legions under Augustus and his successors extended their dominion over all the Alps during the next three centuries. Throughout their great empire, the Romans built amphitheaters, baths, bridges, aqueducts and especially "the mighty Roman road . . . marching on and on irresistibly, huge stone joined to huge stone . . . over ramparts of mountains" (Hamilton 1932, 116). Sections of Roman paving and columns remain to this day near the summits of the St. Bernard, Maloja, Julier, Hochtor and other high Alpine passes. The Romans gradually lost their momentum to invaders of the Alps from the north and east, until Rome itself was sacked by the Visigoths in A.D. 410 and finally by the Vandals in A.D. 455, when the Western Roman Empire came to an end (Gibbon 1952). One of its successors was the Gothic king Theodoric the Great (493–526).

Feudal Fief Fights

The Middle Ages

During the Dark Ages that followed, the Alpine region split up into feudal fiefdoms owned by various kings, barons, bishops and monasteries. The Alps were then reunited for the last time under the reign of Charlemagne (742–814), who became emperor in the year 800, but his empire began to come apart in 817, during the reign of his immediate heir, Louis the Pious (814–40). Six imperial reigns later, the Holy Roman Empire, mainly a German entity, became nominally sovereign over parts of the Alps and other parts of Europe, from 962 to 1806.

Still visible as medieval relics are the ruins of many Alpine castles built by the various robber barons, especially in Austria, eastern Switzerland and the Valle d'Aosta. Also a medieval legacy are the many hereditary titles of nobility that are still prominent in the monarchies and former monarchies of Europe.

An unpleasant medieval occurrence in the Alps was the incursion of Saracen pirates, who were shipwrecked in 887 and established themselves in the Montagnes des Maures, named after them, in Provence (Coolidge 1908). For the next 108 years, they terrorized much of the Alps as itinerant bandits. In 906, they overran the southern and northern Piedmont. In 916, they held the Montgenèvre and Mont Cenis Passes. In 936, their attacks ranged as far as Chur in eastern Switzerland and St. Maurice in the Valais. Finally, in 975, they were exterminated, in their original headquarters, by the count of Provence and the marquis of Turin.

The Hapsburgs

The Hapsburg family came from Alsace in the tenth century and built a minor castle in northwest Switzerland. After the Roman imperial crown became vacant in Germany in 1254, Rudolph of Hapsburg, who had distinguished himself by subduing the local robber barons, was elected Holy Roman emperor in 1273. In 1282, he made his sons dukes of Austria and Styria. Thus the Hapsburgs were Alsatian before they became Swiss and were Swiss before they became Austrian.

They steadily added to their domains—mainly through various dowries and treaties, rather than by conquest—until they developed what became the Austrian Empire. During most of the 645 years of their dynasty, they controlled the eastern Alps, including those which now belong to Italy and Slovenia, but not Bavaria, whose rulers were among their greatest rivals, though it was from them that the Hapsburgs had early acquired Tirol as a dowry.

Swiss Independence

The rule of Emperor Rudolph was not oppressive, but at that time, the junior branch of the Hapsburg family, from its base in Zurich, had been harsh in its treatment of its vassal communities around the south end of Lake Lucerne. The elders of these communities—Uri, Schwyz and Unter-walden—declared themselves to be a free confederation (under the emperor) on August 1, 1291, which is the official Swiss independence day.

Twenty-four years later, their descendants won a decisive victory (Rambert 1889). After a protracted dispute about pasture rights, the men of Schwyz sacked the great monastery at Einsielden, which was under the protection of the Hapsburgs. To punish them, Duke Leopold of Austria, the elder son of Rudolph, set out to attack Schwyz with 4,000 armored cavalry followed by 5,000 men on foot and a large supply of rope to hang the culprits. The men of the Swiss Confederation numbered less than 3,000. No other Swiss came to help them, while those of Zurich, Zug and Lucerne even sided with the duke. The confederates had to separate into smaller forces to cover three easy routes into Schwyz from the west and north. They did, however, have a spy in the enemy camp who warned them to be ready at the pass of Morgarten, south of little Lake Egeri, on the Feast of St. Othmar, November 15, 1315.

The duke's cavalry went ahead as a point of honor, which was a fatal mistake. Above the pass (which is rather insignificant), fifty exiles from Schwyz, who were eager to be reinstated, had prepared an ambush. They allowed half of the cavalry to pass and then split the line in two by rolling boulders and tree trunks down the slope, after which they charged, armed with halberds and scythes. The mounted men, in armor, were thrown into confusion. The foot soldiers, who alone could have helped, were on the narrow path 2 miles behind, between the lake and the mountain. The horses were a hindrance rather than a help. When the rest of the confederates joined the battle, the cavalry was devastated. Many jumped into the lake and drowned. The survivors retreated, and the duke himself barely escaped.

The confederation was joined by Lucerne (1332), Zurich (1351), Glarus (1352) and Bern (1353), followed by other Swiss cantons. After two more victories over the Hapsburgs, the Swiss, flush with their military prowess, engaged in foreign military conquest for the next 200 years and in mercenary service after that. They invaded Italy, where they acquired their present ownership of the Ticino west of Lake Como, being stopped only by the French at the battle of Marignano in 1515.

Swiss Wars

The Rhone Valley, upstream from Lake Geneva, was ruled by the bishop of Sion from 999 to 1798 (though from 1384 to 1569, the land between Lake Geneva and Sion was held by the duke of Savoy). To repel perennial armed incursions by the bishop of Sion, the twelfth-century Bernese dukes of Zahringen built two still-existing castles in the Kander Valley, which rises to the Gemmi and Lötschen Passes across the northern Alpine chain. Several of the battles between Bern and Sion took place at the top of the Lötschen Pass. In the battle of 1419, the Bernese prevailed because they had slept on the Lötschen Glacier below the pass and were less frozen than the Valaisans, who had slept at the top of the pass (Coolidge 1908). Today, the 120-kilometer (70 mi.) border between Bern and Valais follows the main crest of the northern Alps except where pastures north of the Grimsel and Gemmi Passes, captured during the wars with Bern, still belong to the Valais.

In 1519, the Reformation began in Switzerland under Zwingli at Zurich. In 1536, Geneva also became Protestant upon the arrival of Calvin. In 1528, the Catholic cantons of Uri, Schwyz, Unterwalden, Lucerne, Zug, Fribourg and Solothurn fought the battle of Kappel against the Protestant cantons of Zurich, Bern and Basel, in which the Catholics prevailed and Zwingli was killed. The ensuing religious split paralyzed the Swiss Confederation until the end of the Thirty Years' War in 1648. In 1712, the Bernese won a decisive victory over the Catholic cantons at Villmergen, and the dominance of the Protestant cantons was thereafter firmly established.

Thirty Years' War

At the beginning of the Thirty Years' War in 1618, the Catholic valley of Valtelline, which rises east from Lake Como, belonged to the mostly Protestant Grisons. At that time, the Milanese, the territory of Milan, was held by Spaniards, who, in 1620, invaded the Valtelline up to the Umbrail

Pass, into Austria. This established a link between the Spanish and Austrian Hapsburg monarchies, which were the Catholic imperial powers in the Thirty Years' War. In 1635, France, though Catholic, joined the war on the opposite side. Richelieu then sent the duc de Rohan, a Huguenot, to enter the Valtelline and break the Hapsburg link. In this he was brilliantly successful, arriving inconspicuously through Switzerland and repeatedly repelling the more numerous Austrian and Spanish troops at opposite ends of the valley.

De Rohan was assisted by the Grisons under the command of Col. Jurg Jenatsch, a Protestant pastor who became a formidable warrior and who had killed eight men in duels during his military apprenticeship. The Grisons, however, were dismayed when the French army, which was largely one of Swiss mercenaries, decided to stay in the Valtelline. Jenatsch then joined the Austrians and the Catholic faction of Grisons, even adopting their faith patriotically, and he succeeded in driving out the French. In 1637, the Spaniards reappeared from Lake Como and once again linked up with the Austrians. The following year, de Rohan was killed in the battle of Rheinfelden, and in 1639 Jenatsch was anonymously axed to death in a wine shop at Chur (de Beer 1945).

Waldensians

The valleys of the Vaudois, or Waldensians, a group whose first 500 years were a relentless tragedy, descend into the plains of Piedmont from the main crest of the Alps southwest of Turin. They are members of the oldest surviving Protestant movement, founded in the year 1170 at Lyon by a man named Pierre, variously surnamed Waldo or Le Vaudois. Some thirty years before Saint Francis, he got rid of all his possessions to live a life of poverty according to the Gospels, but he was excommunicated when he refused to stop preaching the Gospel without his bishop's permission. His followers, who ranged as far as Bohemia, then had to worship secretly, but many of them were burned at the stake during the Inquisition (including Joan of Arc, who was accused of being a Waldensian). In 1487, to exterminate the Waldensians, the papal legate Albert Cattanée led his troops into the valley of Vallouise west of Briançon. The Waldensians living there, true to their tradition of nonviolence, fled into the caves of Mont Pelvoux, where 3,000 of them died, mostly from asphyxiation when the papal troops burned wood at the mouths of the caves.

However, in 1561, the Waldensians, greatly outnumbered by several thousand troops of the duke of Savoy, decided to resist, placing the defense of their truth above their nonviolent tradition. The Waldensians prevailed and, in the extraordinary treaty of Cavour between the duke and a religious group that had no political status, they obtained the right to practice their faith within the limits of their valleys. When they exceeded those limits, a ducal force of 4,000 destroyed several of their valley villages and massacred much of the population with sadistic torture, after which the surviving Waldensians fled into the mountains. This massacre of 1655 was a subject of protest throughout Europe and in Milton's famous sonnet.

In 1686, Duke Victor Amadeus II of Savoy, under pressure from his uncle Louis XIV of France, declared that, contrary to the treaty of Cavour, no Protestants would be tolerated in any of the Alpine valleys. After a year of fruitless negotiation, the Waldensians, numbering 2,700, agreed to emigrate to Switzerland, which they did under harrowing January conditions. After a few years, however, many became homesick for their Alpine valleys. In August 1689, 900 men, of whom 60 percent were Waldensians and the rest Huguenots organized by King William of England, secretly crossed Lake Geneva at night and began forced marches over less-frequented mountain routes. The men who survived the journey, only three hundred of the Waldensians, arrived one week later at Susa near their Alpine valleys. There they were attacked by 4,000 French dragoons and were about to be annihilated when a sudden fog enabled them to escape into the mountains at night. A few days later, Victor Amadeus II broke his alliance with France, sided with England, and the Waldensians were safe thereafter.

In 1989, in their chief town of Torre Pellice, which includes their main church and seminary, the Waldensians celebrated the tercentenary of their return from Switzerland. The tradition of English assistance to the Waldensians has been active to this day. Because of the tercentenary, we had trouble finding lodgings until Miss Beerbohm, who had been an English missionary to the Waldensians for twenty-five years, arranged for us to stay at the Park Hotel, where the ambience, plumbing, furniture, servants' uniforms and even some of the guests seemed to be of authentic Victorian English vintage.

Savoys

The Savoy dynasty was founded in 1025 by Humbert, count of Aosta, and thus was only one century younger than that of the Hapsburgs (Coolidge 1908). In 1050, the family inherited the region known, then and now, as Savoy, with its capital at Chambery. They became dukes of Aosta in 1238. Also in the thirteenth century, they acquired the lower part of the Valais, with their castle at Martigny, and thereby became lords of major territories on all three sides of Mont Blanc (now French, Italian and Swiss). In 1418, they inherited the Piedmont section of Italy, and in 1559, they transferred their capital from Chambery to Turin. They became kings of Sardinia in 1720 and kings of Italy in 1861.

Illustrating the complexity of the history of the Savoys and the reality of feudal authority during those centuries is the story of Chamonix. It belonged to the house of Savoy from 1253 to 1268, from 1355 to 1792 and from 1814 to 1860; to France from 1268 to 1355, from 1792 to 1814 and from 1861 to the present. Most of these changes had little effect on the valley's population of several hundred, who were serfs under a fiefdom held by the local priory from 1091 to 1786. The priory belonged to a Benedictine monastery near Turin until 1519, when the pope transferred it to the church at Sallanche, which did not improve the people's lives under the oppressive rule of the priors.

Many of the serfs, mostly the women, were burned at the stake as heretics, after which their property was divided between the prior, the inquisitor, and the bishop of Geneva, an arrangement that obviously did not encourage disinterested judgment. In 1283, Jacques Boutillier, "for the repose of his soul" (Whymper 1908), gave his serf Nicholas of Chamonix and the descendants of Nicholas to Richard de Villette, then prior, after which Madame Boutillier sold the three sons of Guillaume Bezer of Chamonix to the prior for fifty sous (two and one-half francs). Already in the sixteenth century, the people began to rebel, sometimes violently. Finally, in October 1786, after 700 years as chattels of a religious institution, they bought their freedom by paying 58,000 livres, each worth ten francs, to the church in Sallanche. A few years later, under the French Revolution, they would have been free without paying, but this was a mixed blessing. When Chamonix again became part of France in 1792, it suffered two years of violent de-Christianization and two decades of war.

Arrival of Modern War

Napoleon

In 1796, Napoleon, as heir to the French Revolution, entered Italy via Nice and conquered the areas of both Hapsburgs and Savoys. He formed the Ligurian and Cisalpine Republics, both controlled by France, and annexed the Valtelline and Italian Bregaglia. In February 1798, Napoleon established the Helvetic Republic in Switzerland, with headquarters in Aarau. Bern was concerned by this threat to its oligarchy and declared war, but it promptly lost to the French under General Schauenberg.

Schwyz and part of Unterwalden, of the original Swiss Confederation, organized an impromptu army that set off to liberate Switzerland from the French, preferring their local form of freedom to that imposed from Paris. A few miles from Morgarten, where their ancestors had defeated the Hapsburg duke five centuries earlier, the valliant Schwyz, commanded by Aloys Reding, repelled the advancing French army at Rothenthurm on May 1–2, 1798 (Rambert 1889). It was analogous to the earlier victory but this time inconclusive. Schauenberg was preparing to return with a larger force that would prevail. Further Swiss heroism would be futile. In Schwyz, at a *Landesgemeinde* (an outdoor meeting of all male members of the canton, which was the basic local form of democracy), the population voted to join the Helvetic Republic. In 1803, Aloys Reding became the first chief of state over all of Switzerland. That year, under Napoleon's edict, the Grisons joined Switzerland as its physically largest canton.

In May 1800, Napoleon and his army crossed the snows of the Great St. Bernard Pass into Italy, and in the following years, he conquered almost all the Alps, except Styria and upper Carinthia. Although he did not conquer the Alps as completely as the Romans and Charlemagne, the influence of his system of government endures, in large areas, up to the present time.

In 1809, Archduke Charles of Austria tried to arouse Austria and Bavaria to revolt against the French and began an invasion of Bavaria. Only Tirol responded, in a rebellion led by its folk hero Andreas Hofer. Napoleon hurried back from Spain and defeated the Austrians using German troops. Napoleon's forces captured Andreas Hofer and shot him at Mantua in November 1809. Hofer is now honored in a personal shrine at Innsbruck.

Suvorov

In 1799, Switzerland was again a battleground, this time with the French under the great General André Massena during Napoleon's war against the Second Coalition (Austria, Russia, England, Turkey, Portugal, Naples and the Papal States). The seventy-year-old field marshall Alexander

Suvorov, the "tiger" of Catherine the Great, was recalled from retirement with the assignment of leading an Austro-Russian army and removing the French from Italy (Napoleon was then in Egypt). Suvorov literally cowed some of the French by threatening to massacre them, as he had done to the Turks in Bessarabia, and caused others to retreat after a series of engagements. He and his army entered Milan and were welcomed as liberators. Suvorov then turned north to join his Russian flank under Korsakoff in Zurich.

In September 1799, after storming the St. Gotthard Pass and defeating the French at the Devil's Bridge (see chap. 9), Suvorov took his men across the difficult Chinzig Pass into Muotathal. There he learned from his Cossack scouts that Massena had annihilated Korsakoff's army and was already in Schwyz, about to attack the invading Russians. After a council of war with his generals, including Bagration of *War and Peace* fame, Suvorov belatedly agreed to retreat. While fighting a rearguard action against the French, he crossed the mountains into Glarus and Elm. From there he led his hungry and frozen Russians over the 2,404-meter (7,887 ft.) roadless and icy Panixer Pass, arriving at the safety of the upper Rhine Valley on October 8, 1799, with a remnant of 15,000 men out of his original 25,000.

From Vienna to Caporetto

After Napoleon's defeat in Russia in 1812 and at Waterloo in 1815, followed by the Congress of Vienna, the Swiss Confederation was reestablished and joined by the Valais, Geneva and Neuchatel, which until then still nominally belonged to the king of Prussia. The confederation's new central government ended the internal religious wars that had plagued Switzerland for centuries. After 1815, Austria controlled all of Italy until 1848, when Kaiser Franz Joseph had to flee to Tirol because of the revolution in Vienna. That was the start of a series of wars in the eastern Alps between Austria (the Hapsburgs) and Italy (the Savoys) in 1848, 1859, 1866 and 1914–17.

In December 1917, at the battle of Caporetto (now Kobarid in Slovenia), also known as the eleventh battle of the Izonzo (Soca) River, the Italians lost some 300,000 men as prisoners and casualties and more than that as deserters. A few months later, the Austrian army also collapsed. Italy then acquired Venice, Trieste and South Tirol from Austria, but after World War II, it lost the outskirts of Trieste to Yugoslavia

(Slovenia), though Italy retains the city's center and port. The two world wars ended the centuries-old dynasties of the Hapsburg and Savoys, who at various times had feuded with each other like royal Hatfields and McCoys.

Episodes of World War II

In 1944, the highest of all battles in the Alps was fought at night on the Glacier du Géant in the Mont Blanc range, between the Col du Géant held by the Germans and the Aiguille du Midi held by the French Resistance. Since the ski troops on both sides were dressed in white, it was impossible to tell friend from foe in the dark until the Germans used tracer bullets, which the French did not have. The outcome was a draw, with both sides retreating to their respective posts in the morning. Among the prominent men of Chamonix who took part in the battle were Gaston Rébuffat, André Bossonay and ski champion James Coutet.

Also in 1944, an American patrol in the French Alps almost met disaster at the hands of German machine gunners in Briançon, as described in the following (abridged) letter of November 17, 1989 we received frrom W. M. Thompson.

> Your article in *Military History* [Shoumatoff 1989] and its accompanying photo of the forts at Briançon brought back memories of 45 years ago. As a member of the O.S.S. Jedburgh team Novacaine I have vivid recollections of those forts. We operated with a Maquis group based near Vallouise with several missions to accomplish when the 7th army invaded from the south. A small group of American infantry reached Briançon just ahead of us and were then replaced by a reinforced battalion of Chemical Warfare troops with 4.2 mortars. We set up a base in the hotel in Briançon awaiting orders. After several days, the Germans mounted an offensive against Briançon, hitting us hard early in the morning.
>
> An Army communications van, parked just outside the hotel door, took a direct hit from an 88 shell. Lt. Gennerick and myself were sent to the roof of the hotel where there was a tourist type telescope mounted. Our mission was to try to find where the Germans were located that they were getting such accurate artillery spotting. We discovered the Germans looking at us through field glasses from an aperture in one of the old forts. At about that time

we found heavy machine gun fire coming in just overhead and we went headfirst down through the hatch and prepared to leave with headquarters company. . . .

Fortunately the Germans did not pursue their advantage and we retreated to a place whose name is something like Cole de Lauterate [Col de Lautaret] (a winter ski resort before the war) which had been completely leveled by the Germans and the owners murdered. Many of our Maquis were trapped in one of the other forts and held out for several days after we fell back but eventually were all killed, we were told. . . . Thanks for the memories! Incidentally all members of the team I was on are now deceased.

Once in Yugoslavia

The termination of World War II in 1945 brought peace to the Alps and the rest of Europe, except in the realm of the ancient Illyrians. The 1990s, through armed conflict in the Julian and Dinaric Alps, brought peaceful independence to Slovenia but tragedy to Bosnia and parts of Croatia.

At the upper end of the long Vrata canyon in the Julian Alps, at the foot of Triglav's great north face, a unique memorial has been erected. It consists of a gigantic steel mountaineer's piton, about twelve feet high and pointing downward, with an enormous carabiner hanging from its upper end. On the stone base below, a bronze plaque commemorates the Alpine partisans who fought the Germans in these mountains in World War II.

In the late 1970s, we spent several days at Aljazev Dom, a hut of the Yugoslav Alpine Club, also near the upper end of the Vrata. During the days, we wandered around the canyon photographing the fabulous alpine flowers beneath the great peaks. In the evenings, we sat in the dining room with mixed groups of climbers from Belgrade, Trieste, Ljubljana and other towns, as they joined in lusty singing of many mutually familiar songs, including a newly popular one called "Yugoslavia!"

One evening, as we talked with a professor from Belgrade, coauthor Nina asked him, a bit daringly, if he thought Tito was a great man. By way of reply, the professor grandly raised his arm toward the large photo of Tito that hung on the wall in a corner near the ceiling, like a religious icon, and said, with exquisite irony, "Well, there he is!" This oblique encounter with the prevailing anticommunist dissidence was the only tension of any kind that we felt during our five visits, between 1964 and

1990, to what was once Yugoslavia (our last visit was just before the federation collapsed). We also visited Belgrade, Banja Luka, Ljubljana, Lipica, Dubrovnik and other towns in the interior and along the Adriatic coast, all with a similar lack of any belligerence in the atmosphere.

Under the federation, as Yugoslavs of all groups have vividly recorded, Serbs, Croats, Bosnians and others of all religions intermingled harmoniously as neighbors and intermarried with each other, as various people do in the United States. In tragic contrast, these same Yugoslavs, differing only in religion, savagely massacred each other in so-called ethnic cleansing during the years of relentless siege and shelling of cosmopolitan Sarayevo from the once peaceful hills of the 1984 Olympics—with blessings, rather than protests, from their religious clergy. Now, in what is hopefully the aftermath, enforced essentially by American troops, the residual traumas in Bosnia and parts of Croatia will take years—perhaps generations—to heal, while, with little hope, grieving survivors search for their dead among thousands of bodies in hundreds of mass graves.

Chapter 12

To the Summits

Climbs before 1800

Mountains of Antiquity

Forty-nine thousand years ago, a group of Neanderthals reached an altitude of 2,445 meters (8,022 ft.) on a sheer rock face, at a cave where they buried seven bear skulls (see chap. 7). This is the only known example of significant mountain climbing from prehistoric time. The historic tradition of climbing mountains is also ancient, beginning with the ascent of Mt. Sinai by Moses (Exodus 19). The ancient Greeks thought of their highest peaks, Olympus and Parnassus, as homes of gods but apparently did not climb them to find out. Nor did they climb Kazbek or Elbrus in their colony of Iveria in the Caucasus, where, on one of these peaks, both higher than anything in the Alps, they thought that the immortal god Prometheus had been eternally chained, in punishment for having revealed to humankind the secret of fire.

The Romans, in contrast, did plenty of climbing in their campaigns and travels over high Alpine passes but showed no attraction or even interest for the summits. Two of their names for passes, which they called mountains, have survived: Mont Cenis and Montgenèvre. One Latin poet, however, considered summits to be impressive: "In the cloudy kingdom of the Alps, the altar of Hercules still stands among snowy peaks. There rises the venerable white summit that neither the rays of the sun nor the warm winds of springtime will ever melt. It rests forever in its envelope of ice as though it carries the weight of the universe on its shoulders. From the top of that peak, Caesar contemplates from afar the plains of Italy" (Petronius *Satyricon,* first century A.D.).

First Recorded Alpine Climb

Petrarch's climb of Mont Ventoux in 1336 was the first *recorded* ascent of an Alpine peak, achieved by one of the brightest stars in the firmament of European culture. At a height of 1,909 meters (6,263 ft.), Mont Ventoux is just east of the village of Malaucene in Provence, from which the ascent was made. With his brother Gherardo and two servants, he started out for the mountain early on April 26. While his companions scrambled up the rocky slope, Petrarch looked for an easier way and found one, which he thought "almost inaccessible." He wrote in a letter to a friend: "At the summit is a small plateau where we rested from our fatigue. At first, smitten by an unfamiliar wind and by the vastness of the spectacle, I was motionless with stupor. Beyond the Alps, which were covered with snow, I then directed my gaze to that part of Italy where my heart beat the fastest" (Gos 1934, 25).

The last sentence refers to his overpowering love for Laura, an Italian woman who dominated his poetry, though he never mentioned her surname. She remains a mystery woman for whom scholars have proposed at least four different Lauras as candidates. His climb of Mont Ventoux, which he characterized as a "voyage of the soul," was primarily an act of devotion to her. At the summit, Petrarch read from the *Confessions* of St. Augustine, which he opened by chance to the page stating, "Men go off to admire the summits of the mountains . . . and neglect themselves." Thus, for more than a thousand years before Petrarch, mountain beauty had not been a novelty. "Poetry and love, religion and beauty are the values which drew men toward the summits when mountaineering began" (Gos 1934, 26). All four of these elements were clearly involved in Petrarch's ascent of Mont Ventoux.

The sun was already setting when Petrarch's group began its descent. They found the way by moonlight, which "lent its agreeable aid to our march." At the Malaucene Inn, while supper was being prepared, Petrarch described his experience in a long letter to a friend, the text of which has been preserved. It mentioned that "In the gorges of the mountain we met an aged shepherd who tried to deter us from the ascent. Fifty years ago, inspired by the same ardor of youth, he had climbed to the top and brought back nothing but regret, fatigue and clothes torn by the rocks" (Gos 1934, 26). Thus the recorded ascent was not the first one, a circumstance that applied to many ascents in the Alps, including the very next one.

First Recorded Snow-Peak Climb

Only twenty-two years later, on September 1, 1358, Bonifacio Rotario of Asti climbed Rochemelon, 3,538 meters (11,608 ft.) high, east of Mont Cenis and just north of Susa. This is regarded as the first climb of an Alpine snow peak (Gos 1934). It has permanent snow and a glacier on its north (French) side, but neither on its south (Italian) side. Rotario climbed it alone from the south, carrying a heavy bronze triptych, which he placed at the top, propped up with stones. Unlike the great Petrarch, his biography is uncertain. He is thought to have been a returning Crusader who had been imprisoned by the Saracens and had vowed to the Virgin Mary that if he should be freed, he would place an image of her on a high Alpine peak. Some say it was a penitential vow. An unlikely version is that he stayed on the summit for the rest of his life as a hermit.

There is evidence here, too, of an earlier ascent. Even after the time of Rotario, Rochemelon was known as Mons Romuleus. A Benedictine chronicle at Novara states that a former King Romulus, for whom the peak was named, had spent some time on the summit (and therefore had climbed it) hoping for a cure from leprosy and had left a treasure there. Soon after his death, in the eleventh century, Count Clement and Marquis Arduin attempted the climb, but both turned back because of bad weather. Rotario's ascent was not difficult except for carrying the bronze triptych, the story of which is significant. It shows the Virgin Mary and Christ Child between St. George and St. James, who present to Mary a kneeling warrior identified by the inscription "Hic me apportavit Bonefacius Rotarius astensis in honorem D.N. J.-C. et beatae Virginis, anno Domini MCCCLVIII die I septembris," where "hic" refers to the summit of the mountain.

The custom gradually became established for pilgrims to climb the peak from both north and south, where a mass was said before the triptych every year on August 5, the feast of the Virgin of the Snows. The pilgrims built stone walls and a roof around the tablet, forming a small chapel. Charles-Emanuel II, duke of Savoy, made the pilgrimage in 1659 and ordered that the triptych be brought down to the Cathedral of Susa, where it is now kept except for every August 5, when it is carried in a procession to the chapel on Rochemelon. In *Voyages dans les Alpes*, de Saussure described Rochemelon as a sharp-pointed peak where the path leading to the chapel was so treacherous that nearly every year it claimed the life of an exhausted pilgrim who fainted and fell. Nearby Mont

Thabor (3,425 m, 10,440 ft.) also has a chapel at the top, where a mass is said each year at the end of August. These are perhaps the only Alpine peaks that are objects of regular active pilgrimage like Mt. Kailas in Tibet and Fujiyama in Japan.

First Extreme Rock Climb

From the mountaineering viewpoint, the most remarkable by far of the early events in the Alps was the ascent of Mont Aiguille near Grenoble on June 26, 1492, by a group led by Antoine de Ville, lord of Domjulien and Beaupré in Lorraine (Gos 1934). The appearance and reality of Mont Aiguille are more formidable than its height of 2,097 meters (6,880 ft.). Its summit is a grassy plateau some 100 meters wide and 800 meters long, completely surrounded by near-vertical limestone walls more than 1,000 feet high, rising from a conical base of erosion debris. W. A. B. Coolidge, who rarely exaggerated, wrote in 1908 that it "even now can only be scaled (without ropes) by a good cragsman." Before it was climbed, its name was Mons Inascensibilis. The king of France, Charles VIII, considered that as long as it was inaccessible, it was not actually a part of his realm, and for this reason he commissioned his chamberlain and gallant warrior, Antoine de Ville, to make the ascent.

In those days, mountains were generally regarded as ominous and mysterious and Mont Aiguille especially so. De Ville, who had never set foot on any mountain, was worried but undaunted when he undertook to carry out the royal command. To him, it was not a rock-climbing exercise but a professional military task. He chose, for one of his companions, the officer in charge of siege engines for the king's army, who came with a large quantity of ropes, hooks and ladders. The party included several local montagnards, as well as two priests to provide the needed divine blessing.

After choosing the most promising route, which de Ville described as "the most horrible and terrifying passage that I or any of my company have ever seen" (Gos 1934), they began the ascent on June 26, 1492, before the great voyage of Columbus. By the end of the first day, they had set up ladders halfway up the cliff and secured them in the modern manner by hooks (pitons) driven into the rock. They spent the night in a bivouac at the base of the cliff. On the second day, they installed ladders the rest of the way up, and the entire party climbed to the top, except for de Ville's lackey, who stayed below as a messenger.

De Ville then immediately wrote a letter to the president of the Grenoble Parliament, reporting their success and asking him to inform the king. He also requested an official delegation that would testify to the presence of the men on the summit, at the edge of which they erected three wooden crosses that were visible from below.

The climbing party waited at the top until the witnesses came and confirmed that they saw the men there. Two groups, one led by Gigue de la Tour and the other by Pierre Liotard, signed affidavits that they climbed to the top, where they saw de Ville and his men and heard the priests say mass. While waiting for the witnesses, the men erected a small stone chapel on the summit, the remains of which are still there. De Ville was surprised and delighted to find a large herd of chamois on the plateau, where one of his men also noted having seen three different kinds of sparrows, a red-footed chough and a large variety of fragrant flowers, especially lilies—a nice touch in a report for the king whose emblem was the fleur-de-lis. These observations were a pleasant contrast to the dragons that they might have expected to see. The letter of Antoine de Ville and the affidavits of the witnesses are preserved in the archive at Grenoble. The climb of Mont Aiguille was not repeated until more than 300 years later, in 1834, by another priest, a lawyer and several local men.

Leonardo da Vinci's Alps

Chronologically, the next historically important ascent was by Leonardo da Vinci. Far more than any of his contemporaries, he was curious about phenomena at high altitude. That is why he was drawn to Monte Rosa, which was clearly visible, in those preindustrial times, from his base in Milan. A famous and somewhat mystifying passage in his notes describes his observations on that mountain.

> I say that the blue which is seen in the atmosphere is not its own color, but is caused by the heated moisture having evaporated into the most minute imperceptible particles, which the beams of the solar rays attract and cause to seem luminous against the deep intense darkness of the region of fire [i.e., of the stars] that forms a covering over them. And this may be seen, as I myself saw it, by anyone who ascends Mon Boso, a peak of the chain of Alps that divides France from Italy, at whose base spring the four rivers which flow as many different ways and water all Europe, and there is no other mountain

that has its base at so great an elevation. This mountain towers to so great a height as almost to pass above all the clouds; and snow seldom falls there, but only hail in summer when the clouds are at their greatest height; and there this hail accumulates, so that if it were not for the infrequency of the clouds thus rising and discharging themselves, which does not happen twice in an age, there would be an enormous mass of ice there, built up by the various layers of the hail; and this I found very thick in the middle of July. And I saw the atmosphere dark overhead, and the rays of the sun striking the mountain had far more brightness than in the plains below, because less thickness of atmosphere lay between the summit of this mountain and the sun. (Lunn 1914, 28)

Since there is no peak now officially named Mon Boso, its identity has been hotly disputed. The most convincing evidence, pointed out by both Lunn (1914) and Uzielli (1890), is that on old maps as late as 1740 Monte Rosa was called Monte Bosa, and Uzielli notes that even in 1890 the mountain was called Mt. Biosa by the natives of Val Sesia, beneath the south slopes of the peak. Leonardo undoubtedly made an important ascent, even though we do not know which of Monte Rosa's summits or saddles it may have been. He made several important observations in the passage just quoted, about the thickness of the ice, the power of the sun, and the darkness of the sky, all of which show that he had reached high altitude, probably higher than anyone else had reached before. He added a poetic touch when he described the dark sky "of a blue like that of the gentian." He also observed that the alpine plants were "short, thin and mostly pale and dry because of the low humidity" (Gos 1934, 53).

From Leonardo to Mont Blanc

The rest of the sixteenth century marked two interesting first ascents. The first recorded climb of Mt. Pilatus (2,129 m, 6,985 ft.) above Lake Lucerne was made in 1518 by Joachim von Watt, who used the humanist pen name Vadianus, and by three other Swiss scholars (Lunn 1914). The six clergymen who had attempted to climb it in 1307 were jailed because they had violated regulations regarding the legend of Pontius Pilate, but Watt had no such problems. In 1585, the legend was disproved by Johann Müller, pastor of Lucerne (see chap. 8). "It appears that the mountain was climbed before the beginning of the fourteenth century," and "by the beginning of the sixteenth century the ascent of easily accessible mountain tops was of not infrequent occurrence" (Lunn 1914, 31).

A different Johann Müller, professor of theology at Berne, made the first ascent of the Stockhorn (2,190 m, 7,185 ft.) above the Lake of Thun in 1536, with "a jovial company of learned men reveling in the spirit of the ancients." He "left a long report of the expedition written in Latin hexameter, composed as a humorous account parodied from ancient writings," in which, "for the first time, alpine flowers are described" (Grosjean 1969).

The seventeenth century was almost a blank in the history of mountaineering. The eighteenth century culminated in the ascent of Mont Blanc preceded by noteworthy climbs that ranged from 2,864 meters (9,396 ft.) at Triglav in the Julian Alps to 3,765 meters (12,353 ft.) at Mont Velan near the St. Bernard Pass, with summits of intervening height at Piz Beverin and Titlis in Switzerland, Buet and Dent du Midi above Lake Geneva, and Ankogel in Austria. A great climber of that period was Placidus a Spescha, a pastor of the Grisons, who made several first ascents in what is now eastern Switzerland (Lunn 1914).

Mont Blanc to the Matterhorn

First Ascent of Mont Blanc

Four men of Chamonix, three of whom were guides, made the first major attempt to climb Mont Blanc (4,807 m, 15,771 ft.) in July 1775. After climbing the Montagne de la Côte, a rocky ridge between the great glaciers of Bossons and Taconnaz, they surmounted all obstacles and attained the top of the Dome du Gouter (4,303 m, 14,118 ft.), probably the highest point reached until then in the Alps. From there it was an easy 2-kilometer walk over the snow to the Mont Blanc summit. However, being unaccustomed to the high altitude and intense sunlight, which made them almost snow-blind, they felt ill and turned back. Moreover, they thought it essential to get back the same day, because it was then supposed that sleeping on the glaciers would be fatal.

In 1783, Michel-Gabriel Paccard, who was Chamonix's medical doctor, began examining possible routes to the top of Mont Blanc through a telescope from the Brevent across the valley. The following year, he explored possible approaches from the upper part of the Mer de Glace and from St. Gervais via the Aiguille du Gouter, whose summit he almost reached. In June 1786, Jacques Balmat, a crystal hunter, attached himself to three guides, who climbed from Chamonix to the north summit ridge at 4,362 meters but turned back frightened by the narrow ridge above, leaving Balmat to look for crystals. He was caught by a storm on the way down and slept on the glacier, proving that this was not fatal. Paccard engaged him as a porter, and on August 8, 1786, they made the first ascent of the main summit. On the way up, Balmat wanted to turn back, but Paccard pressed on and reached the summit, from which, as Balmat wrote two months later, "He called me; I followed." They had climbed the glaciers on the north face of the mountain via the rocks of the Grands Mulets and from there to the east ridge as Paccard had planned (Lunn 1914).

Later, encouraged by Marc-Theodore Bourit (who was jealous of Paccard and wanted to climb Mont Blanc but did not get higher than 3,000 meters [9,843 ft.]), Balmat spread the falsehood, which was popularized by Dumas (see chap. 13), that he had led the climb and had dragged an exhausted Paccard to the top. Bourit even managed to suppress the publication of Paccard's book about the climb, the manuscript of which has been lost, though its prospectus has been found. Only in 1913 was the truth fully established, in a book by Heinrich Dubi based on the diary of Baron von Gersdorf, who had watched the whole climb through a telescope. Further information was developed by Graham Brown and Gavin de Beer in their scholarly work *The First Ascent of Mont Blanc* (1957), which finally gave Dr. Paccard the full acclaim that he had earned (Lunn 1914). In 1986, on the bicentennial of the ascent, Paccard's statue was finally erected in Chamonix. (Paccard had earned his medical degree at Turin, the capital of the kingdom of Sardinia to which Chamonix then belonged, because of which some Italians claim that an Italian first climbed Mont Blanc.)

De Saussure and Mont Blanc

Horace-Bénédict de Saussure (1834) made his famous ascent of Mont Blanc in 1787, at the age of forty-seven. In 1760, he had offered a large reward for those who would make the first ascent. His own attempt in 1785 via the Aiguille du Gouter was unsuccessful. (This is now the standard route.) During sunset on that occasion, he saw, at the opposite end of the sky from the sun, a set of purple rays converging into a point. This was the high-altitude phenomenon now known as "the Glory." He wrote that the first ascent was made in August 1786 by Paccard and Balmat. De

Saussure tried immediately to follow their footsteps but turned back because of bad weather and postponed his climb until the following year. Meanwhile Balmat collected the reward from de Saussure in Geneva after Paccard relinquished his share, but, tragically, Balmat was robbed of the whole amount on his way home to Chamonix.

When de Saussure made his ascent in 1787 by the Paccard-Balmat route, his method, by the concepts of today, was more Himalayan than Alpine. He was accompanied by his valet and eighteen guides, nominally headed by Jacques Balmat. De Saussure's purpose was not primarily just to climb the mountain but rather to make meteorological measurements at the top, which he did for three and one-half hours using bulky instruments that the guides had carried up. They spent two nights on the way up, first in a crude stone hut prepared for the occasion, and afterward in tents. The ascent was extremely strenuous, over steep glaciers with large crevasses and seracs. (De Saussure was the first to use the word *serac* for huge blocks of ice perched on the slopes. In normal French it means a chunk of cheese.) Near the summit, they were terrified by the noisy impact of an enormous serac that fell into a wide crevasse and got stuck halfway down. With disarming frankness, de Saussure tells of the guides placing a ladder at a "bad step" where he thought it was not needed, and he made a point of not touching it because he was "afraid to give the guides a bad opinion [of himself]."

Among de Saussure's observations on the summit, he noted that the sky had become so dark that he could dimly see the stars throughout the day. He attributed this to "the great purity and transparency of the air," though he also referred to its "rarety," which he measured at about one-half of sea-level barometric pressure. The darkness of the air frightened those guides who had not seen it before, because it gave an illusion of a great abyss over the edge of the snow. To bring back a "sample" of the dark sky, he painted a piece of paper with an appropriate shade of Prussian blue. The Mont Blanc summit offered no place where he could directly observe the depth of the snow, but he estimated it was 186 feet by extension from an exposed place on the adjacent Dome du Gouter. (There was no metric system at that time, and he expressed most of his measurements in fathoms or feet.) The only living things he saw near the summit were a small moth, apparently a noctuid, flying over a snowfield, and a butterfly that he thought might be a "myrtil" (probably a blue lycaenid), flying across the summit ridge.

Because he had seen the view for almost two hours while climbing, he was almost disappointed when he actually reached the highest point. Mainly, he was relieved that for the next few hours, the guides could stop worrying about him. He was eager to set up the instruments and get on with his measurements. He recalled how Mont Blanc, which he had seen often from Geneva (in the days before industrial smog), had been his obsession—almost an illness—for so many years, but now that he had arrived, he was not completely satisfied and even less so when it was time to go back without his having made all the desired observations. That night, in the silence of his tent on the way down, he relived the impressions of the day with majestic views engraved in his memory, and he at last experienced unmixed satisfaction. At Chamonix, he was greeted by a large crowd of family, friends and well-wishers, including his wife, all of whom had been watching the ascent through telescopes. He was glad to have brought back all of his guides without their having had any accident.

His climb was the most celebrated mountaineering event in the Alps. An early statue in the center of Chamonix shows the tall de Saussure standing beside the guide Jacques Balmat, who points dramatically to the summit of Mont Blanc that towers 3,760 meters (12,300 ft.) above the village. That statue, so familiar in guidebooks and posters, is almost an emblem of Chamonix. Paccard's undramatic seated statue is at the opposite side of the same square.

Aftermath of Mont Blanc

Seven days after de Saussure climbed Mont Blanc in 1787, Colonel Beaufroy made its first English ascent and began a long line of British climbers in the Alps. In 1808, Marie Paradis of Chamonix was the first woman to climb Mont Blanc, thereby starting the era of woman mountaineers, who are now as numerous as the men. In 1819, Messrs. van Rensselaer and Howard made its first American ascent. In 1822, the British first ladies, Mrs. and Miss Campbell, arrived in Chamonix and made an impressive crossing of the Col du Géant into Italy. In 1838, Henriette d'Angeville, dressed in spectacular pantaloons, made the first climb of Mont Blanc by a visiting lady (an important distinction in those days).

Franz von Salm, bishop of Gurk in Austria, organized the first ascent of the Grossglockner, the highest peak in his diocese. This was the first large-scale expedition that followed in the style of de Saussure. After von Salm provided a comfortable hut partway up the mountain, five of his men, out of a party of more than thirty, reached its summit on July 28, 1800 (Lunn 1914). He was then fifty-one years old, and a few years later he climbed it himself. Archduke Johann commissioned Dr. Gebhard of Vienna to arrange an ascent of the Ortler (which was Austria's highest peak until after the Treaty of Versailles). Three chamois hunters engaged by Gebhard, led by Joseph Pichler, reached its summit on September 28, 1804, and Gebhard climbed it in 1805 (Lunn 1914). By the middle of the nineteenth century, his compatriots had climbed other important peaks of the eastern Alps, including the Dachstein, Zugspitze, Watzmann, Weiss-kugel and Grossvenediger.

Monte Rosa

During the late eighteenth and early nineteenth centuries, the ancient German-speaking colonies in Italy's Val Gressoney and Val Sesia com-peted with each other to explore Monte Rosa. On August 15, 1778, three years after the first attempt on Mont Blanc, seven men from Gressoney tried to climb Monte Rosa and reached a height of 4,343 meters (14,249 ft.) at the Rock of Discovery just west of the Lysjoch Pass. In 1801, Dr. Pietro Giordani of Val Sesia made a remarkable solo climb to the 4,046-meter (13,274 ft.) south summit of Mont Rosa, which now bears his name. (Therefore, Leonardo da Vinci, a man of exceptional physical strength, could have done something comparable three centuries earlier.)

On July 31, 1820, a group from Gressoney including Joseph Zum-stein climbed the Rock of Discovery and the next day ascended the 4,563-meter (14,970 ft.) Zumsteinspitze, just south of the highest point. The highest summit, which is the 4,634-meter (15,203 ft.) Dufourspitze, was first reached on July 31, 1855, by a party of nine via the west ridge from Zermatt. Among them was Rev. Charles Hudson of later Matterhorn fame.

Also a distinguished climber on Monte Rosa was Achille Ratti, who became Pope Pius XI. In 1889, he made its first traverse by the Zumstein-joch. After climbing to the highest summit of the mountain via its vast and sheer east face on their historic traverse from Macugnaga to Zermatt, he and his two companions spent the night a few meters below. They had not planned to bivouac and had no sleeping bags. Ratti wrote: "Who would have slept in that pure air, which pierced our marrow, and in the face of such a scene as we had before us? At that height, in the centre of the grandest of all the grand Alpine theatres, under that sky of deepest blue, lit by a crescent moon and sparkling with stars as far as the eye could reach, we felt ourselves to be in the presence of a novel and most imposing revelation of the omnipotence and majesty of God" (Ratti 1923, 80).

Toward the Golden Age

In 1811, Johann Rudolf Meyer and his brother Hieronymus, both of Aarau in Switzerland, made the first ascent of the Jungfrau by the now standard southeast ridge, after a roundabout approach via the Grimsel Pass, Rhone Valley, Lötschental and Aletsch Glacier (Lunn 1914). In Switzerland, most of the major first ascents before the middle of the nineteenth century were made by all-Swiss groups, including Mont Velan, Dents du Midi, Dents de Morcles, Oldenhorn, Wildhorn, Altels, Finsteraarhorn, Jungfrau, Wetterhorn, Titlis, Todi, Piz Corvatsch and Bernina.

When the English and other visiting climbers arrived in the Alps in the 1850s, most of the Swiss mountain men were glad to be employed as guides, preferring to take their clients on the lucrative first ascents (Lunn 1914). On Desor's "first ascent" of the Wetterhorn's Hasle Jungfrau in 1844, he directed his guides to make the climb first, to establish the route. Alfred Willis's climb of that peak in 1854, which ushered in the golden age of mountaineering, turned out to have been its fifth ascent. In 1855, when a Rumanian countess collapsed from exhaustion just below the summit of the Mönch, her Swiss guide, Christian Almer, refrained from completing the climb, which he could easily have done; then, in 1857, he guided a Viennese doctor on the official first ascent. Other great Swiss guides of that period were Melchior Anderegg, Alexander Burgener, Joseph Knubel and Franz Lochmatter. Great Swiss climbers of that time were Heinrich Dubi, F. J. Hugi and Eugene Rambert.

First Ascent of the Matterhorn

Like Mont Blanc and Monte Rosa, the Matterhorn was first attempted by a local group: Jean-Jacques Carrel, Jean Antoine Carrel and Aimé Gorret, all from the Italian valley of Valtournanche. In 1858, they reached a height of 3,723 meters (12,215 ft.) on the Italian ridge. Competing attempts to climb on that ridge were later made by John Tyndall and Edward Whymper. Whymper tried it seven times from 1861 to 1863, mostly with Jean Antoine Carrel as his guide (Whymper 1871). Whymper also climbed entirely alone to a record height of 13,500 feet and barely survived a 200-foot fall on a snowfield.

In 1865, he decided to try the Swiss side of the mountain. On July 8, he arrived at Breuil on the Italian side to find Jean Antoine Carrel, whom he could not engage because Carrel was committed from the eleventh. Whymper then learned that Carrel's new clients were members of the Italian Alpine Club who were planning to climb the Matterhorn. On the twelfth, Lord Francis Douglas arrived from Zermatt and agreed to join Whymper on the Swiss-side climb. That day, they crossed the Theodule Pass back to Zermatt. There they ran into Whymper's former guide, Michel Croz, and his new clients, Rev. Charles Hudson and Hudson's friend D. Hadow, who were also planning to make the climb the next day. Douglas had engaged Peter Taugwalder of Zermatt as guide and Taug-walder's son Peter as porter.

To avoid confusion, the two groups joined forces, even though Hadow was inexperienced and lacked suitable boots. On the thirteenth, they left Zermatt and found easy going on the Hörnli ridge, which was much less steep than they expected. After a bivouac, they reached the top with no problems the next day. Looking down the Italian side, they saw Carrel and his party about 1,000 feet below and attracted their attention by throwing stones. Unfortunately this caused Carrel to turn back, though he made the climb the next day.

After Whymper left their names on the summit, all seven roped up together and started down. To assist Hadow, Croz went first, though for security he should have been last. Hadow then slipped and caused all except Whymper and the Taugwalders to fall to their deaths. These three were saved because the elder Peter held to a protruding rock, but the rope broke in its weakest part, which was just below him (Whymper 1871). Stunned by the tragedy, the three survivors were transfixed by the appari-tion of three crosses in the sky. Actually, this was a natural fogbow, like that de Saussure witnessed on Mont Blanc.

Climbs after the Matterhorn

In the second half of the nineteenth century, Englishmen were the leading climbers of the Alps, making 301 first ascents of major peaks out of a total of 663, or out of the grand total of 803 made from 1358 to 1907 (Coolidge 1908). Well-known British climbers of that time were J. Tyndall, A. W. Moore, H. Walker, E. Whymper, E. S. Kennedy, W. Matthews, L. Stephen,

D. W. Freshfield and A. F. Mummery. Most of the important peaks were first climbed by them and fellow members of the Alpine Club, which was founded in London in 1857. They were almost always accompanied by guides. In chronological order, their first ascents included Monte Rosa, Dom, Eiger, Grivola, Aletschhorn, Bietschhorn, Gran Paradiso, Monte Viso, Weisshorn, Lyskamm, Dent Blanche, Barre des Écrins, Mont Dolent, Balmhorn, Aiuguille Verte, Matterhorn, Piz Roseg, Piz Badile, Grandes Jorasses, Mont Maudit, Grand Dru, Grepon and Aiguille du Géant (see table 7).

The only outstanding first ascents made by Frenchmen during the nineteenth century, which left few peaks still unclimbed, were those of Boileau de Castelneau, who climbed the Meije in 1877, and E. Javelle, who climbed the Tour Noire in 1876. Famous guides of the Chamonix Valley were J. M. Coutet, J. Balmat, M. Payot, Z. Cachat, M. Croz and F. Devouassoud.

A. F. Mummery, a nonmember of the Alpine Club, for most of his

TABLE 7.   Major First Ascents

Peak	Height: Meters	Feet	Date	Party
Monte Viso	3,841	12,602	1861	Matthews, Jacomb, Croz
Barre des Écrins	4,102	13,459	1864	Moore, Walker, Whymper, Coz
Meije	3,983	13,068	1877	B. de Castelnau, Gaspard
Gran Paradiso	4,061	13,323	1869	Cowell, Dundas, Payot
Mont Blanc	4,807	15,771	1786	Paccard, Balmat
Aiguille Verte	4,122	13,524	1865	Whymper, Almer, Biener
Weisshorn	4,506	14,783	1861	Tyndall, Bennen, Wenger
Matterhorn	4,478	14,692	1865	Whymper, Hudson, Hadow, Douglas, Croz, Taugwalders
Monte Rosa	4,634	15,203	1855	Hudson, Stevenson, Smyths, Birbeck, Lauener
Dom (Mischabel)	4,545	14,911	1858	Davies
Finsteraarhorn	4,274	14,022	1812	Volker, Bortis, Abbuhl
Aletschhorn	4,195	13,763	1859	Tuckett, Bennen, Tairraz
Junfrau	4,158	13,642	1811	J. and H. Meyer
Mönch	4,099	13,448	1857	Porges, Almer, Kaufmann
Eiger	3,976	13,045	1858	Barrington, Almer, Bohren
Bernina	4,049	13,284	1850	Coaz
Ortler	3,905	12,812	1804	Pichler, Leitner, Klausner
Weisskugel	3,739	12,267	1846	Two local men
Grossglockner	3,797	12,457	1800	Bishop of Gurk's party of five

life, was the outstanding climber of his time, specializing in difficult rock, rather than snow-peak, climbs. In 1881, at age twenty-six, he made the first ascent of the formidable Grepon above Chamonix, using his knee in the celebrated Mummery Crack. In 1893, he climbed it again with Mr. Hastings and Miss Bristow, without a guide. In his famous chapter "An Easy Day for a Lady," he tartly observed that "Miss Bristow showed the representatives of the Alpine Club the way in which steep rocks should be climbed" (1895, 159). He was even irreverent, though poignantly so, about the next world: "I should still wander among the upper snows, lured by silent mists and the red blaze of the setting sun, even though physical or other infirmity, even though in after aeons the sprouting of wings and other angelic appendages, may have sunk all thought of climbing and cragsmanship in the whelming past" (331).

W. A. B. Coolidge, an American living in England, made eighteen first ascents in the Alps, more than any other person before him. Several of these were made with his aunt Meta Brevoort and his dog Tschingel. In 1871, just six years after the first ascent of the Matterhorn, Miss Brevoort planned to make its first ascent by a woman, but her English rival Lucy Walker beat her to it by one day. Miss Brevoort then traversed the peak from Switzerland into Italy, being only the fourth person to achieve that feat. In the 1870s the "tigress" Kathleen Richardson made 116 major and 60 minor climbs in the Alps. In the 1880s Mrs. Aubrey Le Blond was president of the Ladies' Alpine Club. In the Alps, when her maid eloped with a porter, Le Blond had to put on her own boots for the first time.

Twentieth-Century Mountaineers

Early Twentieth Century

Out of the thousands of major achievements in the history of world mountaineering, only five stand out as authentic landmarks, being the ascents of Mont Blanc in 1786, the Matterhorn in 1865, the Eiger north face in 1938, Annapurna in 1950 and Everest in 1953. Their sequels represented two dominant trends still continuing today: the quests for difficult climbs on rock and for mountains higher than the Alps. Both trends became evident in the last years of the nineteenth century, when Mummery, Guido Rey and Kugy achieved extreme rock climbs, while Whymper, Freshfield and Mummery climbed in the Andes, Caucasus and Himalayas, where Mummery perished on Nanga Parbat. In the 1920s

Least primrose (*Primula minima*), Defereggental. (Photograph by N. and N. Shoumatoff.)

Moth (*Parnassius apollo*) on a mountain thistle in the Val d'Herens. (Photograph by N. and N. Shoumatoff.)

Helicigona arbustorum (left) and *Gentiana clusii* (right), Kandersteg. (Photograph by N. and N. Shoumatoff.)

Scarce copper *(Heodes virgauresa)* on Alpine goldenrod *(Solidago virgaurea)*, Lötschental. (Photograph by N. and N. Shoumatoff.)

Mountain fritillary (*Boloria pales*) on *Sanguisorba officinalis*, Oschinensee. (Photograph by N. and N. Shoumatoff.)

Erebia sudetica on *Taraxacum alpinum* in the Kander Gorge. (Photograph by N. and N. Shoumatoff.)

Snowfinch *(Montefrigilla nivalis)* in Gornergrat, with Monte Rosa in the background. (Photograph by N. and N. Shoumatoff.)

Young and mature Capra ibex on the Col d'Entrelor, Val Savranche. (Photograph by N. and N. Shoumatoff.)

Gasterntal goats returning to fold beneath Kanderfirn. (Photograph by N. and N. Shoumatoff.)

Haflinger horses in Timmelsjoch in the Otztal Alps. (Photograph by N. and N. Shoumatoff.)

André, David, and Werner Wandfluh in front of the Blümlisalp peaks. (Photograph by N. and N. Shoumatoff.)

French shepherds and sheep above Ceillac-en-Queyras. (Photograph by N. and N. Shoumatoff.)

Italian cowherds making cheese on the south slope of Monte Visto. (Photograph by N. and N. Shoumatoff.)

Slovene group bringing hay to drying rack, Triglav south. (Photograph by N. and N. Shoumatoff.)

Bregaglia hayfield with view of Sciora and Cengalo peaks. (Photograph by N. and N. Shoumatoff.)

Austrian group raking hay below Kals, Grossglockner west. (Photograph by N. N. and N. Shoumatoff.)

Grindelwald hay drying on racks beneath Mettenberg peak with base of Wetterhorn in distance. (Photograph by N. and N. Shoumatoff.)

Man carrying hay below Lötschental avalanche trail. (Photograph by N. and N. Shoumatoff.)

Nicholas and Nina Shoumatoff at a stone farmhouse in Val d'Isère. (Photograph by N. and N. Shoumatoff.)

Bernese summer chalet with ranked cowbells, Gasterntal. (Photograph by N. and N. Shoumatoff.)

Farmhouse and stable under one roof in Bohinj, Slovenia. (Photograph by N. and N. Shoumatoff.)

Hay barn with diagonal drying bars in Bohinj, Slovenia. (Photograph by N. and N. Shoumatoff.)

Houses and church with onion-dome steeple in Zug, Lechtal. (Photograph by N. and N. Shoumatoff.)

Castle, church, barn, and house along a Roman road in Bregaglia. (Photograph by N. and N. Shoumatoff.)

Heiligenblut church and hamlet with view of Glossglockner. (Photograph by N. and N. Shoumatoff.)

Chatelard castle, church, houses, and gardens in Valle d'Aosta. (Photograph by N. and N. Shoumatoff.)

Bled lake, village, and castle with view of Karawanken Alps. (Photograph by N. and N. Shoumatoff.)

Halstatt and Halstattersee, Salzkammergut. (Photograph by N. and N. Shoumatoff.)

Les Haudères and Dent Blanche, painted by Joseph Georges. (Photograph by N. and N. Shoumatoff.)

Bernese chalet with carved and painted facade, Lauenen. (Photograph by N. and N. Shoumatoff.)

Store selling house-carved ceremonial masks, Lötschental. (Photograph by N. and N. Shoumatoff.)

Engadine farmhouse with "graffito" of Adam and Eve, Ardez. (Photograph by N. and N. Shoumatoff.)

and 1930s, the British mainly attempted to ascend Mt. Everest, while the Austrians, Germans and Italians sought harder climbs in the Alps, especially the Eiger north face.

Among well-known British climbers of that period were R. L. G. Irving, Arnold Lunn, Eric Shipton, George Mallory, F. S. Smythe and Geoffrey Winthrop Young, the latter of whom established new routes on the Weisshorn, Grepon and Grandes Jorasses and climbed even after losing a leg in World War I. Meanwhile, Switzerland produced such important climbers as Marcel Kurz, Charles Gos, Othmar Gurtner and Adolph Zürchner, the last of whom became vice president of the Alpine Club in London. The Austrian Julius Kugy (1858–1944) was an outstanding climber of his era, specializing in the Julian Alps. In Chamonix, the elite Groupe de Haute Montagne was founded in 1919 to promote guideless climbing.

Eiger North Face

From 1935 to June 1938, in four unsuccessful attempts to climb the Eiger north face, eight men perished and two, including Ludwig Vorg, withdrew safely. The first ascent was achieved from July 21 to 24, 1938, by the Germans Andreas Heckmair and Vorg and the Austrians Fritz Kasparek and Heinrich Harrer. They made the climb mostly in that order after the Germans overtook the Austrians about halfway up. They proceeded as two separate ropes with the Germans leading, but they finished as a single rope of four (Harrer 1995). Conditions on the face, including rockfalls, water, snow and ice, were unfavorable much of the way. In their worst moment, on an exit crack from the White Spider, near the top, they were hit by two separate avalanches of increasing strength. Already all roped together, they were nearly swept away, yet both times each climber managed to hold his stance. The Austrians made the climb in eighty-five hours with three bivouacs, while the Germans made it in sixty-one hours with two bivouacs.

By 1963, forty-one out of sixty-one attempts to climb the face were successful, with 114 climbers reaching the top and returning safely, one climber doing it twice. One of these groups made the ascent in winter and another in a single day, all others requiring at least two days. In the twenty unsuccessful attempts, fourteen climbers fell to their deaths; eleven died from exposure or exhaustion; two were rescued; and twenty-two, including two women, withdrew safely. The unsuccessful attempts included four solos, of which three were fatal, while the fourth, by Walter Bonatti, led to a safe withdrawal. In 1963, the Swiss Michel Darbellay made the first solo ascent. In 1964, Daisy Voog of Munich, accompanied by Werner Bittner, made the first ascent by a woman. After that, until August 1981, more than fifty more successful ascents had been made on the Eiger north face, which "remains an important yardstick of ability for ambitious alpinists" (Harrer 1995, 302). In 1974, during Clint Eastwood's filming of *The Eiger Sanction*, featuring multiple bivouacs, the Tiroleans Peter Haberler and Reinhold Messner arrived unexpectedly and made the ascent by the 1938 route in a record ten hours, returning the same day.

Sequels to the Eiger North Face

In the half century since the first ascent of the Eiger north face, mountaineers in the Alps as elsewhere (especially in Yosemite and Patagonia) have tackled more and more difficult climbs, on both rock and ice, with less and less protective equipment. The trend toward free climbing was initiated in the late nineteenth century by Kugy (1934), who did not carry pitons even on extreme climbs, except once on a particularly difficult one, when he brought some wooden pitons but forgot to use them. This trend has led to totally free climbs of vertical rock and overhangs with minimal holds and maximum exposure, involving increasingly acrobatic ability by both men and women.

Among leading French climbers in the second half of the twentieth century were Armand Charlet, Maurice Herzog, Louis Lachenal, Lionel Terray and Gaston Rébuffat. The last four of these were heroes of the first ascent of an 8,000-meter peak, the Himalayan giant Annapurna, in 1950, which pointed the way to the ascent of Mt. Everest three years later. Rébuffat was an outstanding pioneer in developing and describing modern rock and ice techniques, with the aid of magnificent photos in the Mont Blanc Range (Rébuffat 1959). He climbed six great north faces of the Alps (Rébuffat 1975), including that of the Eiger with Hermann Buhl and others in 1952.

A leading American mountaineer of the twentieth century was John Harlin, who perished on his attempted "directissima" climb of the Eiger north face in 1966, after which the rest of his party reached the top. One of Harlin's assistants at his climbing school at Leysin near Montreux, the long-haired 6′3″ American Gary Hemming was known as the beatnik mountaineer. In Chamonix, he endeared himself by a feat of rescue on the formidable west face of the Dru. In 1966 two Germans reached a narrow ledge on that face above 200 feet of smooth vertical wall and below an overhang, from which they were unable to go either up or down. Hemming and François Guillot, under helicopter direction from René Desmaison, made an extremely delicate and dangerous climb, reached the Germans and brought them down to safety (*Paris Match* 1966).

Bonatti

Walter Bonatti, according to Herzog, "symbolizes the superhuman limits of Alpine climbing." Among his great solo climbs in the Alps were the southwest pillar of the Dru in 1955, "one of the most remarkable achievements in mountaineering" (Neate 1980), and the Matterhorn north face in 1965. Unlike other solo climbers, he tied in at all times, first securing himself at the top of a pitch then going down to release the rope below and climbing back up with his rucksack, thus making the whole climb twice. Bonatti is honored for his unselfish heroism on the first ascent of the world's second highest peak, K2, in 1954, when he slept near the top without using oxygen so that he could save it for the two who did go on to the summit.

Even the greatest, however, can face defeat from the fury of mountain weather on Mont Blanc. One of its "last problems" was the Central Pillar of Freney at the top of the south face. Bonatti, Oggioni and Galliani started the climb and on the way joined forces with four Frenchmen led by Pierre Mazeaud (Bonatti 1962). Halfway up the pillar, at its most difficult part, they were hit by a sudden, violent electrical storm and then by a blizzard during which they bivouacked for four days on a narrow ledge. Those four frigid days tied to the rock left them with no food or drink. Weakened, frozen and desperate with no letup in the storm, they tried to go down through the blinding snow and wind, which required fifty rappels and plowing through steep powder that was often over their heads. In spite of efforts by their companions, four of them died from exhaustion, one by one along the way, and only three made it to the Gamba Hut: Bonatti, Galliani and Mazeaud. Numerically, it was a tragic parallel to the first ascent of the Matterhorn where four perished and three survived.

Messner

During the last decades of the twentieth century, Reinhold Messner (1998) achieved the status of the world's leading mountaineer. (Messner believes that the greatest living climber today is the Slovenian Tomo Česen, who specializes in impromptu, unsupported solo ascents of the most difficult routes in the Alps, Himalayas and Karakorams, including the south face of Lhotse in 1990.) Messner, the son of a farmer, is a native of the Dolomites in Italy, where, like most of his neighbors, his mother tongue is German. Messner is an exponent of free and solo climbing in the Dolomites, Bernese Alps and Mont Blanc Range and of Alpine-style and solo climbing in the Himalayas and other great mountains. In the Dolomites, he achieved hundreds of historic first ascents of extreme climbs, including winter ascents, with his brother Gunther and others or solo. The "crazy solos" included the north faces of the Civetta and Langkofel (Sasso Lungo) and the south face of Marmolada. In the Mont Blanc Range, he made the first solo climb of the north face of Les Droites and the first ascent of the right-hand buttress on the Grandes Jorasses.

On their descent from the summit of Nanga Parbat in 1971, Reinhold lost track of Gunther, who apparently disappeared under an avalanche without a trace. After four days of hopeless searching, Reinhold lost his first four left toes and first two right ones to frostbite. Yet within a year he was climbing again, with his greatest feats still to come: the first oxygenless and the first solo ascents of Everest and the first climb of all fourteen of the 8,000-meter peaks. He also ascended Elbrus, Aconcagua, McKinley, Kilimanjaro, Carstenz and Vinson, thus completing the highest points on all seven continents.

Chapter 13

Around the Alps

Travels before 1800

Leonardo da Vinci

Possibly the earliest of those who both traveled widely in the Alps and wrote extensively about them was Leonardo da Vinci (Uzielli 1890). He could see the skyline of these mountains on clear days from his workshop in Milan. That was his base from 1482 to 1499 and again from 1506 to 1512, during the major part of his life, from when he was thirty until he was sixty. His excursions from Milan often brought him into the Alps. He wrote about them mostly in the discursive style of his private notebooks, from his scientific and artistic points of view (see previous chapters), rather than in narratives intended for general readers. He referred to some of his trips, such as those to Valle d'Aosta, briefly, but he described a few, such as those to Monte Rosa and Bregaglia, of which he wrote:

> Above Lake Como in the direction of Germany lies the valley of Chiavenna where the river Mera enters the lake. Here the mountains are barren and very high with huge crags. In these mountains the water birds called cormorants are found; here grow firs, larches and pines, and there are fallow deer, wild goats, chamois and savage bears. One cannot make ascents there without using hands and feet. In the season of the snow the peasants go there with a great trap in order to make the bears fall down over these rocks. The river runs through a very narrow gorge: the mountains extend on the right and the left in the same way for a distance of twenty miles. From mile to mile one finds good inns there. Higher up the river there are waterfalls six hundred braccia [about 1000 ft.] high, which are very fine to see, and you may find good living at four soldi for your bill. (1938, vol. 1, 379)

Impressed by the towering crags of the Piz Badile, Cengalo and Sciora, which dominate to upper Mera Valley, he chose them as models for the background of his favorite painting, the Mona Lisa.

A younger contemporary of Leonardo was Aegidius Tschudi of Glarus in eastern Switzerland. He crossed the Great St. Bernard, St. Bernardino, Furka, St. Gotthard, Lukmanier, Septimer, Splügen, and Theodule Passes a few years before 1528, as outlined in his book of 1571. In 1734, his descendant Giles Tschudi was the principal author, and perhaps the inventor, of the story of William Tell. Between 1702 and 1711, Johann Jakob Scheuchzer of Zurich made ten expeditions throughout Switzerland, which were the basis for his book, published in 1723, on the natural history of the Alps (including his famous description of four types of dragons).

De Saussure in Chamonix

During the last decades of the eighteenth century, Horace-Bénédict de Saussure, a patrician scientific scholar of Geneva, explored the Alps extensively. He wrote of his travels and observations not only at great length and in meticulous detail (1879–96) but also with modesty and charm. Nothing escaped his attention, from the largest to the smallest things, including mountains, people and insects. Throughout his travels, which included the Bernese Oberland and southern Alps, he identified rare alpine flowers, which he collected for the botanist Albrect von Haller, author of the poem "Die Alpen" that had inspired their Geneva contemporary Jean-Jacques Rousseau. De Saussure made the first ascents of four Alpine peaks (Coolidge 1908). The accounts of his travels, even after two centuries, offer a wealth of relevant information about the people, geography and natural history of the Alps.

When he first visited Chamonix in 1760, the village had no inns, but eighteen years later, it had three. Even over the course of those few years, he found that the "antique simplicity and purity" of the local customs had been altered by the influx of tourists, but he noted that the people of the valley remained honest, faithful, and devout in their Catholic religion. He found them "lively and gay, grasping with singular finesse the ridiculousness of the strangers, and bantering pleasantly among themselves . . . in their old French speech dressed up with a bit of Italian and many words of Celtic origin" (1834, 152). At the upper end of the valley of Chamonix, he enjoyed being followed by "a troop of extremely sprightly young girls for whom our trip, clothing, speech and slightest movements were occasions for immoderate explosions of laughter. They even imbued us with part of their gaiety" (73).

From the 3,076-meter (10,092 ft.) summit of the Buet, he was impressed by the view of the immense north slope of Mont Blanc, draped in snow and ice, and "of the vast district of the high Alps of Chamonix," which "excites a profound emotion in the soul" (82). On the bowl-shaped Glacier de Talèfre, deep within the heart of the range, he saw rare alpine flowers on the unique flat rock now known as Le Jardin but then called Le Courtil, which also means "a garden." He described the valley of Chamonix, its climate, inhabitants, and huge glaciers that then descended into the valley beneath the soaring granite spires.

At that time, the women of Chamonix were left to do all the work in the valley while their men hunted for chamois and rock crystals in the mountains, where both had thus become quite scarce. As described by de Saussure, this merely incited them to greater efforts, making them "so carried away by their passion for the chase that they lost all sense of danger, crossing snowfields without thought for hidden crevasses, and jumping from rock to rock without knowing how they would get back" (135). Often they were away for days at a time, armed with two-shot one-barrel carabines, sleeping on piles of rock debris without warm clothing, and without food or drink except for rock-hard bread and a flask of brandy.

Too many perished, leaving their wives to wait for them to appear in a dream to tell where to find their bodies and to beg for last rites. The few men who survived these ordeals were permanently affected and rarely lived to a ripe old age. One young woman had thus lost her father, husband and brothers. In her grief, she remarked, "It is strange that of all those who have gone away, none have ever come back" (153). She also said to de Saussure, a Geneva Protestant, that she "could not believe that all Protestants are damned, because many are honest and God is too good and just to make indiscriminate judgments." De Saussure was deeply moved by her noble demeanor and "singular combination of reason and superstition" (153).

De Saussure around Mont Blanc

In his trek around Mont Blanc in 1778 (his third such tour), he continued from Chamonix around the south end of the mountain, crossing the Col du Bon-Homme and the Col de la Seigne. The region of arid mountains between these two passes was "extremement sauvages" with a "tristesse insipide." At the hamlet of Chapiu, which belonged to the Tarentaise, he was "amused by the unfamiliar costumes of the sherpherdesses" (1834, 162), so different from those of Faucigny between Geneva and Mont Blanc. The Tarentaise women plaited their hair and twisted it at the back into "a sugar loaf in the form of a snail." From the Col de la Seigne, he descended the Allée Blanche and Val Veni to the French-speaking, now Italian village of Courmayeur, which was already a popular health spa renowned for its mineral waters. From there he made the first ascent of one of the lesser mountains, the Crammont, and obtained a glorious view of the overpowering south face of Mont Blanc. A bit dubiously, he speculated that "since the secondary mountains had been formed in the bosom of the waters, it follows that the primitive mountains, such as the chain of Mont Blanc, also had the same origin" (182). De Saussure has been called the father of Alpine geology (Collet 1974).

From Courmayeur, De Saussure returned to Geneva via the St. Bernard Pass and gave a detailed description of its dismal landscape, morgue and hospice and of the rigorous life of the monks, especially in winter. Great quantities of wood had to be carried up in advance by mules to heat the huge hospice and care for travelers. He explained the role of the dogs in guiding as well as rescuing travelers in the snow, but he noted that because of the depressive effect of alcohol, the brandy that the dogs carried in little casks around their necks could harm or even kill the half-frozen travelers.

De Saussure on Col du Géant

The best-known part of de Saussure's writing is his account of climbing Mont Blanc in 1787 (see chap. 12). The following year, accompanied by his older son and a smaller group of faithful guides, de Saussure accomplished an even more significant feat, which was to stay for seventeen days on the Col du Géant on the crest of the Mont Blanc range at an altitude of 11,000 feet. There, with less discomfort from high altitude, he and his son made all the measurements they wanted, using more elaborate equipment. On the way up via the Glacier des Bois (now called the Mer de Glace), his guides commented on the dangers of the route, but he did not take them seriously, because of their tendency "to flatter the travelers by telling them of the great perils that they had escaped" (1834, 270).

During their stay at the top of the pass, not an hour went by without their "seeing or hearing an avalanche of rocks plunging with the noise of thunder to the flanks of Mont Blanc" on the Italian side. While making their observations with the instruments in special tents, both he and his son felt that they "were significantly more free in spirit, more active, and even more inventive than they were in the lowlands, and less easily fatigued" (276). The guides, however, were eager to get back down and ate as much as possible of the available food to make sure that the stay would not be extended. The expedition descended by the steep but not dangerous Italian side of the pass and returned to Switzerland over the Col Ferret.

De Saussure around Monte Rosa

Another year went by, and in the summer of 1789, de Saussure set off with his son and three Chamonix guides to make a circular tour of Monte Rosa, which at that time was less familiar to northern travelers than Mont Blanc. (Actually, until then, no one except de Saussure and his group, not even Italians, had ever trekked around either of these two great mountains.) Using mules, de Saussure crossed the Simplon Pass into Lombardy and ascended the Val Anzasca to Macugnaga, a village at the foot of the stupendous sheer east face of Monte Rosa. From there he measured its highest point and satisfied himself that it was the second highest mountain in the Alps.

Even well-to-do inhabitants of the valley subsisted on extremely simple fare, consisting of six-month-old rye bread that had to be cut with an ax and softened in hot milk to produce a "species of soup." Cheese and cured meat were reserved for special occasions, while fresh meat was not eaten at all. From Macugnaga, de Saussure climbed to the pasture of Pedriolo below the highest point of Mont Rosa, where he and his group spent the night in their tents. They decided that the mountain itself was impractical to climb from that side. No man could be found who was strong enough to carry de Saussure's rock samples down to a large village for shipment to Geneva, but the local women were stronger and equal to the task.

The Monte Moro Pass from Val Ansazca to Saas Fee in Switzerland had been extensively used by commercial travelers in earlier centuries, but at the time of de Saussure's trip the trail was in bad shape, difficult for pedestrians and impossible for mules. Therefore, to make the tour of

Monte Rosa, de Saussure set off westward for the Theodule Pass into Switzerland. This involved crossing four ridges, first into Alagna in Val Sesia and from there into three valleys in the province of Aosta—Gressonay, Ayas and Tournanche—all of which at that time belonged to the house of Savoy. De Saussure visited the gold mines in Val Sesia, but although some of the mines were still operating, they were all for sale because their richest veins had been exhausted. He noted that the inhabitants of Gressonay, Alagna and Macugnaga all spoke German, and he theorized, correctly, that their ancestors had settled there centuries ago by crossing the Alps from Switzerland. He assumed that the Italian- or French-speaking people had not wished to live in the cold upper ends of these valleys.

De Saussure and the Matterhorn

While crossing the Theodule Pass, both the mules and the men, who had dismounted, kept sinking into the snow at every few steps, "forming an allure which was equally fatiguing and ridiculous" (de Saussure 1834, 322). De Saussure was impressed by the Matterhorn, which he saw in passing (and he resolved to come back for a longer look). This route brought them into Zermatt, where he found the people to be extremely inhospitable. No one, not even the priest, was willing to put them up for the night, until one of his guides arranged the needed lodging with great difficulty (another example of xenophobia; see chap. 7). From there they descended to St. Nikolaus and Visp and down the Rhone to Geneva.

When de Saussure returned in August 1792 for a week at the top of the Theodule Pass, he carefully avoided the unfriendly Zermatt and arrived from the Italian side via the St. Bernard Pass, returning the same way. In the Val Tournanche, from the town of Chatillon on the way to the Theodule Pass, he noted that many serpentine rocks were scattered on the valley floor, but with their normal green color oxidized to pink on the outside. He was impressed by the evidence that the Matterhorn had been carved into its obelisk shape by erosion, but he could not explain what had happened to the resulting rock debris, virtually all of which had been somehow washed away (see chap. 3). From the Theodule Pass, he made the first ascent of the Klein Matterhorn, which he called the "Brown Breithorn." Among his observations at the top of the pass were many insects, including butterflies, damselflies and snow fleas.

Goethe

In 1777, Johann Wolfgang von Goethe visited Lake Lucerne and the St. Gotthard Pass. In 1779, after consulting de Saussure, he arrived at Chamonix after dark and wrote: "Above the summits before us a light was revealing itself, the source of which we could not understand. It shone through the night like a glow-worm and we realized at last that it was none other than Mont Blanc. It had a strange, supreme beauty; it covered us with light and the stars were massing round it. It had not their twinkling glimmer, but it looked like a vast shining body, belonging to a higher sphere. It was difficult to believe that it had earthly roots" (Engel 1965, 69).

He traveled up the Chamonix Valley and over the Col de Balme to Martigny. From there, he traveled up the whole length of the Valais and out of it across the Furka Pass in November. As he wrote:

> We paid our muleteer for the hire of his beast, since the route we were to follow would not be practicable for a mule. . . . Our guide came back with another fellow who looked even bigger and more powerful than himself, and who, with the strength and courage of a horse, hoisted our luggage on his shoulder. . . . After crossing a small footbridge, we had a view of the Rhone glacier. It is the largest we have yet seen. It extends right across the opening in the mountains and flows down in an uninterrupted stream to the point where the Rhone issues from it. The local people say that the snout of the glacier has been receding for several years, yet the diminution is nothing in comparison with the vast mass of ice that remains. Every hollow was filled up with snow, yet we could still distinguish the broken cliffs of ice which the wind had put bare of snow, with their fissures glassy blue, and we could clearly see where the glacier ended and the rocks under the snow began. . . . The great danger is from avalanches, which may start rolling down when the snow is deeper than we found it. . . . In about three-and-a-half hours we reached the saddle of the Furka, close to the cross which marks the boundary between Valais and Uri. . . . We pushed on in single file as before; the track-maker in front often sank into the snow up to his waist. . . . The willing spirit of these mountain guides, the light-hearted way they talked of the difficulties of our route, did much to maintain our spirits. (Irving 1938, 154)

Nineteenth-Century Travels

Dumas

In 1832, more than a decade before writing *The Three Musketeers* and his other famous novels, Alexandre Dumas traveled extensively, partly on foot, through the French and Swiss Alps, as told in the 850 pages of his *Impressions de Voyage en Suisse*. At the Mer de Glace above Chamonix, his guide Payot (whose descendant Jean Payot took coauthor Nicholas to the top of Mont Blanc) asked Dumas if he wished to cross the glacier to see Le Jardin, which he described as "a small tongue of vegetation, in the form of a triangle, in the north of the Glacier de Talèfre." Dumas: "Very well; and what does one do there?" Payot: "Nothing at all." Dumas: "Then why does one go there?" Payot: "To say that one has been there" (perhaps one of the main reasons why people climb mountains). Dumas: "Well then, my friend, I'm not going to say it, and that's that." However, since he "knew how to skate," Dumas agreed to a few steps on the glacier, which he then described as "an ocean of ice, frozen in the middle of a tempest, with waves of a thousand shapes rising to sixty or eighty feet high"—an exaggeration. "After an instant of this view, you are no longer in France, no longer in Europe, you are in the Arctic Ocean. . . . A cold sweat broke out on my forehead, my voice changed, and I was about to faint. Of course I was not afraid, since there was no danger. Nevertheless, with those crevasses at my feet and those waves hanging above my head, I grasped the arm of my guide and said: Let's get out of here." Payot: "Really, you look pale. What's the matter?" Dumas: "I feel seasick." ("mal de mer" on the Mer de Glace!) Payot and Dumas both burst into laughter (Dumas 1982, 141–42).

Dumas was decidedly less interested in mountains than in stories about them, to which he added long fictional dialogues with William Tell, Pontius Pilate, Charlemagne and Napoleon. He also wrote of eating a bear steak at Martigny, of the Devil's Bridge and of Schwarenbach (see chap. 8). On his visit with Jaques Balmat, which was the centerpiece of his trip, he gave a fulsome development of Balmat's false story that he had climbed Mont Blanc first and later dragged a dazed and exhausted Paccard to the summit. Dumas ends with Balmat's comment that when Paccard died in 1831, his eyes were red, not because of climbing, but because of alcohol, "upon saying which Balmat finished his third bottle" (1982, 132). Despite this deft Dumas touché, his Balmat story was almost universally believed, even by Whymper (1908), and by some today, though it was conclusively disproved by Brown and de Beer (1957).

Tyndall

John Tyndall traveled and climbed widely in the Alps (Tyndall 1871). He made the first ascent of the mighty Weisshorn, made early attempts on the Matterhorn, and initiated modern concepts of glacier movement (see chap. 4). One of his dramatic moments was a close encounter with an ice avalanche on the Glacier du Géant in the Mont Blanc range.

> We had reached a position where massive ice cliffs protected us on one side, while in front of us was a space more open than any we had yet passed; the reason being that the ice avalanches had chosen it for its principal path. We had just stepped upon this space when a peal above us brought us to a stand. Crash! crash! crash! nearer and nearer, the sound becoming more continuous and confused, as the descending masses broke into smaller blocks. Onward they came! boulders half a ton or more in weight, leaping down with a kind of maniacal fury, as if their sole mission was to crush the seracs to powder. Some of them on striking the ice rebounded like elastic balls, describing parabolas through the air, again madly smote the ice, and scattered its dust like clouds in the atmosphere. Some blocks were deflected by collision with the glacier, and were carried past us within a few yards of where we stood. I had never before witnessed an exhibition of force comparable to this, and its proximity rendered that fearful which at a little distance would have been sublime. (1871, 34)

George

In 1866, H. B. George published his magnum opus, *The Oberland and Its Glaciers, Explored and Illustrated with Ice-Axe and Camera,* with twenty-eight historic photographs by Ernest Edwards, who accompanied him on this trip. It is the account of a single extended trek over glaciers of the Jungfrau, Eiger, Wetterhorn, Finsteraarhorn, Aletschhorn, Blümlisalp and interconnecting glacier passes, with six relevant essays and a report of the first ascent of the Nesthorn. (Much of his itinerary coincided with ours on our twelve-day glacier trek, with a climb of the Finsteraarhorn, in

1961.) George was a staunch disciple of John Tyndall's glacier theories. During this trip, George employed three Grindelwald guides, all of whom were named Almer or Almen, so that the only way to tell them apart was by their given names. In his book, George mentions having made the acquaintance of Christian Almen's female dog Tschingel, who at that time was one year old and later earned fame as an alpinist who climbed with W. A. B. Coolidge and Miss Brevoort. Coolidge later wrote a biography of the dog (1912).

Edwards

In 1873, Amelia B. Edwards first published her book *Untrodden Peaks and Unfrequented Valleys: A Midsummer Ramble in the Dolomites*, written at a time when tourists in that part of the Alps were few. Here, in abridged form, is her description of the Val di Canali.

> No glaciers find a resting place among these precipices. Only a narrow ledge outlined in white, or a tiny intermediate plateau sheeted with dazzling snow, serves here and there to mark the line of eternal frost. The path lies for a long way in the shade of the fir-woods, with openings here and there through which the great mountains are seen to be ever closing in, nearer and loftier, till the whole culminates in a scene of savage grandeur. Green pastures, and above these, dark fir woods, climb to about one third of the height of the Cima di Canali; while innumerable threads of white waterfall are seen leaping from ledge to ledge and wavering down the cliffs in every direction. The sound of them fills the air like the roaring of the sea upon an ironbound coast. The fir trees shiver, as though a storm were at hand. I doubt if a more lonely, desolate, and tremendous scene is to be found this side of the Andes.

Twain

In *A Tramp Abroad,* published in 1880, Mark Twain wrote in his usual semisatirical style of his extensive journey through the Swiss and French Alps. Except for his Himalayan-style alleged climb of the Riffelberg, a smooth alp just above Zermatt, this can probably be classified as a nonfiction travel book. He clearly disliked mountains, as indicated by his description of the trail between Schwarenbach and the Gemmi Pass.

All about us rose gigantic masses, crags, and ramparts of bare and dreary rock, with not a vestige or semblance of plant or tree or flower anywhere, or glimpse of any creature that had life. The frost and the tempests of unnumbered ages had battered and hacked at these cliffs, with a deathless energy, destroying them piecemeal; so all the region about their bases was a tumbled chaos of great fragments which had been split off and hurled to the ground. Soiled and aged banks of snow lay close about our path.

I have just said that there was nothing but death and desolation in these hideous places, but I forgot. In the most forlorn and arid and dismal one of all, where the racked and splintered debris was thickest, where the ancient patches of snow lay against the very path, where the wind blew bitterest and the general aspect was mournfulest and dreariest, and furthest from any suggestion of hope, I found a solitary wee forget-me-not flourishing away, not a droop about it anywhere, but holding its bright blue star up with the prettiest and gallantest air in the world, the only happy spirit, the only smiling thing, in all that grisly desert.

Conway

In *The Alps from End to End* (1895), Martin Conway described what was probably the longest journey over the Alps on foot up to that time. Together with an English friend, two Italian guides and two Gurkas (the ruling Hindu caste in Nepal), his party walked more than a thousand miles from the Col de Tende in the Maritime Alps to Bad Gastein in Austria. They did this in eighty-six days, of which sixty-five were spent in actual walking and the remainder were days of rest, either voluntary or enforced by storms. Their aim was to climb and preferably traverse as many peaks as possible along the way. He wrote: "We climbed in all twenty-one peaks and thirty-nine passes. If the weather had been better, the peaks would have been more and the passes fewer" (1895, 8).

The summits they reached included Monte Viso, Mont Blanc, Monte Rosa, Jungfrau, Weisskugel and Grossglockner, while at several others they were forced to turn back below the summit or pass them up completely, including the Matterhorn, which was covered with snow. Conway describes their passage through Martin's Loch, a natural tunnel above Elm in the Glarner Alps (see chap. 3), and gives a detailed account of the disaster from the mountain fall at Elm in 1881. A number of climbers' huts had already been built at the time of Conway's trek and provided his group with shelter. The most pleasant of these by far were those in Austria, offering the most comfortable accommodations, good food, wine and convivial company. The book concludes with a chapter by Conway's friend Coolidge, "The Western and Central Alps," about the Alps from the Maritimes to the Bregaglia and the Silvretta. Coolidge describes many interesting places not included on Conway's route.

Twentieth-Century Travels

Lunn

In the early part of the twentieth century, Arnold Lunn, who is credited with having invented the Alpine slalom, was an exponent for the use of skis equipped with sealskins for mountain travel and for the ascent of major peaks. He was also a prolific writer of books, especially about Switzerland. He wrote: "The details of glacier passes crossed on foot are blurred in my memory, but I can recall with meticulous accuracy every phase of those snow passes which I have crossed on ski. And I remember not only the changing tactics that each slope demanded, but also the details of the surrounding country, which never seems more beautiful than when it borrows from the ski something of the ski's own magic motion" (1925, 35).

In 1908, Lunn climbed the Wildstrubel solo on skis from Montana across the vast Plaine Morte Glacier, reaching the summit at 4:30 P.M. Afterward he wrote of "the mystical value of moments which are the unique reward of the solitary climber . . . When you are alone and have no friends to recall you to a proper sense of the insignificance of mankind, you can forget the scale of man and mountains and can lose the sense of your own individuality, merged for the moment in the larger life of Nature" (1925, 43).

In May 1918, after a glorious ski tour on the Unteraar Glacier with ascents of several "skiable peaks," Lunn also climbed and descended the Eiger on skis. He was chided for this "reckless" enterprise and afterward wrote, "The Eiger is not an ideal ski tour" (1925, 179).

Irving

In 1938, R. L. G. Irving published a small book called *The Alps,* which describes a virtually continuous eastward trek through the French, Swiss,

Italian and Slovenian, but not the Austrian, Alps—not always where there were actual trails. Here is an excerpt on the Bernese Alps.

> From the Zanfleuron [Glacier] the man who keeps to the highest standard will cross the Wildhorn to the Wildstrubel hut; it should not take more than eight hours. About the same time will be needed by the lower route to Montana. Having made your way over the Col de la Selle you will cross a bare plateau, which has been described as a petrified glacier and then strike a bisse. The bisses are the watercourses on which the Rhone Valley depends to bring fertility to its sunbaked hillsides. They go through tunnels and over bridges; they cross precipices, sometimes in a channel carved in the rock, sometimes by propping from below or even suspension from above. In difficult country they are exciting things to follow. This particular bisse should bring you on your way to the Lake of Luchet, and beyond and below this you strike the path to the Rawyl Pass. (76)

Smythe

Frank B. Smythe wrote several books about his travels in the Alps and Himalayas. In February and March 1946, after years of absence during World War II, he returned for two months of travel on skis through the Bernese and Pennine Alps, as described in his book *Again Switzerland* (1947). Here are some snatches from his description of the Haute Route between Zermatt and Chamonix, which he traveled with his friend James Belaieff.

> To begin with, the route led us into the impressive glacier cirque which is bounded by the Stockje, the Tete de Valpelline, the Dent d'Hérens and the Matterhorn. . . . What a queer yet beautiful little glacier is the Tza de Tzan. Its uppermost limit under the rocks of the Dents des Bouquetins forms one of the smoothest and most secluded little snow-fields imaginable, yet a few yards away it falls in a savage torrent of shattered ice. (179)

> The slopes below the Col du Mont Brulé are very steep, and the snow, as already mentioned, was in poor shape. Belaieff, ever a bold and skillful runner, essayed successfully several spectacular downhill turns. As for me, on crusted snow at a high angle I am well content to

make kick turns at the end of each traverse, the traverses being as long as I can make them. . . . The trouble with high Alpine ski-ing is that it ruins the mountaineer for those long glacier trudges which are an inevitable feature of summer mountaineering in high ranges. . . . Once you have tasted the magic of ski-ing on the high snows you are ruined for foot-slogging over them. (180)

Unlike so many places that have been irretrievably changed, Zermatt retains an ancient charm. The spirit of the past is perpetuated in the old portion of the village, in the familiar façade of the Monte Rosa Hotel, and the low wall outside where generations of guides have sat awaiting employers. And when these are gone, as they will be some day, there will still be the Matterhorn. (140)

Around Mt. Bego

One day in July 1989, when both seventy-two, we set off for a remote wilderness valley in the Parc National de Mercantour of the Maritime Alps. The valley is called Vallée des Merveilles because of its famous petroglyphs. From an alpine wildflower garden at 5,700 feet, near the hamlet of Casterino, we started our walk on a mule path to Refuge Valmasque of the French Alpine Club at 7,300 feet. This was the first leg of our four-day 24-mile circular trek around the 9,400-foot Mt. Bego— over an 8,400-foot pass to the valley of petroglyphs at 7,500 feet, then down to 4,600 feet at the Lac des Mesches and back up to the alpine garden (see our 1991 article "The Way to Shangri-La in the Alps"). We had virtually nothing in our tiny packs except toothbrushes, flashlight, plastic raincoats, light parkas and extra sweaters. For security we had light steel-pointed bamboo canes, made from children's ski poles.

At Refuge Valmasque, we watched three male ibex moving gracefully on the vertical rocks above. The burly hut-keeper, Robert Zartariem, said it was full, but he found a place for us in one of the bunk rooms. A group of trekkers were setting up tents when it began to rain hard, and they retreated into the hut. Dinner was hearty, with a bracing red wine poured generously to all the moderately sober guests. We sat with a loquacious Italian group including a lady named Nina, and the hut had a pack mule named Nina who didn't like the rain and kept opening the door with her nose all through the meal, with everyone shouting her name. Including our coauthor, it was a three-Nina dinner.

Robert woke us up at 5 A.M. The weather had cleared, and we were soon on our way. After skirting around three lakes of increasing size and height, with a pass before each one, the trail climbs the steep 700 feet to the final 8,400-foot pass and an even steeper 900-foot drop into the valley of the petroglyphs.

The thousands of images engraved into the granite of Mt. Bego, mainly of hunting weapons, animals and fantasies, are about 4,000 years old. Most are high on the crags of the mountain. We found one of the finest petroglyphs about 100 feet above the trail, the famous face called Le Christ, made long before Christ's time. We did not, however, find one called the Sorcerer, with hands growing weirdly out of the sides of its face. In this high and desolate landscape, our prehistoric ancestors left a legacy of their cherished thoughts addressed to the spirit of this sacred place.

We completed the 24 miles of our circular walking tour around Mt. Bego, with overnight stops at the Refuge des Merveilles and at a hostel called Neiges et Merveilles, in the buildings of an abandoned mining establishment. The hostel has an intellectual health-conscious atmosphere, with a grand piano, a large library, an exercise gym, modern plumbing and two long refectory tables, one of which is for vegetarians, who missed out on our rabbit stew, *lapin aux pruneaux*. We sat next to a black-bearded man from Provence, who, we thought, looked and talked just like Daudet's Tartarin de Tarascon would, and who knew more about alpine flowers than anyone we ever met.

In the morning, a herd of sheep and goats, led by a boy in his early teens and his dog, rushed up between two buildings to a flowering pasture swarming with *Parnassius apollo* butterflies. Including the ibex, the lakes, the crags, the convivial French huts and the musical-literary hostel, this was a microcosm of the local mountain world. Dominating it was the aura of the mysterious petroglyphs from thousands of years ago, which will endure for thousands more, outlasting many other works of Alpine art of the past and the future.

Chapter 14

Alpine Attractions

Psychological Interactions

As recorded in prose and poetry, the power of mountains, especially the Alps, to inspire a variety of emotions is an experience that many have shared. The recorded reactions range from enjoyment to grief, from elation to fear, from curiosity to amusement and from wonder to reverence and awe. Whether shared or in solitude, the emotional power of the mountains is a psychological reality that shapes human perceptions of the Alpine world and that motivates much of what happens there, not just to human beings. This reality is one key to the linkage between the natural and human realms in the Alps.

Emotions Not Merely Human

One can only dimly perceive how the Alpine world is a matrix of effectively innumerable, highly interdependent and changing relationships among inanimate and living things, among which human beings are only one of the many kinds. One's ability to understand what goes on in the lives and feelings of all sentient beings is limited indeed. Moreover, as Henry Beston saw, the human propensity to look down on other animals is highly inappropriate: "In a world older and more complete than ours they move, finished and complete, gifted with extensions of the senses we have lost or never attained, living by voices we shall never hear" (1928; see the end of chap. 6 for a lengthier quotation of the same passage).

The great Swiss mountaineer and Alpine scholar Eugene Rambert had a rare opportunity to observe an exciting episode in the private lives of a group of young chamois (see chap. 6). They repeatedly raced each other down a steep snow slope and stopped abruptly at the top of a cliff, where with great enjoyment they looked over the edge, in defiance of mortal danger, but fully confident in their ability to prevent a fatal fall.

In a different situation, a group of chamois expressed almost palpable terror from an inanimate Alpine source. One day, when Julius Kugy was walking up the Trenta Valley in Slovenia, his companion and guide Andreas saw "a great boulder come away high up on the Jalouc";

> it had already swept down the couloir, and was now rushing upon us through the steep corrie. At any moment it would be here. We ran forty or fifty paces aside, and watched in breathless suspense. Then, a few seconds later, the monster appeared. It was as big as a house. It rolled down, thundering, crashing in gigantic leaps through the forest, till at length its journey ended far down the valley. All the mountains seemed to look down in amazement and disapproval at the disturber of their peace. A fleeing chamois-herd rushed from terrace to terrace, and it was a long time before the wild uproar ended. (1934, 56)

Like those of chamois, the emotions of ibex (see chap. 6) can also be inferred.

> You who live so high in the world,
> what do you think of us men?
> You watch us, perched on your mountain tops,
> or leaning on the grey rocks or the green of an alp
> which must taste so good after a winter of snow,
> and of eating lichen and wood below.
> I envy you and your peace in this silence without end.
> Even when you are hungry, your eyes are calm, without fear,
> for they have seen the immensity of Nature,
> and the sublimity of beauty which changes but is always there.
> And we? We seek this peace
> which to us has not yet been given.
>
> (Nina Shoumatoff)

The French say of the birds and of their "bird brains" that "ils n'ont que de l'ame" [they only have souls]. This, however, underscores their ability to feel emotions. In the French Alps, at the lofty central summit of the Meije, Julius Kugy had a close encounter with an eagle (see chap. 6): "wings wide-outspread, eyes turned keenly on us, talons stretched forward, bent upon attack. . . . But just in front of us it turned aside, and soared away in a superb curve. A confused swarm of choughs followed in pursuit, and scattered screaming in its rear" (1934, see chap. 6). In this episode, the emotions of both eagle and choughs were obvious. When we watched a flock of choughs cavorting and shrieking below the Blumlisalp (see chap. 6), we seemed to be witnessing a similar emotional outburst on their part.

Scientists still know virtually nothing about possible emotions felt by lowlier creatures, such as insects, beyond the alleged "hard wiring" of their instincts. Even in recent decades, most biologists disdained any thoughts of insect emotions as being anthropomorphic (a major scientific sin). From this viewpoint, they ascribed the playful behavior of butterflies to such imperatives as search for mates or food plants or just to turbulent winds. However, more recent studies in the molecular biology and neurobiology of insect brains (Dyar 1997) reveal their previously unsuspected complexity. Thus, their ability to experience enjoyment and other emotions no longer seems such a naive idea. The essential affinity of high-altitude butterflies with their mountain world quite possibly has an aesthetic component, which remains to be defined.

Attractions for Visitors

Among prominent attributes of the mountain world, its healthfulness and aesthetic grandeur have for centuries offered major attractions for visitors to the Alps. Both provided forms of physical recuperation, psychological basking and spiritual inspiration around which local people have developed services of hospitality and pathways for enjoyable and invigorating walks, often following ancient trails. During the past two centuries, these attractions have increasingly centered on opportunities for mountain sports of skiing, climbing and trekking.

In the fifteenth century, according to Paracelsus, St. Moritz was already a thriving health spa. More than a thousand years before that, the hot spring at Monétier near Briançon was a favorite place where Roman soldiers came to nurse their battle wounds. Health consciousness continues to be a major goal that attracts visitors to Alpine facilities, which include clinics, sanatoriums and New Age inns that feature mineral waters and herbal and innovative medicine.

In Chamonix, in contrast, the attraction after the examples of Rousseau, Haller and Gessner was primarily mountain grandeur. People came to admire majestic Mont Blanc, its towering spires and its impressive *glacières*. Already in 1778, de Saussure reported that visitors were coming there in increasing numbers and that inns, of which there had been none eighteen years before, were being built for them. Slyly, he remarked how the local people were "grasping with singular finesse the ridiculousness of the strangers" (1834, 152).

This mild early reaction grew into a significant impact along with a steadily increasing flow of visitors. John Murray, in his 1838 guidebook to the Swiss and French Alps, observed how numerous visitors to Chamonix misunderstood one of the earth's sublime places by inappropriately exclaiming, "How rural!" Since then, the flow of visitors has grown into a torrent, and the torrent keeps growing. After 1924, the establishment of seven Winter Olympic sites and their satellites throughout the Alps has visibly affected architecture, amenities and infrastructure. Nevertheless, according to a study of Bätzing et al. (1996), the actual economic and demographic impact of development for tourism has been concentrated in relatively small areas, mainly in Tirol, having bypassed other large parts of the Alps.

Fatal Attractions

More than two centuries ago, fear was the main emotion that high peaks inspired among Alpine people. They expressed this fear through their belief that the heights were the homes of dragons. Meanwhile, the highest mountains irresistibly attracted a few intrepid individuals. Their motivation was perhaps instinctive acrophilia or the challenge of the ever present hazards, even unto mortal danger. These mixed feelings underlie one of the best-known poems about the Alps, which describes their strange fatal attraction.

> The shades of night were falling fast,
> As through an Alpine village passed
> A youth, who bore 'mid snow and ice,
> A banner with the strange device,
>   Excelsior!
> His brow was sad; his eyes beneath,
> Flashed like a falcon from its sheath,

And like a silver clarion rung
The accents of that unknown tongue,
    Excelsior!
In happy homes he saw the light
Of household fires gleam warm and bright;
Above, the spectral glaciers shone,
And from his lips escaped a groan,
    Excelsior!
"Try not the Pass!" the old man said;
"Dark lowers the tempest overhead,
The roaring torrent is deep and wide!"
And loud the clarion voice replied
    Excelsior!
"O stay," the maiden said, "and rest
Thy weary head upon this breast!"
A tear stood in his bright blue eye,
And still he answered with a sigh,
    Excelsior!
"Beware the pine-tree's withered branch!
Beware the awfyl avalanche!"
This was the peasant's last Good-night;
A voice replied, far up the height,
    Excelsior!
At break of day, as heavenward,
The pious monks of Saint Bernard
Uttered the oft-repeated prayer,
A voice cried through the startled air,
    Excelsior!
A traveler, by the faithful hound,
Half-buried in the snow was found,
Still grasping in his hand of ice
That banner with the strange device,
    Excelsior!
There in the twilight cold and gray,
Lifeless, but beautiful he lay,
And from the sky, serene and far,
A voice fell, like a falling star,
    Excelsior!

                    (Longfellow 1893, 19)

In the Alps, one is often just one step away from danger. During a four-day August blizzard in the course of a twelve-day Bernese glacier trek, we rescued a group of eleven English Boy Scouts and their scoutmaster. They all would have perished had not coauthor Nina noticed, in the evening outside the Mutthorn Hut, that a weakly calling group was in trouble at the bottom of a cliff two-hundred feet below. One by one, we pulled them up the cliff by a rope with a flashlight tied to the end and treated them for exposure, hypothermia and shock. At Interlaken, at the end of our trek, we met them again, and they surrounded Nina to say good-bye, which has left a warm memory in our hearts.

Two days earlier, at the Eiger Glacier Station, after descent from the Eiger's icy west ridge, "the ordinary tourist route," we enjoyed a convivial supper with the exuberant Austrian guide Adi Mayr and his Australian client Bill Parer. The next morning, they left to climb the Matterhorn. Back in London, we read in the newspaper that a man named Adi Mayr was making the first attempt to climb the Eiger north face solo, and the next day we read that he fell to his death from the ramp above the notorious White Spider near the top. We did not believe it was he, knowing that he had gone to Zermatt to climb the Matterhorn. However, when we met Bill Parer in London, he told us that the newspaper story was true (see Harrer 1995). After coming down from the Matterhorn to the Hörnli Hut, Adi Mayr said, "Bill, I am leaving you now. I have a date with the Eiger." Then he ran down the ridge and kept his rendezvous with fate.

Two Magic Mountains

Byron wrote long dramatic poems about the Alps but just one elegant quatrain about their highest peak.

> Mont Blanc is the monarch of the mountains;
> They crowned him long ago
> On a throne of rocks, in a robe of clouds,
> With a diadem of snow. (Murray 1938)

Gaston Rébuffat, a French hero of Annapurna and a pioneer of modern rock and ice technique, whose writings about the Alps are prolific and often poetic, found a simpler way to express his feelings: "Suppose for a moment that Mont Blanc—it is absurd—was called something else. No other mountain has a name of such beauty, clarity, and rigorous precision. What purity and richness in those two words. Crossing its summit, they define for our soul the mountain as a whole and reverberate like an echo: MONT . . . BLANC" (1962, 10)

For Julius Kugy, and for the thousands who have read his account or followed in his trail, his first approach to Mont Blanc was unforgettable.

> So it came about that in August, 1887, I traveled up the Aosta valley. . . . Monks from the Great St. Bernard were traveling in our diligence, their clever dark eyes set in weatherbeaten faces, regarding all nature in joy and gratitude. At one point about half way up, where the beautiful valley of the Dora Baltea makes its great bend, there was a sudden stir among the company. Something had arisen before us, and it filled the background of the valley. . . . A fabulous structure of cloud, rock, ice and snow, a picture great beyond the richest fantasy, a cathedral borne on giant granite columns, an altar lit by the glory of heaven, a dome standing brilliant in the firmament. "Ah! le Mont Blanc," cried one of the monks. It was a cry from the inmost heart, with a ring of ecstasy. He bent forward with arms upraised and a light in his eyes, as in prayer, to greet this vision from another world. All of us had risen. And in solemn tone, as if to proclaim honor and praise to the highest, his voice trembling with inward emotion, the eldest among them turned to us all: "Oui, c'est le Mont Blanc, Messieurs, le Mont Blanc dans toute sa majesté!" There was not one of us but would have bowed himself in reverence. (1934, 235)

Guido Rey, a great mountaineer, was a contemporary of Julius Kugy. One day, when they still did not know each other, their paths crossed at Breuil (Cervinia), at the foot of the Matterhorn. Each of them then immediately knew, almost by instinct, who the other one was. Guido Rey devoted his life to climbing and studying the Matterhorn and retained a sense of awe about it. He even speculated about the emotions that the mountain itself might have.

> I think that few Alpine peaks can create so sublime, so stern an impression as this one does, when it is seen from this point [Breuil], at sunrise or at sunset, when the walls of the valley that frame it are sunk in shadow, and the whole towering pyramid is wrapped about with light and seems to shine in glory. At such times we have before our eyes no reality, but an apparition. No other mountain is revealed

in so personal a manner to our gaze; we are tempted to expect to find it has a countenance, like a man or a monster, to believe that head contains a conscious thought, to read upon its stony brow the expression of its pride and its strength; and if the clouds, chasing one another around it, assist the optical illusion ever so lightly, our fancy seems to see it move, bending its head in sorrow, or raising it with a Titan's pride, and we think with terror what its power would be if it moved indeed. (1897, 169)

For two thousand vertical feet beneath the "hanging" Matterhorn Glacier that stretches across the bottom of the mountain's sheer north face, a meadow rich in alpine flowers serves as a pasture for sheep, among anomalous boulders that look like sheep. Below the meadow, a legally protected forest of ancient arolla pines has the highest tree line in the Alps (see table 5). Just above it, the crumbling Stafelalp "hotel" still offered daytime refreshments on its terrace. Having walked down the meadow, we lingered on the terrace, just the two of us alone, long after all staff and clients had left for the night. We were unable to part from the dark peak that towers above the landscape with its curving top, guarding it like a reared-up cosmic cobra. In the golden fading light, its strange power transfixed us, until the sun went down behind the Col de Valpelline and the Haut Glacier de la Tza de Tzan. Then the Matterhorn's summit disappeared in the clouds, we too were on our way.

Mona Lisa and the Alps

Until the end of Leonardo da Vinci's life as a guest of King Francis I at Amboise in France, the one painting that the artist treasured above all others was the Mona Lisa, and he never parted from it. (It was on that condition that he sold it to the king, which is how it came to be in the Louvre.) As depicted by Leonardo, the timeless beauty of the lady in this painting, also known as La Gioconda, which was her married name, still fascinates and mystifies millions. It is unquestionably the best-known, most copied and most caricatured painting ever produced.

Walter Pater wrote of the Mona Lisa's "subdued and graceful mystery . . . defining itself on the fabric of his dreams . . ."

The presence that rose so strangely beside the waters is expressive of what in the ways of a thousand years man has come to desire. . . . It is a beauty wrought . . . of strange thoughts and fantastic reveries and exquisite passions. . . . All the thoughts and experience of the world have etched and molded there . . . the animalism of Greece, the lust of Rome, the reverie of the Middle Ages with its spiritual ambition and imaginative loves, the return of the pagan world. . . . She is older than the rocks among which she sits . . . and as Leda, was the mother of Helen of Troy, and as Saint Anne, the mother of Mary. (1878, 89)

The background of the painting has mostly escaped explicit attention, except for general tributes, such as "This is aerial perspective at its finest" (Wallace 1966, 140). It is an immense mountain landscape viewed from a marble loggia perched at an enormous height, probably Leonardo's own mountain, the Monte Rosa. From there, one looks down—far down—on the summits of major Dolomite spires, separated from each other by a winding river that flows through a deep gorge. The river emerges from a lake below a group of soaring crags that strongly resemble those of the Bregaglia, from the Sciora to Piz Badile, which Leonardo described (see chap. 13). The lake is fed by a large glacier coming from a snow peak that towers on the far horizon, in the distant mist. Another winding river flows from the lake and under a three-arched Florence-type bridge, whose apparent smallness is a measure of the landscape's vastness.

This is not a real Alpine scene. It is dream landscape, but not from an ordinary dream. Precisely because of its strangely evocative power, Leonardo presented it in the cryptic, imaginative manner that he did and placed it within his most beloved painting, around the lady of his dreams. It is a vision in which the Alps spoke to him in dimensions commensurate with those of his own towering genius. A close examination of its details reveals that he not only saw, like John Muir, "the young rivers flow rejoicing from the glacial caves," but that he also understood, and was able to express, how and why they rejoice. This painting embodies a powerful interaction of the most gifted exponent of the Renaissance with the woman and the mountains that he loved. If one were to imagine the Mona Lisa without its Alpine background, it would be an impoverished work indeed.

Three Who Loved the Alps

Leonardo da Vinci's extensive writings about mountains, while phrased in a sober, scholarly idiom appropriate to his scientific concerns, have enriched the literature of the Alps. Meanwhile, his emotional attraction to these mountains comes through most powerfully in his art, not only in the Mona Lisa and in his great paintings of the Madonna, but also in his preliminary studies for future paintings that he had in mind and described in his notes.

Horace-Bénédict de Saussure, a learned man of the eighteenth-century Enlightenment, wrote more extensively about the Alps than almost anyone else, in a typically charming and often amusing manner. His deep personal love for these mountains is expressed in a few short passages only. After finding a small grassy plateau on the slopes of Mont Blanc above Chamonix, he wrote: "I would keenly wish to own a fairly comfortable dwelling at that spot, where I could collect and cultivate the most gorgeous alpine plants, and calmly study the mountains which rose before my eyes, during deep meditations which alone can reveal to us the great secrets of nature" (1834, 118).

Leonardo da Vinci and H. B. de Saussure, who symbolized the great Italian and French-Swiss traditions, were two of three men who have contributed deeply through both their knowledge and their love for the Alps. It remained for the third member of this trio, Julius Kugy, a pioneer of extreme rock climbing and an exponent of two other great traditions, Austrian and Slavic, to express most powerfully his emotional attraction to the Alps. In his first book, Kugy wrote that his aim was "to describe those benefits which the mountains have poured upon my life; a thank offering, or even, if it might be so, a Canticle sung to the glory and praise of the hills" (1934, 1). Near the beginning of his narrative, he describes a nostalgic recollection of his earliest years in the mountains: "It is as if spring were then eternal, spreading its gentle splendor over those paths, over valley and height, where a magician's hand weaves a fine veil of earliest green. Thrushes' songs echo through the awakening woods, while brooks pour downward in music; the air is filled with the intoxicating fragrance of primroses, and a solemn sound of Easter bells comes from the distant Land of Youth" (22)

A few years later, at the height of his great physical powers, his feelings after a difficult climb on Triglav brought into play his love for music and for night in the Alps, particularly with moonlight on the mountain snows: "The heavens sang a hymn of unimagined glory. A night of magic moonlight succeeded the magic day. The moon, high in the heavens, shone on our path, and kindled a thousand lamps among the icy slopes on either side, now dancing like will-o'-the-wisps, now seeming to move in solemn procession. It was as if ghostly companions of mountain spirits passed over the cliffs with burning torches, and we had caught their voices" (52).

In his later years, when no longer active in making difficult ascents, he often wandered alone up the gentle south slope of the same mountain, also experiencing the special emotion of nocturnal Alpine solitude: "I put out the lantern and sat waiting. How much there is to hear! Through the stillness of the night, the waters of Triglav, free from their rocky fetters, sing in the valleys. It is a nocturnal music of overwhelming beauty, when from the solemn night, a sombre chorale goes up to the trembling stars" (364).

Floral Inspiration

The flowers in the Alps have been an inspiration for many. Julius Kugy, a great mountaineer who loved his numerous bivouacs in the mountains, recalled especially one on the Peuterey Ridge, the most gigantic of what he called the "giant granite columns" of Mont Blanc. "We slept," he wrote,

> not in the damp upper cave, but thanks to the beauty of the night, in the open, on moraine-debris and scanty tufts of grass. St. Bruno's lily was blossoming in multitudes, and whenever I woke during the night, the slender white blooms fluttered and danced about me. I love it more than any other flower of the Alps. It is for me a symbol of unsullied purity in the everlasting hills. It is no flower of earth, such as edelweiss, nigritella, artemisia, alpenrose. Stand in reverence before the flower of Paradise *[Paradisea liliastrum]*, and think upon the serene celestial peace, for which the soul may yearn in life's fitful fever. Give it quiet greeting and go on your way. (1934, 280)

The creator of the world-famous Sissinghurst garden, who conversed with flowers in dialogues, wrote of her walks in the French Alps: "One found oneself above the line of trees, in complete, high solitude, on the slopes of short grass blowing with the bright Alpine flowers. How amazing are their delicacy! they grow with no fear of the imposing summits around them, these bright tiny things, intimidated neither by the space and emptiness nor by the storms which stalk over these lonely heights, the lightning dancing along the ground, for these are the places where the elements have things to themselves" (Sackville-West 1940, 212).

Some alpine flowers, such as the butterfly orchids, are shaped like insects, presumably to attract the real ones as pollinators. This was among the things noted by one of the "forty immortals" of the Academie Française:

> These alpine plants all have distinct habits when you observe them. Some look like birds or insects. Some know how to protect themselves against the rain or the sun. Others know how to flee an enemy. What enemy? Probably civilization. They have a stem and a foliage the color of lichen or crumbling rock. It is a real quest to discover them. No matter how small their petals, they remind you of the immensity of the sky—the same blue, the same silvery grey. These flowers make you think of a chapel built on the slopes of a mountain, consecrated to the strictest order of monks, and like them they are drunk on solitude and abstinence. The wind is their friend, and a ground too fertile would make them perish and die. (de Lacretelle 1956)

It was snowing hard on the St. Bernard Pass one morning in August. We walked down the Italian side, along the old Roman road to the Alpe des Baux, below the snowstorm. Dark, low clouds still covered the sky. A ray of reflected sunlight from far down in Italy lit up the surrounding spires, including the tall Tour des Fous that leans precariously downhill, like a gigantic Tower of Pisa. In the eerie upward light, the landscape resembled an immense stage set. Tall purple gentians with closed, globular flowers rose through a layer of mist that clung to the ground. These hundreds of floating black dots gave the landscape an unearthly look. Afterward, Nina wrote in her diary: "Today we walked in celestial meadows on the Great St. Bernard Pass full of anemones and gentians, and while we photographed them, the Mercedes, Fiats, and Alfa Romeos never looked at them nor wondered why we were there. Only the flowers understood."

Alpine Enchantment

Rosa Bailley, a prolific French poetess who spent her vacations in the Haute-Savoie, had the unusual thought of the physical mountain world being at the receiving end of an emotional interaction: "Wayfarer, give life to the mountains! Lend your joy to the winds, and to the storm your passions. Listen, in the voice of the brook, to the echo of your footsteps on the path, and of your songs" (1935, 73). She also wrote on her personal interactions with the mountains and their butterflies.

> The black worries lay in wait for me at your entrance, little valley. When I return, they will attack me with open claws. But they dare not follow me on the tiny path, bristling with nettles. There, free at last, my soul sings at the leaping of your brook beneath your scarped walls, crumbling into chaos. A song of children, an exultant round, from the days when I danced, holding hands in the village with my companions. How serene those evenings were! Dance around me, butterflies of the mountains. (105)

In a more Gothic style, Algernon Blackwood characterized the emotional impact of the Alpine environment on a fictional visitor to the Swiss Alps.

> He knew that the spell of Nature was greater for him than all the other spells in the world combined—greater than love, revelry, pleasure, greater even than study. . . . His pagan soul dreaded her terrific powers. . . . Like a forest rose the huge peaks above the slumbering village, measuring the night and the heavens. They beckoned him. And something born of the snowy desolation, born of the midnight and the silent grandeur, born of the great listening hollows of the night, something that lay 'twixt terror and wonder, dropped from the vast wintry spaces down into his heart—and called him. Very softly, unrecorded in any thought his brain could compass, it laid its spell upon him. (1962, 236)

Ruth Rudner, an American woman who walked widely in the Alps, mostly alone, treasured all the different ways that they affected her feelings.

> "I walk along the edge of a mountain. The abysses there are real, a part of the order of nature and no invention of my mind. I have faith in the strength of my legs, my boots and the open sky. I sling my pack over my back, set off along a mountain road and become a vagabond. Lying at noon in a field of wildflowers, I do not remember any other noons. Lying at night on a thin mattress in a dark and primitive

hut, I have no knowledge of soft beds. I wander through hours of hot sun pouring down on me, pouring down on the rocks that are warm to my touch, on the crystal clear water tumbling down jagged walls above and around me and sparkling, sparkling in that sun. It is ice cold water that slakes all thirsts, ice cold crystal water I kneel to drink. I walk through fog, through rain—a drizzle, a torrent. Thunder shakes the mountains. The earth is slippery, dark, oozing beneath my feet. I take shelter on the porch of a shepherd's hut. Damp, sweating, cold, I wait out the lightning. I go on and walk through hail that stings my face and lift my face to its sting. Soft new snow falls. The trail above is covered. Mine are the first footsteps in eternity." (1972, 4)

Surrounded by flowering meadows and jagged crags, the Alpine peaks are wildly sculptured by the battle between upheaval and erosion, while their huge white shapes are etched against a dark blue sky. Their wildness is punctuated by the boom of cracking glaciers that serve as trails to the snows above. These are places where one sometimes feels the presence of distant ibex even before they can be seen with binoculars. The silence is also broken by the piercing whistles of marmots, who require no such telepathy to make their presence known.

Despite the high altitude, or perhaps because of it, we have found that one can feel the peace of centuries as one walks over the rocky slopes, on meadows that are the most beautiful carpets on earth. Within a few hours in that rarified air, one's nerves unwind and one's negative thoughts depart. The strains of one's life seem far away and unimportant up there. Each day, one becomes more enthralled by the beauty and wildness of the mountain slopes, where glaciers boom, gentians bloom, wild goats play, and butterflies dance in the wind.

> God watch over our mountains
> And protect them from people's loudness
> But please guide them where our souls
> Will find You in this silence without end.
> Here in the flowers of Your Alps
> Our hearts beat slowly and our souls are calm
> As they turn to the author of this heaven.
> Our earthly problems diminish at every step
> And our bad thoughts fall into the streams nearby.

Every day we become dazzled with all Your beauty,
And when we get home
We will feel blessed by You.

                    (Nina Shoumatoff 1979)

Geoffrey Winthrop Young, the most poetic of major mountaineers, who lost a leg in World War I but continued climbing thereafter, came close to describing the joy of the Alps.

There is a region of heart's desire
free for the hand that wills:
land of the shadow and haunted spire,
land of the silvery glacier fire,
land of the cloud and the starry choir,
magical land of hills.

                    (1927, 62)

Bibliography

Agassiz, Louis. 1847. *Glaciers: Nouvelles Etudes et Experiences.* Paris.

Aiby, Irene, ed. 1986. *Gressoney e Issime i Walser in Valle d'Aosta.* Aosta: Walser Kulturzentrum.

Audisio, Aldo. 1992. *Le Montagne della Fotografia.* Turin: Museo Nationale della Montagna.

Audisio, Aldo. 1997. *The Mountain: The Event, the Book, the Film.* Turin: Museo Nationale della Montagna.

Audisio, Aldo, and Angelica Natta-Soleri. 1995. *La Cordata delle Imagini: La Montagna, L'Alpinismo e L'Esplorazione Nei Manifesto del Cinema.* Turin: Museo Nationale della Montagna.

Aulitsky, H. 1974. *Les regions menaces des Alpes et les mesures de prevention.* Strasbourg: Conseil de l'Europe.

Bailly, Rosa. 1935. *Alpes.* Paris: La Force. Poetry.

Barneby, T. P. 1967. *European Alpine Flowers in Colour.* London: Thomas Nelson and Sons.

Bätzing, Werner, et al. 1996. "Urbanization and Depopulation in the Alps." *Mountain Research and Development* 16, no. 4 (November): 335–50.

Berger, John. 1983. *Once in Europa.* New York: Pantheon.

Berger, John. 1987. See Marzorati 1987 (interview with Berger).

Berlin, Isaiah. 1957. *The Hedgehog and the Fox.* New York: Mentor.

Berlioz, Hector. 1986. "Program Notes for Symphonie Fantastique, 1831." In *Dictionary of Composers and Their Music,* ed. Eric Gilder. New York: Holt, Rinehart and Winston.

Bernt, Ernst. 1986. *E. T. Compton und Sohn Harrison.* Garmisch-Partenkirchen: Galerie Pritschow.

Bersezio, L., and P. Tirone. 1995. *Grand Paradiso, Vanoise, Oisans: Les grandes traces.* Grenoble: Glenat.

Beston, Henry. 1928. *The Outermost House.* New York: Holt, Rhinehart and Winston.

Blackwood, Algernon. 1962. *Tales of the Uncanny and Supernatural*. London: Spring.

Bocherel, J. 1952. *Le Patois et la Langue Francaise en Vallee d'Aoste*. Neuchatel: Victor Ottingen.

Bonatti, Walter. 1962. *A Mes Montagnes*. Paris: Arthaud.

Brandli, P. 1975. "Warum steigt der Mensch auf hohe Berge?" *Les Alpes: Revue du Club Alpin Suisse* 51, no. 2:80–83.

Briand, Frederic, et. al. 1989. *The Alps: A System under Pressure*. Gland, Switzerland: World Conservation Union.

Broad, William J. 1996. "Strange Slab Atop Swiss Alps Puzzles Theorists." *New York Times*, April 9, C1, C12.

Brown, Thomas Graben, and G. R. de Beer. 1957. *The First Ascent of Mont Blanc*. London: Oxford University Press.

Bryk, Felix. 1935. *Das Tierreich: Parnassiinae*. Berlin: de Gruyter.

Cerlogne, Jean-Baptiste. 1907. *Dictionnaire du Patois Valdotain*. Aoste: Imprimerie Catholique.

Chanu, Tersilla Gatto. 1988. *Il Fiore del Leggendario Valdostano*. Turin: Emme.

Christoffel, U. 1963. *La Montagne dans la Peinture*. Zurich: Club Alpin Suisse.

Club Alpin Suisse. 1909. *Chansonnier des Sections Romandes*. Lausanne: Duvoisin.

Collet, Leon William. 1974. *The Structure of the Alps*. London: E. Arnold, 1935. Reprint, Huntington, N.Y.: Krieger.

Conway, William Martin. 1895. *The Alps from End to End*. London: Constable.

Coolidge, W. A. B. 1908. *The Alps in Nature and History*. London: Methuen.

Coolidge, W. A. B. 1912. *Alpine Studies*. New York: Longmans, Green.

Cuvelier, Andre. 1965. *Contes et Legendes de Suisse*. Paris: Nathan.

Daudet, Alphonse. 1885. *Tartarin sur les Alpes*. Paris: Flammarion.

Da Vinci, Leonardo. 1938. *Notebooks*. Ed. and trans. E. MacCurdy. 2 vols. New York: Reynal and Hitchcock.

De Beer, G. R. 1945. *Escape to Switzerland*. Hammondsworth: Penguin.

De Beer, G. R. 1952. *Speaking of Switzerland*. London: Eyre and Spottiswoode.

De Beer, G. R. 1955. *Alps and Elephants: Hannibal's March*. London: Bliss.

De Beer, G. R. 1967. *Early Travellers in the Alps*. London: Sidgwick and Jackson.

De Lacretelle, Jacques. 1956. Preface to de Vilmorin 1956.

De la Harpe, Eugene. 1910. *Les Alpes Valaisannes*. Lausanne: Bridel.

De Maupassant, Guy. 1957. *L'Auberge, in Contes et Nouvelles*. Paris: Michel.

De Saussure, H.-B. 1834. *Voyages dans les Alpes precedes d'un Essai sur l'Histoire Naturelle des Environs de Geneve*. 8 vols. Geneva, 1786–96. One vol. (selected ed.), Geneva.

De Vilmorin, Roger. 1956. *Plantes Alpines dans les Jardins*. Paris: Flammarion.

Dobrzhinetskaya, Larissa, H. W. Green, and S. Wang. 1996. "Alpe Arami: A

Periodite Massif from Depths of More than 300 Kilometers." *Science* 271 (March 29): 1841–45.

Dobzhansky, Theodosius. 1937. Genetics and the origin of species. New York: Columbia University Press.

Dougedroit, Annick. 1978. "Timberline Reconstruction in the Alpes de Haute Provence and Alpes Maritimes." *Arctic and Alpine Research,* 10, no. 2 (May): 505–17.

Du Bois, Jean, et al. 1969. *Das Bild der Schweiz im Biedermeier.* Basel: Pharos.

Dumas, Alexandre. 1982. *Impressions de Voyage en Suisse.* 2 vols. Paris, 1834. Reprint, Paris: Maspero.

Durant, Will, and Ariel Durant. 1967. *Rousseau and Revolution.* New York: Simon and Schuster.

Dyar, Fred C. 1997. "The Seat of Insect Learning." *Natural History* 9, no. 97:58–59.

Dyurgerov, Mark B., and Mark F. Meier. 1997. "Mass Balance of Mountain and Subpolar Glaciers." *Arctic and Alpine Research* 29, no. 4:379–91.

Edwards, Amelia B. 1890. *Untrodden Peaks and Unfrequented Valleys.* London: Routledge.

Engel, Claire Eliane, ed. 1965. *Mont Blanc.* Chicago: Rand McNally.

Farrer, Reginald. 1911. *Among the Hills.* London: Waterstone.

Faverger, C. 1972. "La Vegetation." In Schaer et al. 1972.

Field, William O., ed. 1975. *Mountain Glaciers of the Northern Hemisphere.* Hanover, N.H.: U.S. Army Corps of Engineers.

Flemwell, G. 1910. *Alpine Flowers and Gardens Painted and Described.* London: Black. Translated into French as *Sur L'Alpe Fleurie* (Paris: Marret, 1914).

Fliri, F. 1975. *Der Klima der Alpen in Raume von Tirol.* Innsbruck: Univeritats Verlag Wagner.

Fowler, Brenda. 1991. "Scientists Enthralled by Bronze Age Body." *New York Times,* October 1, C1, C10.

Fowler, Brenda. 1992. "Man in Glacier Offers Rich Trove from the Stone Age." *New York Times,* July 21, C1, C6.

Fowler, Brenda. 1997. "Following Stone Age Footsteps." *New York Times,* August 3, 13, 20.

Fraser, James George. 1996. *The Golden Bough.* New York: Touchstone.

Freshfield, Douglas William. 1896. Exploration of the Caucasus, by Douglas W. Freshfield. With illustrations by Vittorio Sella. London, New York: E. Arnold.

Friedl, John. 1976. "Swiss Family Togetherness." *Natural History,* February.

Frison-Roche, Roger. 1949. *Premier de Cordée.* Paris: Arthaud. Translated into English as *First on the Rope* (New York: Prentice-Hall, 1950).

Gaussen, Henri, and Paul Barruel. 1955. *Montagnes: La Vie aux Hautes Altitudes.* Paris: Horizons de France.

George, H. B. 1866. *The Oberland and Its Glaciers, Explored and Illustrated with Ice-Axe and Camera.* London: Bennett.

Gereben, Barbara-Amina. 1995. "Co-occurrence and Microhabitat Distribution of Six Nebria Species (Coleoptera: Carabidae) in an Alpine Glacier Retreat Zone in the Alps, Austria." *Arctic and Alpine Research* 27, no. 4: 374–79.

Gibbon, Edward. 1952. *The Decline and Fall of the Roman Empire.* 8 vols. London, 1776–88. one vol. abridged ed. New York: Viking.

Giono, Jean. 1985. *The Man Who Planted Trees.* Chelsea, Vt.: Chelsea Green.

Glassberg, Jeffrey. 1993. Butterflies Through Binoculars: A Field Guide to the Butterflies in the Boston-New York-Washington Region. Oxford University Press.

Gos, Charles. 1934. *Alpinisme Anecdotique.* Neuchatel: Attinger.

Grodinsky, Caroline, and Michael Stuwe. 1987. "A Prolonged Close Call for Alpine Ibex." *Smithsonian* 18, no. 9 (December): 68–77.

Grosjean, Georges. 1969. "Man and Mountain through the Ages." In *The Mountains of Switzerland: The Adventure of the High Alps,* ed. Herbert Maeder, 10. New York: Walker.

Guex, Jules. 1976. *La Montagne et Ses Noms.* Martigny: Pillet.

Guichonnel, Paul. 1986. *Proverbes et dictons de Savoie.* Paris: Rivazco.

Guillaume, A. 1986. *Le Queyras.* Gap: Societe D'Etudes des Hautes Alpes.

Guiton, Paul. 1929. *Switzerland: Northern and Eastern.* Boston: Hale, Cushmen and Flint.

Häfeli, Peter. 1970. "The Alpine Salamander." In *The Water World,* 166–74. London: Allen and Unwin.

Hambrey, Michael, and Jurg Alean. 1992. *Glaciers.* New York: Cambridge University Press.

Hamilton, Edith. 1932. *The Roman Way.* New York: Norton.

Harrer, Heinrich. 1995. *The White Spider.* London: Flamingo.

Harris, Moses. 1766. *The Aurelian; or Natural History of English Insects; Namely Moths and Butterflies.* London: Printed for the author.

Heierli, Hans. 1983. *Geologischer Wanderfuhrer Schweiz.* Vol. 1, *Die Geologische Grundlagen.* Thun: Ott.

Heimberg, Bert. 1986/87. *Okologie der Alpen—eine kritische Literaturubersicht.* Brunswick: Zoologische Institut, Technische Universitat Braunschweig.

Hemingway, Ernest. 1929. *A Farewell to Arms.* New York: Scribner.

Hemming, Gary, and Rene Desmaison. 1966. "Dans la Tourmente du Dru, Un Hero Est Ne." *Paris Match,* 3 September, 30–47.

Higgins, L. G. 1941. *An Illustrated Catalogue of the Paleoarctic Melitaea.* London: Transactions of the Royal Entomological Society, 17 November.

Higgins, L. G., and N. D. Riley. 1970. *A Field Guide to the Butterflies of Britain and Europe.* London: Collins.

Hofmann, Paul. 1994. "Sherlock Holmes, Inc.: Meiringen, Switzerland." *New York Times,* May 1, 35.

Hoinkes, Herfried C. 1969. "Surges of the Vernagtfern in the Otztal Alps since 1599." *Canadian Journal of Earth Science* 6, no. 4: 853–61.

Hugo, Victor Marie. 1898. *The Alps and Pyrenees.* London: Bliss, Sands.

Hutter, Kolumban. 1982. "Glacier Flow." *American Scientist,* January–February.

Hutter, Pierre, and Michel Glauser. 1974. *Les Chamois et les Bouquetins.* Lausanne: Payot.

Huxley, Anthony. 1967. *Mountain Flowers.* London: Blandford.

Ichac, Marcel. 1960. *Les Etoiles du Midi.* Paris: Arthaud.

Ingwersen, Will. 1978. *Manual of Alpine Plants.* Eastbourne: Dunnsprint.

Irving, R. L. G. 1938. *The Alps.* London: Batsford.

Irving, R. L. G., ed. 1936. *The Mountain Way.* London: Dent.

Ives, Jack D., and Roger C. Barry, eds. 1974. *Arctic and Alpine Environments.* London: Methuen.

Jaberg, K., and J. Jud. 1928. *Linguistic and Ethnographic Atlas of Italy and Southern Switzerland.* Zofingen: Ringier.

Jean, Louis. 1939. *Fleurs des Alpes.* Gap: Ophrys.

Kariel, Herbert G. 1989. "Socio-cultural Impacts of Tourism in the Austrian Alps." *Mountain Research and Development* 9, no. 1:59–70.

Kelley, Michael. 1998. "Letter from Bosnia: Where Are the Dead?" *New Yorker,* February 16, 36–41.

Kitti, Robert. 1971. *2000 km per Ski uber die Alpen.* Wels, Austria: Landesverlag.

Knight, Max. 1978. *Return to the Alps.* San Francisco: Friends of the Earth.

Kohlhaupt, Paula. 1966. *Fleurs des Alpages.* 2 vols. Paris: Hatier.

Kraege, Charles. 1987. *Lexique de Toponomie Alpine.* Lausanne: CAS Diablerets.

Kugy, Julius. 1934. *Alpine Pilgrimage.* London: Murray.

LaChapelle, Edward R. 1969. *Field Guide to Snow Crystals.* Seattle, WA: University of Washington Press.

Ladurner, J., et al. 1970. *Die Welt der Alpen.* Innsbruck: Pinguin.

Landolt, E., and R. Corbaz. 1969. *Notre Flore Alpine.* Zurich: Club Alpin Suisse.

Leach, Maria, ed. 1984. *Funk and Wagnalls Standard Dictionary of Folklore, Mythology and Legend.* New York: Harper and Row.

Lieberman, Marcia R. 1991. *The Alps.* New York: Stewart, Tabori and Chang.

Löbl, Robert. 1968. *Die Alpen in Farben: Vom Wienerwald bis zur Cote d'Azur.* Munich: Suddeutscher Verlag.

Lockington Vial, A. E. 1952. *Alpine Glaciers.* London: Batchworth.

Longfellow, Henry Wadsworth. 1893. *The Complete Poetical Works of Longfellow.* Boston: Houghton Mifflin.

Lubbock, John. 1896. *The Scenery of Switzerland.* London: Macmillan.

Lunn, Arnold. 1914. *The Alps.* London: Williams and Norgate.

Lunn, Arnold. 1925. *The Mountains of Youth.* London: Oxford University Press.

Lunn, Arnold. 1963. *The Swiss and Their Mountains.* London: Allen and Unwin.

Mani, M. S. 1968. *Ecology and Biogeography of High Altitude Insects.* The Hague: Junk.

Mann, Thomas. 1927. *The Magic Mountain.* New York: Knopf.

Marzorati, Gerald. 1987. "Living and Writing the Peasant Life: John Berger, Working in the French Alps." *New York Times Magazine,* November 29, 39, 46–54.

Maurer, Joseph. 1981. *Giovanni Segantini—Maler der Alpen.* Trento: Manfrini.

Maurice, J.-P.-M. 1987. *Les Alpes Vues par les Peintres.* Lausanne: Edita.

Mehr, Christian. 1989. "Are the Swiss Forests in Peril?" *National Geographic,* May.

Menardi, Herlinde. 1990. *Hausgewerbe, Hausindustrie.* Innsbruck: Tiroler Volkskunstmuseum.

Messerli, Bruno, et al. 1978. "Fluctuations of Climate and Glaciers in the Bernese Oberland, Switzerland." *Arctic and Alpine Research* 10, no. 2 (May): 247–60.

Messner, Reinhold. 1998. *Free Spirit: A Climber's Life.* Seattle: Mountaineers.

Miller, Peter. 1987. "Mont Blanc." *Smithsonian,* June.

Milton, John. 1899. *Complete Poetical Works.* Boston: Houghton Mifflin.

Morton, Friedrich. 1953. *Halstatt und die Halstattzeit.* Halstatt: Musealverein.

Müller, Juerg Paul. 1988. *Das Murmeltier.* Disentis: Desertina.

Müller-Guggenbühl, Fritz. 1958. *Swiss Alpine Folk Tales.* London: Oxford University Press.

Mummery, A. F. 1895. *My Climbs in the Alps and Caucasus.* London: Fisher Unwin.

Murray, John. 1829. *Glance at Some of the Beauties and Sublimities of Switzerland.* London: John Murray. Quoted by Esther Singleton in *Switzerland Described by Great Writers* (New York: Dodd, Mead, 1909), 336.

Murray, John. [1838] 1970. *Murray's Handbook for Travellers in Switzerland.* Reprint, New York, Humanities Press.

Mützenberg, G. 1974. *Destin de la langue et de la literature rheto-romanes.* Lausanne: Editions L'Age d'Homme.

Neate, W. R. 1980. *Mountaineering and Its Literature.* Seattle: Mountaineers.

Netter, Thomas W. 1985. "Swiss Language Gap Widens as Germanic Dialect Thrives." *New York Times,* August 19.

Neustadtl, Sara. 1990. "Glarus Thrust: Giving the Lie to Geology's Theory of the Shrinking Apple." *Summit,* summer, 90–92.

Nidegger, Jules. 1984. *Ayoba por Ario—Etude Detaillee du "Ranz des Vache" de la Gruyere.* Bulle: Musée Gruerien.

Niederer, Arnold. 1972. *Alpine Folk Cultures.* Zurich: MS.

Niederer-Nelken, Loni. 1982. *Haus und Wohnung im Lotschental.* Kippel: Lotschentaler Museum.

Nietzsche, Friedrich W. 1954. *The Portable Nietzsche.* New York: Viking. Includes *Thus Spake Zarathustra* and "Nietzsche contra Wagner."

Paccaud, O. 1972. "Economie humaine." In Schaer et al. 1972.

Parker, Stephen C., and Giuseppe Orambelli. 1981. "Alpine Rockfall Hazards." *American Scientist,* January–February.

Pater, Walter. 1959. *The Renaissance.* 1873. New York: Mentor.

Patzelt, Gernot. 1970. *Die Langenmessungen an der Gletschern den Oster-reichische Alpen, 1890–1969. Zeitschrift* fur Gletscherkunde und Glaziologie, vol. 6, nos. 1–2.

Patzelt, Gernot. 1976. *Statistische der Langenmessungen an der Osterreichische Gletschern, 1960–1975.* Zeitschrift fur Gletscherkunde und Glaziologie vol. 12, no. 1, 91–94.

Patzelt, Gernot. 1978. *Die Gletscher in Osterreichischen Alpen, 1979–1984.* Zeitschrift fur Gletscherkunde und Glaziologie: vol. 18, no. 2.

Patzelt, Gernot. 1987. *Die Gletscher im Osterreichischen Alpen, 1985–1986.* Zeitschrift fur Gletscherkunde und Glaziologie, vol. 23, no. 1, 173–89.

Penz, H. 1978. *Die Almwirtschaft in Osterreich.* Studien zur Soziale und Wirtschaftliche Geographie, vol. 15. Munich.

Peterson, Roger, et al. 1954. *A Field Guide to the Birds of Britain and Europe.* London: Collins.

Pitelka, Louis F. 1997. "Plant Migration and Climate Change." *American Scientist* 85 1997, no. 5:464–75.

Polunin, Oleg. 1969. *Flowers of Europe.* London: Oxford University Press.

Price, Larry W. 1981. *Mountains and Man.* Berkeley: University of California Press. Includes ibex photo by Nicholas and Nina Shoumatoff.

Priuli, Ausilio. 1984. *Gravures Rupestres dans les Alpes.* Grenoble: Glenat.

Pyatt, Edward. 1984. *The Passage of the Alps.* London: Hale.

Rambert, Eugene. 1875. "Deux jours de chasse dans les Alpes vaudoise." Reprinted in *Anthologie Romande de la Littérature alpestre,* ed. Edmond Ridoux, 69–81 (Lausanne: Bibliothèque romande, 1972).

Rambert, Eugene. 1888. *Les Alpes Suisses—Etudes D'Histoires Naturelles.* Lausanne: Rouge.

Rambert, Eugene. 1889. *Les Alpes Suisses—Etudes Historiques et Nationales.* Lausanne: Rouge.

Ramuz, Charles-Ferdinand. 1925. *La grande peur dans la montagne.* Paris: Grasset. Translated into English as *Terror on the Mountain* (New York: Harcourt-Brace, 1967).

Ramuz, Charles-Ferdinand. 1934. *Derborence.* Bienne: Marguerat. Translated into English as *When the Mountain Fell* (New York: Pantheon, 1947).

Ratti, Achille [Pope Pius XI]. 1923. *Climbs on Alpine Peaks.* London: Unwin.

Rébuffat, Gaston. 1954. *Etoiles et Tempetes: Six Faces Nord.* Paris: Arthaud.

Rébuffat, Gaston. 1959. *Neige et Roc.* Paris: Hachette.

Rébuffat, Gaston. 1962. *Mont-Blanc Jardin Feerique.* Paris: Hachette.

Rébuffat, Gaston. 1975. *The Mont Blanc Massif: The 100 Finest Routes.* New York: Oxford University Press.

Renaud, Andre. 1955. *Les glaciers de la region de Zermatt.* Zermatt: Alpine Vereinigung.

Renfrew, Colin. 1928. "Ancient Europe Is Older than We Thought." *National Geographic* 152, no. 5: 615–28.

Rey, Guido. 1907. *The Matterhorn.* London: Fisher Unwin.

Riba, Daniel. 1983. *Mercantour: La Vallee des Merveilles.* Nice: Serre.

Riedler, Michael. 1989. *William Tell: His Story as Told by our Forefathers.* Chapelle-sur-Moudon, Switzerland: Ketty and Alexander.

Riefenstahl, Leni. 1995. *A Memoir.* New York: Picador.

Roberts, David. 1993. "The Iceman: Long Voyager from the Copper Age." *National Geographic* 183, no. 6 (June): 36–57.

Rokitensky, Gerth. 1964. *Tiere der Alpenwelt.* Innsbruck: Pinguin.

Rousseau, Jean-Jacques. 1783. *La Nouvelle Heloise.* Geneve: J.-J. Rousseau. Reprint, Paris: Flammarion, 1967.

Rudner, Ruth. 1972. *Wandering.* New York: Dial.

Ruskin, John. 1860. *Modern Painters.* Vol. 5. London: Smith-Elder.

Rutten, M. G. 1969. *The Geology of Western Europe.* Amsterdam: Elsevier.

Sackville-West, Vita. 1940. *Country Notes.* New York: Harper.

Samivel. 1965. *Sous l'Oeil des Choucas.* Paris: Delagrave.

Sauter, Marc-R. 1976. *Switzerland from the Earliest Times to the Roman Conquest.* London: Thames and Hudson.

Schaer, J.-P. 1972. "Geologie." In Schaer et al. 1972.

Schaer, J.-P., et al. 1972. *Guide du Naturaliste dans les Alpes.* Paris: Delachaux et Niestle.

Schaller, G. B. 1977. *Mountain Monarchs.* Chicago: University of Chicago Press.

Schauer, Th., and C. Caspari. 1975. *Flore et Faune des Alpes.* Paris: Nathan. Includes a chapter on geology.

Schenker, M., and P. Hedinger. 1941. *Reded Schwizertutsch.* Lausanne: Payot.

Schlatter-Rauch, E. 1986. *J'apprends le Romanche.* Lausanne: La Jorette.

Schneider, Adolf. 1981. *Wetter und Bergsteigen.* Munich: Rudolf Rother.

Schumacher, Pierre v. 1925. *Der Geologische Bau der Klaridenkette.* Bern: Stampli.

Seligman, G. 1936. *Snow Structures and Ski Fields.* London: Macmillan.

Sentis, Gabrielle. 1982. *Legende Doree des Hautes-Alpes.* Grenoble: La Tronche.

Shoumatoff, Nicholas. 1989. "Feuding on a Grand Scale." *Military History,* December.

Shoumatoff, Nina. 1979. *Dieu gardez-nous nos montagnes.* La Cordee/Die Seilschaft, CAS Section. Monte Rosa, April.

Shoumatoff, Nicholas, and Nina Shoumatoff. 1978. "Comparative Analysis of Upper Forest Limits in High Mountains of Europe and the United States" (Abstract). *Arctic and Alpine Research* 10, no. 2: 432.

Shoumatoff, Nina, and Nicholas Shoumatoff. 1991. "The Way to Shangri-La in the Alps." *Explorers Journal,* fall.

Smythe, Frank S. 1947. *Again Switzerland*. London: Hodder and Stoughton.

Spectorsky, A. C., ed. 1955. *The Book of Mountains*. New York: Appleton-Century-Crofts.

Spuler, Arnold. 1908. *Die Schmetterlinge Europas*. Stuttgart: Schweizerbartsche.

Spyri, Johanna. 1958. *Heidi*. 1881. New York: Scribner.

Stevens, William E. 1988. "Life in the Stone Age: New Findings Point to Complex Societies." *New York Times*, December 20, C1, C15.

Stutzer, Beat. 1990. *Das Engadin Ferdinand Hodlers*. Chur: Bundner Kunstmuseum.

Sullivan, Walter. 1970. "High on the Jungfrau, Scientists Are Conducting Varied Research." *New York Times*, November 5, 49.

Sullivan, Walter. 1994. Data Give Tangled Picture of World Climate Between Glaciers. *New York Times*, November 1, C4.

Thompson, W. T. 1989. Letter to author, November 17. Re Briancon, World War II, 1944.

Tosco, Uberto. 1974. *The World of Mountain Flowers*. London: Orbis.

Tourn, Georges. 1980. *Les Vaudois*. Valence: Reveil.

Tranquillini, Walter. 1979. *Physiology and Ecology of the Alpine Timberline*. Berlin: Springer.

Troll, Carl. 1972. *Geoecology of the High Mountain Regions of Eurasia*. F. Steiner Verlag, vol. 14. Wiesbaden: Erdwissenschaft Forschung.

Troyat, Henri. 1952. *The Mountain*. New York: Simon and Schuster. See film starring Spencer Tracy.

Trzesniowski, A. 1976. *Logging in the Mountains of Central Europe*. Rome: Food and Agriculture Organization of the United Nations.

Twain, Mark. 1880. *A Tramp Abroad*. London: Chatto and Windus.

Tyndall, John. 1871. *Hours of Exercise in the Alps*. London: Longmans.

Uzielli, Gustavo. 1890. *Leonardo da Vinci e le Alpi*. Turin: Candeletti.

Verity, Ruggero. 1940. *Le Farfalle Diurne D'Italia*. Florence: Marzocco.

Veyret, P. 1972. "Le climat." In Schaer et al. 1972.

Wallace, Robert. 1966. *The World of Leonardo*. New York: Time-Life.

Warren, B. C. S. 1936. *Monograph of the Genus Erebia*. London: Oxford University Press.

Whitehead, Alfred North. 1925. *Science and the Modern World*. New York: Macmillan.

Whymper, Edward. 1871. *Scrambles amongst the Alps in the Years 1860–1869*. London: Murray.

Whymper, Edward. 1908. *Chamonix and the Range of Mont Blanc*. London: Murray.

Wiget, Josef. 1985. *Morgarten*. Schwyz: Kulturkommission des Kantons Schwyz.

Wildhaber, Robert. 1971. *Swiss Folk Art*. Zurich: Pro Helvetia.

Wilford, John Noble. 1998. "Lessons in Iceman's Prehistoric Medicine Kit." *New York Times*, December 3, F3.

Wilton, Andrew. 1980. *Turner and the Sublime*. London: British Museum.

Wolff, Carl Felix. 1927. *The Pale Mountains: Folk Tales from the Dolomites*. New York: Minton Balch.

Wunderlich, Edmund. 1977. *Der Berg in Zeichnung und Malerei*. Bern: Schweizerisches Alpines Museum.

Wurz, Richard, and Thomas Stemberger. 1975. "Wood Supply of the Austrian Cellulose and Paper Industry and Special Consideration of Lower Austria." Vienna, May.

Yoon, Carol Kaesuk. 1994. "Warming Moves Plants up Peaks, Threatening Extinction." *New York Times,* Jun 21, C4.

Young, Geoffrey Winthrop. 1927. *On High Hills*. London: Methuen.

Zeller, Willy. 1976. *Kunst und Kultur in Graunbunden*. Bern: Haupt.

Suggested Further Reading

Ammann, Gert. 1984. *Die Tirolische Nation, 1790–1820*. Innsbruck: Ferdinandeum.

Bach, R., et al. 1966. *Through the Swiss National Park: A Scientific Guide*. Neuchatel: Attinger.

Ball, John, ed. 1859. *Peaks, Passes, and Glaciers*. London: Longmans.

Breeden, R. L., ed. 1973. *The Alps*. Washington: National Geographic Society.

Busch, Richard M. 1993. *Laboratory Manual in Physical Geology*. New York: Macmillan.

Chronic, Halka. 1987. "Our Geological Legacy: Continents That Drift." *Explorers Journal* 65, no. 2: 64–71.

Clark, Ronald. 1973. *The Alps*. New York: Knopf.

Engel, Claire Eliane. 1950. *A History of Mountaineering in the Alps*. London: Allen and Unwin.

Engel, Claire Eliane. 1952. *They Came to the Hills*. London: Allen and Unwin.

Fabjan, Ivan, ed. 1984. *The Triglav National Park*. Bled: Natural Sciences Society of Slovenia.

Frison-Roche, Roger. 1961. *Mont Blanc and the Seven Valleys*. Paris: Arthaud.

Gos, Charles. 1948. *Le Cervin*. Neuchatel: Attinger.

Gos, Francois. 1925. *Zermatt et sa Vallée*. Geneva: Alpina.

Hubbard, Bryn, and Martin Sharp. 1995. "Basal Ice Facies and Their Formation in the Western Alps." *Arctic and Alpine Research* 27, no. 4: 301–10.

Korff, Serge A. 1954. *The World's High Altitude Research Stations*. New York: New York University, Research Division.

Lukan, Karl, ed. 1968. *The Alps and Alpinism*. New York: Coward-McCann.

Lunn, Arnold. 1943. *Mountain Jubilee*. London: Eyre and Spottswoode.

Lunn, Arnold. 1948. *Mountains of Memory*. London: Hollis and Carter.

Lunn, Arnold. 1952. *The Cradle of Switzerland*. London: Hollis and Carter.

Lunn, Arnold, ed. 1947. *Switzerland in English Prose and Poetry*. London: Eyre and Spottswoode.

Neill, J., ed. 1962. *Selected Climbs in the Pennine Alps*. London: Alpine Club.

Nicholas, William H. 1950. "Switzerland Guards the Roof of Europe." *National Geographic* 98, no. 2 (August): 205–46.

Noyce, Wilfrid. 1950. *Scholar Mountaineers.* London: Dobson.

Parker, Malcolm, and Nicole Parker. 1986. *Grand Traverse and the Mont Blanc Tour.* London: Diadem.

Pause, Walter. 1960. *Die 100 Schönste Bergwanderungen in den Alpen.* Munich: Bayerischer Landwirtschaftsverlag.

Pont, Andre. 1965. *Ski Alpin: Alpes Valaisannes.* Sierre: Club Alpin Suisse.

Roch, Andre. 1963. *La Haute Route.* Lausanne: Marguerat.

Samivel. 1985. *The Summits of Samivel.* Port Townsend: Alta House.

Shoumatoff, Nina, and Nicholas Shoumatoff. 1989. "High Points of Climbing in the Alps." *Explorers Journal,* December.

Stephen, Leslie. 1871. *The Playground of Europe.* London: Longmans.

Stoller-Berger, Otto. 1992. *250 Jahre Schwarenbach.* Frutigen: Stoller-Berger.

Sullivan, Walter. 1974. "Geologists Find Snow Rarely Fell in Ice Age." *New York Times,* March 18.

Suro, Roberto. 1988. "New Theories on Early Europe Cite Migration, Not Conquest." *New York Times,* May 10, C4.

Tinner, Willy, Brigitta Amman, and Peter Germann. 1996. "Treeline Fluctuations Recorded for 12,500 Years by Soil Profiles, Pollen, and Plant Microfossils in the Central Swiss Alps." *Arctic and Alpine Research* 28, no. 2:131–47.

Toth-Gonns, Werner. 1939. *Die Grossglockner Hochalpen Strasse.* Munich: Rother.

Tyndale, H. E. G. 1948. *Mountain Paths.* London: Eyre and Spottiswoode.

Vincent, Francois. 1976. *Aspects de Certains Reliefs de la Vallée de Chamonix: Notions de Geomorphologie.* Chamonix: Reserve Naturelle des Aiguilles Rouges.

Von Eltz, Lieselotte. 1964. *Die Alpen in Alten Ansichten.* Salzburg: MM Verlag.

Webster, Bayard. 1982. "Mountains Worldwide Imperiled as Man and Nature Collide." *New York Times,* December 21, C1, C2.

Wendelberger, Elfrune. 1968. *Zauberwelt der Alpenblumen.* Frankfurt: Pinquin.

Wick, Lucia, and Willy Tinner. 1997. "Vegetation Changes and Timberline Fluctuations in the Central Alps as Indicators of Holocene Climatic Conditions." *Arctic and Alpine Research* 20, no. 4:445–58.

Wrangham, E. A. 1957. *Selected Climbs in the Range of Mont Blanc.* London: Allen and Unwin.

Index